MEMORIAL MONUMENT
HONORING THE 9TH DIVISION
CARTERET, FRANCE

Here

June 18 1944

The 9th Division of the 7th Corps

From the 1st American Army

General Bradley

Participated in

The separation of Contentin (Peninsula)

This book contains pages titled, "Veterans' Recollections & Diary." Veterans of World War II can create personal diaries of events they experienced. Veterans of Korea and Vietnam can create diaries of their war experiences. These can be passed along to children and grandchildren as valuable family historical records.

Some of the army terminology has been eliminated so readers of all ages unfamiliar with such expressions may better enjoy this narrative. However, it was felt that obliterating all service 'jargon' would subtract from the realism of THE WAY IT WAS! The Matt Urban Story is a valuable historic document -- Treasure it -- Retell it -- Pass it on. It is timeless and true!

THE
MATT URBAN
STORY

Author: Lieutenant Colonel Matt Urban
Co-Author: Charles Conrad

Printed in
The United States of America
Publisher
The Matt Urban Story, Incorporated
PO Box 2004
Holland, Michigan 49422-2004
USA

THE MATT URBAN STORY

Library of Congress Cataloging in Publication Date

Urban, Lt. Col. Matt
    The Matt Urban Story

1. Education, Military Training
2. World War II, 1941–1945
        North Africa:
            Algeria
            Morocco
            Spanish Morocco
            Tunisia
        Sicily
        England
        Europe:
            Utah Beach
            Normandy
            France
            Belgium
            Germany
3. Post-War Years
        Liberty Magazine, "Old Sarge"
        Recreation Director:
            Monroe, Michigan
            Port Huron, Michigan
            Holland, Michigan
4. Medal of Honor Award
        White House Ceremonies
5. Homecoming Gala
        Holland, Michigan

ISBN: 0-9624621-0-1

THE MATT URBAN STORY

**To Our Daughter Jennifer
"One in a Million"**

LT. COL.
MATT URBAN

US DECORATIONS
(Individual)
Silver Star (1 OLC)
Bronze Star (2 OLC)
*with "V" Device
Purple Heart (6 OLC)

US DECORATIONS
Presidential Unit Citation (1 OLC)

SERVICE MEDALS
American Campaign Medal
European-African-Middle Eastern
Campaign Medal w/1 Silver
and 1 Bronze service star
World War II Victory Medal

BADGES
Combat Infantryman Badge

*1 award of BSM authorized
based upon award of CIB

FOREIGN DECORATIONS
(Individual)
Croix de Guerre with Silver Gilt

FOREIGN DECORATIONS
(Unit)
Croix de Guerre (France)
Fourragere (Belgium)

CIVILIAN AWARD
The New York State Conspicous
Cross w/4 Silver - 1 Gold
Clusters

35-Year Wait for Medal of Honor
29 Medals Awarded for Bravery
20 Months in Front-Line Action
7 Times Wounded in Action
6 Major Battle Campaigns
5 Major Countries:
Algeria - Tunisia - Sicily
France - Belgium

iv

LIEUTENANT COLONEL MATT URBAN
UNITED STATES ARMY, RETIRED
HOLLAND, MICHIGAN 49423

To all of My Military and Civilian Friends:

It is my sincere desire to thank each of you for the support that saved my life during numerous military actions of World War II. Also, I wish to express my gratitude to each Unit of the 9th Division, 60th Regiment, and to my 2nd Battalion, as loyal comrades in arms.

As a recipient of the Congressional Medal of Honor , I wear it with pride in knowing that each of you are represented in that medal by your valor and direct actions that helped achieve victory in World War II.

In civilian life, my gratitude is to the host of friends who supported me in all activities. It was truly a pleasure to work as Recreation Director with young people in Monroe, Port Huron and Holland, Michigan.

The Amateur Soft Ball Association has provided much challenge and pleasure in my years of service as State of Michigan Commissioner and Regional Vice President of the Association.

A special thanks to personal friends and organizations who have made publication of The Matt Urban Story a reality.

With Deepest Appreciation and Affection,

Matt Urban

DEDICATED TO THE HEROIC NINTH INFANTRY DIVISION
TO
HONOR ITS MEN -- LIVING, DEAD, AND THE MIA
OF WORLD WAR II, KOREA, VIETNAM
AND ITS TROOPS NOW SERVING OUR COUNTRY

In 1923 the Ninth Infantry Division -- with War Department approval -- adopted the *Octofoil* as its patch. The design dates back to the 15th century when it was customary for each son to have an individual mark of distinction.

Octo, meaning eight, is confusing to many when speaking of the Ninth Division. But in foiling there are eight foils (positions) and heraldic rules gave the *Octofoil* to the ninth son, since it was symbolic of his being surrounded by eight brothers; which is an explanation of why this eight-petaled insignia is correct for the Ninth Regular Army Division.

The design consists of a red quatrefoil atop a blue quatrefoil, with a white center. The red stands for the artillery, the blue for the infantry, the white denotes the color of numerals found on division flags. Surrounding the Octofoil is a rim of olive drab -- symbolic as nothing else of the US Army.

LIEUTENANT GENERAL OMAR BRADLEY

The "Doughboys General", an infantryman, stubborn, informational, clear-headed, a strategist, son of a Missouri school teacher, West Point graduate, entered with the Class of 1915 --- picture from Time Magazine Cover, May 1, 1944 --- just before "D" Day in Normandy, France.

Troops of the Ninth Infantry Division: 10 May 1945

This May 9th that passed was too big a part of your life to crowd it with recollections. It belongs to you and the world as the day on which the German war was ended. However, May 9th has a greater meaning for men of the First and Ninth Infantry Divisions. In recalling the day in future years, you can remember with great pride that it marks not the first, but the second unconditional surrender of an enemy you fought valorously for thirty long months.

       (continues)

From the waddies of El Guettar where the First and Ninth Divisions fought shoulder to shoulder against crack elements of the Afrika Korps to the final surrender of German forces to the American Second Corps on May 9, 1943, the Tunisian Campaign was an epoch, fashioned largely in the bravery, skill and achievements of your two divisions.

American troops advancing through the minefields of the Sedjenane and on the road to Mateur, gave our Nation its first great land victory of the war, and the world its first great unconditional surrender of large-scale German forces.

Since then I have followed your red numeral of the First Division and your tricolored insignia of the Ninth across the sands of Sicily, past the defenses of Troina, over the beaches of Normandy and through the hedgerows to Sherbourg. Side by side, your two divisions have fought the German army 700 miles across the Continent to the inevitable and final defeat of the German nation.

The American Army is studded with splendid divisions. But rarely have two teamed so expertly; never have two divisions fought longer and harder with greater skill or courage.

Sometimes you may have felt forgotton. Sometimes you may have felt, as fighting soldiers do, the endlessness of our long road to Germany. Now that you're here, however, and now that many of you are ready to go home, I want you to know the gratitude of your Nation.

And as your commander, I want to share with the millions of your friends and champions throughout the Army, their pride in your unsurpassed and monumental achievements.

Omar N Bradley

General, U.S. Army, Commanding

OPENING PAGE

Matt Urban is a hero for all ages. He is one of the greatest combat soldiers that ever donned the khaki uniform of the United States Army. A true hero and patriot, a gentleman who in his combat infantry service during World War II managed, by dint of his sheer bravery and tenacity, to become one of this country's most decorated soldiers .... receiving 29 of the nation's highest awards.

As you read this story you will be able to ascertain the frightening, yet magnificent odyssey of the kind of man and character that most aptly fits the role of a real hero! For those who may find some kind of empathy for the Rambo imagery, the story may well provide a new sense of perspective of what constitutes true heroism.

Andrew J. Sikora
Editor - Publisher
The Polish American

FOREWORD

Blitzkrieg! Catastrophic destruction rained down from Germany in late 1939. Its military forces capitalized on ancient rivalries and created racial hatred. It destroyed country after country. Millions of people lost their homes, families, friends and loved ones. The Wehrmacht crushed all resistance to the cruel dictatorship of Adolph Hitler.

By 1940 the world was at the brink of total domination by the Axis war machine. Following World War I, nations of the world searched for peace 'at any price'. Nazi Germany took complete advantage of that narrow vision. All of Europe and North Africa were either conquered or under attack by Hitler. The Japanese had become the masters of the Orient. Russia was under siege, England was reeling from Hitler's aerial bombardment. The United States was just beginning its urgent task of mobilizing industries, manpower and creating the modern weapons to counter the Nazi threat to civilization. *(continues)*

A WORLD OF WAR
Surprisingly the spirit of the people showed no signs of defeat;
hurting inside but yet smiling and warm in their relationships with
Americans.

German scientists and military planners had designed the first jet aircraft. Bombs were pounding London almost daily. Wernher von Braun began design of the A-10, a two-stage booster rocket conceived in 1940 as a trans-Atlantic missile capable of blasting the heartland of America. Design of weaponry was almost finished by a Nazi government already too ruthless in the mass bombing of civilian populations. Torture and murder were raging throughout the world. In Europe whole neighborhoods of non-German people were being slaughtered. Millions were enslaved at internment compounds. Slave labor was used to construct a gigantic continental fortress. The German armies seemed invincible. U.S. Government officials were aware of these conditions ... but unprepared to react.....

In contrast to the turmoil in Europe in 1939, civilian population of the United States was just emerging from the Great Depression. Americans were primarily concerned with building careers and creating a better world for themselves and their children. The 'Winds of War' seemed far off. Though speculation was rampant, hope continued that

(continues)

xiii

events would take care of themselves. All United States citizens hoped to be spared the ravages of war..

In the 1930's as the bright, hopeful youth of America studied for lives of harmony and peace, an entirely different education was brewing overseas. In Germany, Hitler's youth were preparing to rule a world to be under Nazi domination. Across the Pacific, an ancient Samurai war code was being absorbed by the young people of Japan.

The difference between America's dream of peace and the reality of a world in turmoil was about to be made apparent. The United States of America was in for a hard lesson! The last vestiges of isolationism and the final hopes for peace were blown away by the notorious sneak attack on Pearl Harbor by the Japanese on December 7, 1941. Germany declared war on the U.S. four days later. A reluctant America was thrust into a battle for survival, and a struggle for its foundation of freedom.

By 1944 Allied forces had broken the grip of the Nazi war machine in Europe. Yet some of the bloodiest fighting was still to come. The Ninth Division

(continues)

distinguished itself as a great fighting outfit. Beginning with its invasion and attack on Nazi-held North Africa, it continued through Sicily and into Europe. The Ninth Division was known to the Germans as the most formidable opponent. Poised on the border of Belgium, the Ninth Division was selected to lead the battles into the heart of the Rhineland, culminating in the 1945 unconditional surrender of the Nazis to the Allied Forces.

by Les Murray

-- CONTENTS --

CHAPTER 1

THE CLASS THAT WENT TO WAR
Cornell University

Matt Urban left Buffalo in the late summer of 1937 to begin his studies at Cornell University. The campus is located in Ithaca, N.Y. on the banks of beautiful Lake Cayuga.

Europe was clinging to an uneasy peace. The life style in the United States was changing noticeably. The interest and emotions of the people were affected by hazardous developments in Europe. Civil war had broken out in Spain. The Republicans and Falangists struggled for control. Russia provided military aid to one faction. The Germans were providing aid and military equipment to the other. The British and French governments still believed that Hitler's threats of military aggression could be tamed through compromise and appeasement.

This cartoon by Shoemaker during a European trip in 1938 proved to be most prophetic.

Lying between Russia and Germany, Poland wished to remain neutral. It feared with good reason, that it would be the loser in any next war --- that the victor would either partition Poland or seek to occupy it permanently. Racial antagonisms in Poland offered a fertile field for propaganda by interested major powers.

In 1938 Poland was nominally an ally of France but had come to the conclusion several years before that France was on the downgrade and that Germany would soon dominate Europe. Therefore, Poland signed a 10-year non-aggression pact with Germany. As 1938 came to a close, Germany was stirring up grave trouble among the Ukrainian minority of Poland. In great anxiety Poland was therefore seeking a closer relationship with its other traditional foe, Russia.

Adolph Hitler became Chancellor of Germany in 1933. This was the same year that Urban entered high school.

The world watched in dismay as Hitler dissolved German labor unions, burned books, and outlawed opposition parties. Dismay turned to chagrin when Germany withdrew from the League of Nations. Hitler reintroduced compulsory military service and stepped up weapons production. In 1936, Hitler and his troops occupied the Rhineland.

As Matt Urban began studies at Cornell, Hitler was issuing the Hossbach memorandum outlining his plans for future wars. The world was on the threshold of military disaster as Matt calmly continued his studies at Cornell.

The premonition of war and turmoil festered from 1936. This had the effect of bringing the American people together because of common concern about the future and its uncertainties.

The class of '41 convened under the clouds of war. Their destiny knitted them together throughout the college years. Each classmate was recognized as a fellow student and also importantly as a fellow

FRANK H. T. RHODES
President

CORNELL UNIVERSITY
300 DAY HALL
ITHACA, N. Y. 14853-2801

Office of the President

November 12, 1987

Lieutenant Colonel Matt Urban
352 Wildwood Drive
Holland, MI 49423

Dear Matt:

    Just a brief note to say how good it was to have you back on campus last Friday and how much I appreciated the chance to meet with you.

    We are all immensely proud of your achievements.

    With highest regards,

                    Sincerely yours,

                    Frank

                    Frank H. T. Rhodes

4

patriot. A remarkable comradeship developed as these classmates learned to rely on each other. Closeness and true friendship characterized Matt's class, because its education was gained in the shadow of terrible events developing in Europe. The group became known as THE CLASS THAT WENT TO WAR. This special aura can still be felt whenever the class reunions are held at their beautiful Ivy League Campus in Ithaca, New York.

Cornell University was founded by Ezra Cornell in 1865. This picturesque location in the Finger Lakes region on the shores of Lake Cayuga provided a unique and peaceful setting for the University. In intervening years, the school expanded and prospered under a steady succession of astute presidents. This tradition was preserved by its current leader, President Frank Rhodes.

Matt Urban was awed by the majesty of the setting and serenity of the campus. Deep glacial gorges and the white-water of cascading rivers enhanced its beauty. A slender suspension bridge traversed a rushing waterway. He enjoyed walks on the campus and many trips across the bridge. Cherished friendships were developed and valuable lessons were learned. He considered his years at Cornell as

SIBLEY ENGINEERING BLDG.

MORRILL HALL

BAKER DORMITORY

SAGE CHAPEL

having provided a variety of outstanding experiences. Urban recalls these as the best years of his life.

At one time he held five part-time jobs while balancing classes, study, and running on the cross-country track team. A person with less stamina would have been exhausted by such a work/study schedule. His multiple jobs underscored the gulf between him and students who could afford and enjoy a normal campus life.

Urban's steady job was to serve as a waiter in a fraternity house. He often volunteered (without pay) to fill in for an absent dishwasher. While sweating over a sink full of dirty pots and pans, he could hear the affluent fraternity brothers frolicking on the other side of the door. They seemed to be a world away. His solace came from his only companion in the kitchen, Beulah, the cook. She was a cheerful woman of fifty, who dispensed wisdom, humor and faith along with the hearty meals she served him every night.

CORNELL UNIVERSITY QUADRANGLE
This is Urban's beloved University Campus. His residence in 1941 was Sheldon Court. It is interesting to note that the yearly rate for Matt's room #41 cost only $140.00!

On weekends Matt worked as a coatroom attendant in the Willard Straight Hall of the Student Union. He could see the glitter of the ballroom through the doors and feel the beat of the big bands. On various occasions the music of Glen Miller, Tommy Dorsey, and Les Brown filled the air. Although enjoying his appreciation of the music, Matt felt cut off from the campus life which other students took for granted.

Late each night he walked in solitude back to his cramped room under a stairwell in the Sheldon Court Dormitory. On these walks across the Cornell grounds, he reveled in the profound beauty of the sleeping campus. It was nearly a mile walk to his room. He found ample time to reflect on how great it was to be alive and to be at Cornell University!

Urban's academic accomplishments began rather unimpressively. This was due to time constraints of his heavy working schedule. At mid-term the dreaded pink slip warning arrived. It shocked Matt into reality ... he was determined not to fail. He vowed not to join the ranks of the 'Busted' referenced in the

PROFESSOR FRED MARCHAM
Distinguished Service Award — 9-16-88

"A Students' Pied Piper" --- Whenever there was a need for a
helping hand, Professor Marcham was always there.

Cornell parody sung to the tune of: GIVE MY REGARDS TO BROADWAY —

> *Give my regards to Davy,*
> *Remember me to Teefy Crane,*
> *Tell all the pikers on the hill*
> *That I'll be back again.*
> *Tell them of how I busted*
> *Lapping up the high, highball,*
> *We'll all have drinks at Theodore Zinck's*
> *When I get back next fall.*

Cornell's beloved history professor, Fred Marcham, invited the struggling Freshman to his home for a game of chess. As one game led to another, the compassionate professor wove many lessons of life into the conversation. Matt learned that one can handle a multitude of tasks under pressure if they are completed in a good priority, one at a time. He buckled down with a determination to successfully complete his education.

The class of '41 worked hard and played hard. Although he had to forego his dream of playing football, Matt continued his athletic career. He ran track in the spring and cross-country events in the fall.   He also found that he could participate in

Urban's Cornell Boxing Coach, Allie Wolff, was a friend of World Heavyweight Champion Boxer Jack Dempsey.

He taught many of the techniques picked up from Dempsey when training Matt Urban to become the "Ace" boxer at Cornell University 1940/41.

boxing without taking much away from his limited study time.

As a team sport, boxing demanded the least training time. Much of the training involved roadwork. Matt was already doing this with the cross-country and track teams.

Urban had not boxed before. His showing in the intramural boxing tournament convinced coach Alfred "Allie" Wolff to talk young Matt into joining the varsity team.

Even as a new recruit to the ring Matt was a natural. He felt at home there. His success was based on quickness and agility. Matt proudly recalled that he never had a black eye or a bloody nose in the boxing duals. Boxing was an athletic activity in which Urban could quickly gain respect and recognition for his ability.

Matt baffled ring opponents by boxing equally well as a right-handed or south-paw fighter. Urban won the All-University Championship in the 165, 175, and heavyweight classes during two consecutive years. He was so successful that Coach Wolff called him the one-man boxing team. During inter-collegiate matches, Matt's teammates would sometimes put lead in his pockets so he could tip the scales to qualify for the heavier-weight class boxing matches.

It was a memorable heavy-weight bout at the West Point Military Academy during January, 1941. Matt at one hundred sixty five pounds, knocked out his opponent who had been an outstanding tackle on the Army football team.

This led to another memorable bout at the U.S.Naval Academy in Annapolis, Maryland. The Academy made the Saturday Night Boxing Match an annual affair. It was followed by a prom and homecoming celebration. Midshipmen in dress uniform brought their guests to the boxing event which the Navy traditionally won. The attendance was reported to be a total of five thousand.

Matt fought as a light heavyweight. He weighed in at one hundred sixty lbs. His would be the final and deciding bout of the evening. As the band played 'Anchors Aweigh', Urban's bout started, and he defeated his highly favored opponent from the Navy. That moment was etched deeply into Matt's mind as the midshipmen and their dates rose to give him a rousing ovation.

In March of '41 Matt fought in the light heavyweight division for the Eastern Intercollegiate Championship in Syracuse, N.Y. He defeated all of his opponents through the semi-finals. In the highly touted championship match he faced Americo Woyceisjes, the three-time champion at Syracuse University.

It was said that Woyceisjes (Wow-Jezes) was a part-time steel mill worker. He was known for a blockbuster punch. Matt felt confident going into the boxing match because of his own speed and punching ability.

Everyone had long anticipated the championship match between Woyceisjes and Matt. The action was furious. In Matt's words, "He never hurt me seriously, though he staggered me a couple of times. I was never in trouble. I thought I had earned the decision."

The decision of the three judges came back a draw! After much conferring it was determined that an intercollegiate champion for 1941 must b e recognized. Ten or fifteen minutes elapsed before the questionable decision was returned --- Woyceisjes was declared the winner!!

March 8, 1941

Americo Woyciesjes

Matt Urban

Undefeated Light Heavyweight Boxer, Co-captain of Syracuse University Boxing Team, three years Intercollegiate Champion, Honor Student in Forestry, and a steel worker five nights a week.

After defeating the best in the Midwest, he prepares for his bout with top seed Matt Urban.

Punched his way into the finals of the Mideastern Intercollegiate Boxing Association. Weighing only 160 lbs., Urban won all his bouts—fighting the majority of them in the 175-lb. class.

In this match the crowd thought Urban won, even though the decision went to Woyciesjes. He also agreed that "Matt was robbed."

The arena erupted in catcalls as the boxers left the ring. Matt remembered the pandemonium around him as he made his way to the dressing room. Later, Woyceisjes came into the room with a sympathetic expression. He said, "Some Bull, Matty! They sure did rob you!"

This controversial loss ended Matt's career as a college boxer. This triggered a reaction at Cornell. Shortly after the uproar, the University gave up intercollegiate boxing to place more emphasis on intramural sports. However, Cornell never acknowledged Matt's bout as the motivating factor in giving up varsity boxing, but knowledgeable observers did link the two events.

The closeness and pride of the class of '41 carried its members to outstanding achievement during their college days and long after graduation. Their fighting spirit was evidenced in the sports program by the legendary performance of the Cornell football team.

In these years, Cornell surprised the nation by upsetting such Big Ten powers as Ohio State University and the University of Michigan. For weeks the team was ranked number one in college football.

CORNELL 1940 CHAMPIONSHIP FOOTBALL SQUAD

This is the team that upset the University of Michigan, Ohio State and other Big Ten Teams. Cornell was ranked Number One in College football.

Any lack in size and reputation was made up with spirit and ingenuity. Their accomplishments are still a subject of conversation in Ithaca.

These young men shared the destiny of living in the shadow of war. It bonded them deeply.

Ben Mintz worked in the School Athletic Office and was a sports reporter for the Cornell Sun. He became a close friend of Matt Urban. Other friendships which continue to this day include Fullback Walter Matuszak, Quarterbacks Bud Finneran and Walter Scholl, also Wide Receiver Hal McCullough. Mort Landsburg, Nick Drahos and Bill Murphy are names that still resound in the Cornell Hall of Fame. Lou Conti continued his career as a Marine Aviator and attained the rank of General. Brud Holland became a U.S. Ambassador. Alvin Kelly as a Coach at Yale, Colgate and Rutgers, carried the inspiration and traditions generated by this outstanding group of Cornell athletes.

Several of the Cornell football players could have joined professional teams after graduation. However, they were THE CLASS THAT WENT TO WAR.

URBAN IN ROTC DRESS UNIFORM - 1940
Urban on last day of maneuvers

"ROTC Program's the best training and camaraderie that any young man will ever experience."   To Urban --- It meant survival!

One day as the team returned to the locker room from football practice, they were surprised. Someone (who is unknown to this day) had gone to considerable effort and expense to let the team know they were being called up to active duty in the military service.

As each team member opened his locker, he discovered his civilian clothing missing. In its place someone had hung an old World War I military uniform. Most team members then knew they were being called to active duty. This event occurred about six months prior to graduation.

As Matt boxed future cadets and midshipmen in intercollegiate competition, he continued his preparations for the possibility of war. Matt joined the Cornell Reserve Officer Training Corps (ROTC).

His immediate reason and need was very simple. It was the challenge and need for money to meet college expenses. Urban thought of ROTC as another part time job and a way to pay his way through school. The money was good; the military demands were reasonable. The duty requirements were a breeze for someone In excellent condition. He remembered the summer camps as outings --- as it turned out the ROTC training became the most important part of Urban's education. Survival skills learned and the ability to work as part of a team, were essential to Matt throughout his military and civilian life.

In addition to rigorous survival training, Matt experienced a great camaraderie in the ROTC. He graduated as a leader who had developed that delicate balance of commanding a unit while remaining one of the men. Urban's tendencies toward leadership blossomed into a coherent set of skills supplementing an intuitive sense of what would be required to get a job done.

ROTC military exercises required Matt to combine the best of his athletic ability with other skills such as hunting and shooting that were taught to him by his father. Urban thrived on hard work. Each night he fell into his cot with aching muscles and the peace of mind that comes from a sense of accomplishment.

The ROTC training center was near Plattsburg, New York. It nestled into the Adirondack Mountains on the shores of Lake Champlain. A fast tempo paced the final days of field training for the senior class of '41. Reveille, hiking, rifle range, obstacle course, parade grounds, and retreat each day put the finishing touches to a transition from ROTC Cadet to Commissioned Second Lieutenant in the U.S. Army.

While finishing the last bit of chow on the final Saturday evening of training, bedlam broke out in the mess hall. A couple of outspoken, gambling-tainted cadets were seeking to stir up excitement. They brainstormed a betting challenge. They had to decide on who would be the victim in accepting the challenge. One can visualize the melee that erupted, the bellowing conversations and mass confusion.

Such point-blank bursts as "Any volunteers?" "Delegate -- Who?" Fingers pointed at Urban.

"Hey! How about you, Urbie? A boxer --- track and cross-country guy --- lots of stamina --- you can do it!"

A chant picked up with shouts of "Yeah! Yeah! Yeah! He's the guy! Urb's our man! "

The group pushed its way and surrounded Matt. They nudged him with pats on the shoulders and gentle shoves.

Cheers erupted, "We've got our man!"

Matt was hoisted onto burly shoulders. The surprised young cadet , Urban, had become a victim of circumstances. It was as good a shanghai job as anyone would ever see. He was the designated pigeon in this game.

The pepped-up cavalcade hit town for the closing night. It would bo a night the townspeople of Plattsburg would long remember. At 1800 hours the trek to town began by truck. Groups of cadets also tramped alongside, singing and chattering over the hilly route to town.

The instigator of this betting opportunity grabbed the moment with shouts of "Place your bets here! Urban is capable of drinking twenty schooners of beer in one sitting!" Matt answered by saying that he never refused a dare.

To the cheers of his fellow cadets, Matt sat down with four cold beers lined up in front of him. At first he downed them with machine like regularity. By the 12th the fun had gone out of the contest for Urban. The men around him seemed to be enjoying themselves more and more.

As they drank their beer they loudly cheered and made side wagers. When not watching Matt all eyes focused on the minute hand of the wall clock as it approached the agreed-upon 0100 deadline hour for completion of Urban's challenge. Some cadets acted as messengers. They relayed the countdown to others outside the jam-packed bar.

Matt finally got to the 20th glass of beer. The second hand of the clock was reaching for the deadline. He steeled himself for one remaining swallow. His stomach felt stretched as tight as a drum. Those who had bet on him leaned down and screamed encouragement.

Matt lifted the glass and finished off the last beer amid rousing cheers. He raised the empty glass for all to see.

As quickly as the result was officially recorded on the chalk scoreboard, Matt shoved his way to the men's room. He cleared away the half mouthful and throat of beer that just could not be forced down.

Amid loud cheers and shouts, they hailed Matt's victory in the challenge. In celebration his fans hoisted him on their shoulders. Singing and laughing, arm-in-arm, half-carrying Matt, they marched off to camp.

NOTATION: *In later years in recalling this story, Urban said it reminded him of Paul Newman in the movie, COOL HAND LUKE, and Newman's challenge to down fifty eggs in an hour.*

CHAPTER 2

THE BIRTH OF AN ARMY CAMP
Fort Bragg, North Carolina

As Matt was enjoying life at Cornell, the Nazi war machine crushed one European country after another. Austria and Czechoslovakia fell before the power of diplomacy. Germany used claims of racial superiority and historic precedent. The German armies moved into these countries without firing a shot.

On September 1, 1939, Matt Urban entered his Junior Year at Cornell. Poland was devastated by the Nazi blitzkrieg. The Polish armies were outgunned and overwhelmed by the Nazi Panzer Tank Divisions. Thousands of men and women were killed in the onslaught of the invasion of Poland. The country was conquered in a month of fighting.

Upon the invasion of Poland, England and France declared war on the Third Reich. They were unable

Years before World War II Adolf Hitler wrote "Mein Kampf" —-- He called it "My Struggle". It was a story of his life and his plans for world conquest. Statesmen of other nations could not believe Hitler meant what he said: Annexation of all German-inhabited territories in Europe, a war to the death with France, and a war for partition of Russia.

Hitler took it seriously; the German people took it seriously --- but it all seemed too fantastic for other countries to take seriously prior to 1939.

to provide the needed assistance for Poland to resist the German firepower. Within a year Hitler's troops invaded and crushed Denmark, Norway, Belgium, Holland, Luxembourg, and France. British troops in Europe suffered a humiliating defeat at Dunkirk, France. British ships and civilian boats lifted thousands of troops from the beaches where the Germans had driven them to the sea.

The Dunkirk evacuation and the increased pressure by the Nazi armed forces against France and England raised the possibility of U.S. involvement.

The United States entered a serious phase of disarmament during the 1930's. The U.S. fighting forces were reduced to a total of 174,000 men in all branches of the service. Due to the threat of war, Congress increased the authorized strength of the military to 375,000. Military leaders began to design a new kind of army. It was based upon formation of triangular divisions to replace the outmoded square design.

Matt was preparing to enter his Senior year in September, 1940. At that time, the first cadre of the newly activated Ninth Infantry Division was arriving at Fort Bragg, North Carolina. Army life began in a tent

From
Fort Bragg Post
Wednesday, March 24, 1941

General Manton S. Eddy
New Commander of the 9th Infantry Division
Commissioned from civilian life in 1916. Served overseas in World War I with the 39th Infantry. Became a Major prior to the Armistice. Served many stateside duties in Georgia, Kansas, Kentucky and the Hawaiian Islands. Commanded 'Anti-Airborne Unit No. I' of the First Army in North Carolina maneuvers. Assisted prior Post Commander General H.E.D. Hoyle. General Eddy received his first set of Stars when he was assigned to command the Division on March 16.

city on a desolate insect-infested tract of sandy land. 'Bragg' became the birthplace of the modern American Army.

The first men to arrive for the Ninth Division were ninety three regular army men transferred from the Second Infantry Regiment of Fort Custer, Michigan. The first registrant at 6:00 A.M. on the morning of August 1st was Sergeant John J. Waldrop. He was followed by Sergeant Raymond Duckworth and Sergeant Ralph Bogle.

All ninety three men from Fort Custer were in the area to form the 39th Infantry Regiment by August 2nd. This number increased to 1,881 soldiers from twenty four states within three weeks. It was this group that formed the basis for the build-up of the remaining units of the Ninth Division.

On the 24th of July at Camp Roberts, California, Brigadier General Manton S. Eddy (Later Lieutenant General) was placed in command of the Ninth Division by the War Department.

General Eddy was a tall person and a veteran of World War I. He was serving with the original 39th Infantry when wounded in 1918. General Eddy was a natural born soldier but was not a West Point graduate. He was an efficient and inspiring leader. As General, he led the Ninth Division through Africa, Sicily, England and Normandy. The Ninth Division was considered as being one of the best combat teams in the European Theatre of Operations. Thomas R. Henry of the Saturday Evening Post wrote of General Eddy as the country's most brilliant Division Commander.

General Eddy was a fearless but mild-mannered leader. He believed victory should be won by sweat and surprise rather than by blood and death. This type of leadership resulted in the Ninth Division excellence.

On September 16th, 1940, Congress passed the Selective Service Act. It was necessary to organize the Draft to strengthen the manpower of the extremely weak American forces. Three months later the country implemented its famous FISH-BOWL Selective Service drawing. Thousands of young men were called up for military service that year. The isolation of the United States lent a sense of security in earlier times. Now the protection from the expanse of the Atlantic Ocean seemed to be disappearing.

Preparations for war affected every household in America.

When Urban graduated from Cornell in 1941, over 500,000 men had been called into uniform. Industry was rapidly changing from producing civilian products. Now they were tooling up to produce planes, tanks, bombs, rifles, cannons, etc. Rationing had begun for rubber, gasoline and other essential items.

The German submarines were torpedoing American ships on the high seas. Millions of tons of cargo were sunk each month. This further strained the ability of America to supply the necessary armaments and other products to its European Allies. Direct involvement in the war seemed inevitable. Relations with Japan were becoming increasingly strained. Germany invaded the Soviet Union on June 22, 1941. One by one the voices supporting isolationism in America fell silent.

The summer of 1941 provided Matt's first experience south of the Mason-Dixon line. He loved the tradition at Fort Bragg with its horses, cavalry, and association with men from all walks of life and from the entire United States. However, the romance of the cavalry

FORT BRAGG, N.C. BATTLE TRAINING

This particular battle training course was designed for assault actions. It included a 200 yard obstacle course. Infantrymen were required to cover the distance with rifle and pack in four minutes.

During the week of February 1st to 7th the regiment will go to the McKellar Pond area to practice the landing operation incident to sea-borne attacks. Large rafts and outdoor motorboats will be employed in this exercise. Don't slip men, or it will be a ducking for you—life guards will be posted just in case.

was quickly giving way to the modern armor and weapons of the 1941 army.

Nothing Urban had heard about the army could have prepared him for the mass of humanity and huge quantities of weapons at the greatly enlarged Fort Bragg. The military base already housed 67,000 uniformed personnel. A tenseness pervaded the area. It was a direct result of thousands of individuals performing seemingly endless acts of hard labor and physical training. An esprit de corps developed rapidly as the build-up continued at Fort Bragg.

A swift escalation of good and bad effects soon developed in the quiet North Carolina town of Fayetteville. Some folks felt the expansion was a mixed blessing as the community was overwhelmed by the rapid influx of troops and development.

The reactions at Fort Bragg were specifically focused on preparations for war. Combat training was already taking place. Men from all over the U.S.A. were engaged in tough programs of mental and physical conditioning. They vigorously entered the task of building the mightiest army the world had seen. The soldiers at Fort Bragg sneered at the rumors of Nazi supermen. They didn't hesitate to vocalize what they would do to these Nazis if they encountered them in battle.

Matt Urban enjoyed the variety of faces and accents he encountered. Soft southern drawls, tough Brooklyn street talk and the staccato accent of New Englanders blended as young men from all over the country discovered common bonds and values that made all of them true Americans.

Urban (military protocol required use of last names) was assigned to D Company, 60th Infantry Regiment. He entered Fort Bragg as a 2nd Lieutenant upon graduation with ROTC training at Cornell University.

His first assignment was platoon leader, Company 'D', 2nd Battalion, 60th Infantry Regiment of the Ninth Division. Captain Walter N. Guletsky, a West Point graduate, served as his Commanding Officer. Urban benefited from the leadership and disciplinarian characteristics of his Commander. The Captain was close to 30 years of age. His experience and military professionalism inspired Urban and the new officers.

Colonel (Major General) Frank C. Mahin commanded the 60th Regiment. He was a veteran of the World War I Infantry. The Colonel had first-hand knowledge of the terrible slaughter of American troops during that conflict because of insufficient weapons training. Then the soldiers received their weapons only a few weeks before combat. Mahin was determined to give his troops at Fort Bragg the best training possible. Firing weapons became a priority in training his troops. They would become familiar with the feel and value of the rifles from the beginning of training. His troops accepted the fact that their rifles were the key to combat survival. It became automatic for his troops to keep the rifle within arm's reach at all times.

The direction of Colonel Mahin and the grueling training by Sergeant E. F. Groves soon transformed Urban and his comrades from civilians into a disciplined combat team. This took only a matter of months.

This did not eliminate requirements for KP or 'policing the area'. These activities were as despised as frequent stints on guard duty.

Normal grumbling included, "What does this have to do with fighting Nazis --- just get me to the war!"

MAJOR ROBERT C. ANDREWS

ONE OF URBAN'S TOUGH TUTORS

Urban and his men later were to appreciate their crusty trainers, the discipline to take orders, and trust in leadership that knitted Urban's company and others into highly effective fighting units.

Others complained, "How can constant saluting, marching, standing in line, and Yes Sir! No Sir! get us ready to fight a battle! Get me over there, and we'll be home in a month!"

Major Robert C. Andrews was an old-timer. He had fought in the Spanish-American War. He provided the officers' training. He had a strong muscular body which seemed to have been untouched by time. His energy was unlimited. Few of the younger officers could keep up with him in the field. He was an idealist. He believed men could be trained and tuned to deliver a level of intensity which would allow them to accomplish the impossible.

Matt later compared him to 'Kojak' with his large bald head, bushy mustache and black, piercing eyes. Andrews taught the tricks of the trade so firmly that this training would stick with the young officers for the rest of their lives.

Major Andrews taught that one of the main reasons for officers failing and their being discharged from the army was for lack of proper financial record-keeping. He would yell, "Damn it!" and then would point as he walked through the aisle. He would order each of his young officers: "YOU LEARN THAT NOW! I insist that you initial and record all transactions, or you will find yourself on the way out!".

"Fraternization with the troops is taboo! You treat 'em all alike and keep your distance!"

He ranted against having drinking buddies. Andrews recommended a policy of no pals during wartime. He said, "Young officers must make quick decisions in determining whom to assign on missions with deadly risks. You must remember to treat all soldiers alike. No favorites! " He looked each officer in the eye as he jabbed his finger at them.

Major Andrews taught that camps and bivouacs must be clean, whether it's overnight or for days. Standard latrines must be dug. He insisted that they must have a canvas enclosure. He shouted his pappy had taught him there are two times when a person needs privacy --- and he made it clear in earthy language exactly what he was talking about!

The stubborn and stiff style of Major Andrews made one permanently learn the lessons he imparted. Urban always remembered the Major as a living replica of Teddy Roosevelt's 'Rough-Riders'.

Later, during the weeks and years of World War II battles, Urban and his men were to thank their crusty trainers time and time again. Those habits learned that resulted in dry feet and clean, disease-free camps, were so basic to good health in the front lines. The discipline to take orders and trust in their leadership knitted Urban's group and others into highly effective fighting units.

The lessons of the Civil War times proved the importance of hygiene and proper troop care. More military personnel were lost in the Civil War as the result of dysentery and other diseases from uncleanliness than in any other action in U.S. history. It was not always feasible to explain the importance of seemingly insignificant tasks when training the troops for World War II. Many of the recruits were convinced that these demands were developed as an aggravation and torture. However, every moment of the intensive combat training was designed to build a disciplined team. Its dedicated mission was to effectively function regardless of the intense and complicated problems of army deployment.

The men were also obsessed with thoughts of individual concern, "How will I do? Will I die? Will I be brave? Will I come back in one piece?"

"Fort Bragg Meets Urban"

**2nd Lt. Matt Urban
Platooon Leader Company "D"
2nd Battalion - 60th Infantry Regiment
of the Ninth Division**

Urban also served as morale officer and founded the 'Go-Devil' Newspaper at Fort Bragg.

Instructors drilled into the recruits the encouragement that God Almighty would be there throughout their danger and whenever there is a need. Also, He will give you the deep down strength and will to do whatever must be done.

Combat training was only part of Urban's Fort Bragg experience. He also was assigned the responsibility of Regimental Morale Officer. Not only was he responsible for keeping his platoon alert and efficient but his orders were to keep up the morale of the troops. Urban did this by development of sports and recreational projects. He also started the "Go-Devil" troop newspaper and arranged for entertainment events featuring Martha Raye, Betty Grable and Harry James.

Colonel Fred deRohan, Regimental Commander, insisted that his officers maintain excellent physical condition. He ordered construction of volley ball courts and a gymnasium. Urban set up fitness and running programs for the officers. Baseball diamonds were built for enlisted personnel. Although a great proponent of sports and exercise, the Colonel was not athletic --- in fact he was a bit rotund. He admired champions and naturally gravitated to his outstanding Morale Officer. Urban

60TH REGIMENTAL BASKETBALL TEAM

9TH DIVISION CHAMPIONS
Engler, Steve
Lafferty, Phil "Red" -- Guard
Hoffman, Wm. "Buck" -- Guard
Clark, Frank -- Forward
Thomas, Raymond "Muscles" -- Guard
Lt. Matt Urban -- Coach
Schwartz, Erwin "Futchie" -- Captain
Holmes, Clarence "Reindeer" -- Forward
Held, Shirl "Whitey" -- Center
Klomp, Harry -- Forward
Group, Charlie -- "Life of the Party"
Johnson, Raymond "Whitey" -- Forward

recruited several men who had some basketball experience. He assembled the 60th Regimental Team which played against east coast and midwestern colleges.

Team members were Holmes, Schwartz, Lafferty, Group, Flannagan, Thomas, Ergler, Klomp, Johnson, Hoffman, Held, Kelly, Clark, Mgr. Erickson and Coach Urban. They were the nucleus of an exciting competitive basketball team. There were no individual stars on this team. Often they seemed to be outclassed. Frequently Urban's team came from behind to win. They put together a winning streak of twenty-five games (Six of them won in overtime) and only one loss.

Urban soon became as tough a coach as Sergeant Groves had been a combat drill instructor. Matt was deeply respected by his players and he treated everyone the same regardless of their rank or ability. His compassion developed the best ability in each player. Urban encouraged performance from average athletes with achievements that the men didn't realize was possible. Motivation was Urban's specialty. Everyone worked with him to become an overachiever. Many individuals recall Urban as having a profound influence on their lives.

As morale officer, Urban founded the "Go-Devil" newspaper; he dedicated it to the men of the 60th Infantry Division.

The army crowd loved to see Matt's team emerge from the locker room after half-time. Urban specialized in half-time talks. He challenged his men with demands of, "How can you expect to win a war if you can't even beat these guys!" He would yell, harangue, cajole. He used guilt, inspiration and appeal to logic. Instinctively Urban knew what would work with each of his players. This strategy paid off with many last minute victories!

Winning was the objective and the reward. Winning became as deep a passion for the players as it always had been for Urban.

Although Matt was successful in developing a winning basketball team, he was at his best with the boxing team. Colonel deRohan loved competition. He provided whatever boxers needed. After his Regimental Team won all of its matches, Urban came to the attention of the higher brass. The Ninth Division needed a coach to put together a winning team to compete in the all-army matches. Urban was assigned to this special duty and became the boxing coach for the Ninth Division.

Boxing was a primary attraction in the military. Regimental pride was always on the line. The excitement of a Regimental team win was comparable to that of today's Super Bowl games.

The team was called 'The Fighting Ninth'. It had overcome an outbreak of measles and went on to win the Carolina Golden Gloves Tournament. This do or die effort resulted from the inspiration of Lt. Karl Ingebretson, their coach.

Urban then took over as the boxing team coach. He imparted his personal commitment and creative tactics. The Ninth Division team became consistent winners. They reached prominence as team ohampiono in tho European Thcatrc of Opcrations.

Sergeant Earl Evans became the first of a remarkable group of boxers. He was a handsome New Yorker who was dubbed 'Golden Boy' Evans. He was a 210-lb. heavyweight boxer. His well-groomed brush-cut topped the image of a perfectly developed athlete. In his red and white embroidered Golden Gloves championship robe he looked like the model of the 'All American Boy'.

Ben Murell lacked natural ability, but burst forth with determination and desire to become a winner. He said that Matt Urban had taught him more about boxing and life than anyone he had ever met. In later years he developed a successful political career in Hudson, N.Y. Ben named his only son 'MATT' in honor of Urban.

Al Sebock was rough and tough but with a heart of gold. He resembled the professional boxer, Rocky Graziano. His friendship with Urban lasted until Al passed away in 1985. Their brotherly military attachment was sadly interrupted with Matt Urban performing his last military and personal assignment with Sebock. He met with Al's family, provided consolation and participated in the final rites of laying his dear friend to rest.

Tom O'Mara boxed as a light heavyweight. If any adjective were to describe this Philadelphia Irishmen it would be 'KING'. He would meet any one's face to face challenge with a brazen, "I can beat anyone," and he did!

Although George Albert didn't really look like a fighter, Urban sensed an inner reserve of power. He was the big man who came from the championship ranks of wrestling at Waynesburg College, Pennsylvania.

BEN MURELL

GEORGE ALBERT

Noted for his determination—desire to win—later became Little League Umpire and Professional Wrestling Referee, New York State. Later years Supervisor, Hudson, New York. Named his son "Matt" to honor his friend, Matt Urban. His standard quote, "The Army made me."

Won as Heavyweight Boxing Champion in the European Theater of war. Knocked out the former champ, Vince Kozak, in 1:58 of the first round.

Colonel deRohan issued the order that each company assign two men to coach Urban's boxing team. George Albert was summoned before the Company Commander and told of his new duty. He was listening in disbelief, "But sir, not me!" He started again, "But, sir ...!" His pleadings fell on deaf ears as the company captain led him to the door: "Yes, you! ... The company will be proud of you." Those were the Captain's parting comments.

Although George won as the leading heavyweight in the European Theatre of Operations, to this day he still insists , "I am a lover, not a fighter!"

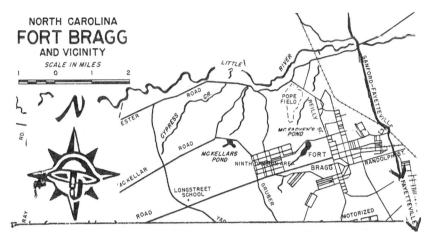

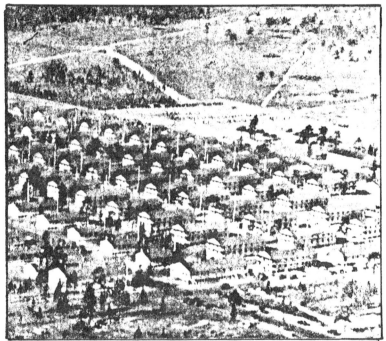

PART OF NINTH'S NEW CANTONMENT AREA

CHAPTER 3

FINAL COMBAT PREPARATIONS
Pearl Harbor!   War Declared!

While Matt Urban and his troops of the Ninth Division were receiving intensive training, Germany continued to perpetrate its 'blitzkrieg' war. To this point no nation could offer serious resistance to roaring onslaughts of Germany's airforce, ground forces or its tough Panzer (tank) Divisions. Russia seemed on the verge of collapse. The Nazi invaders were pounding Russian troops on the outskirts of Moscow. Hitler's Luftwaffe ruled the skies over the continent. Only the desperate defense of the Royal Air Force in the Battle of Britain was preserving England.

Italy entered the war as an ally of Germany. Two hundred thousand Italian troops attacked British outposts in North Africa. General Sir Archibald Wavell's famed Desert Rats counterattacked. They drove back the larger Italian force and captured

THE MATT URBAN STORY

<u>VETERANS' RECOLLECTIONS & DIARY</u>

Name _____

Rank _____

Serial # _____

_____

_____

_____

_____

_____

_____

_____

_____

_____

_____

_____

_____

_____

_____

_____

_____

_____

_____

_____

_____

_____

130,000 prisoners. The 'Desert Rats' by comparison suffered only 1,800 casualties. Hitler sent Rommel's Afrika Korps into the area. Italy attacked Greece, forcing Britain to divert troops from North Africa. The gallant British soldiers who remained were badly outnumbered. They were fighting desperate battles against impossible odds.

Japan terminated diplomatic talks with the U.S. Only two countries remained with enough resources to threaten the Axis program of world conquest. Britain was already in serious trouble and the U.S. was still unprepared! Matt Urban and thousands of other American boys had only begun combat training.

The German/Japanese strategy aimed to immobilize the United States. England could then be forced to surrender. World domination by the Axis powers would be greatly increased.

On December 7, 1941, a dreadful shock engulfed the nation. The United States Navy fleet anchored at Pearl Harbor lost seven of eight battleships. Casualties reached 3,581 ... with 2,403 Americans killed in a treacherous attack. The Arizona and Oklahoma capsized. President Roosevelt declared this 'a date which will live in infamy'. The United

States burst into action. Military preparations and production were abruptly accelerated. The real threat to United States security was unquestionably clear to the entire population.

Hitler declared war on the U.S. on December 11, 1941. The U.S. retaliated by declaring war on Germany and Italy on that same day.

FORT BRAGG:

The rambunctious army recruits of Fort Bragg froquontly opillod ovcr into ncarby towns to celebrate their passes and furloughs. Urban was in one of these nearby cities, Raleigh, N.C. on his first weekend pass. This was a welcome relief from his grueling training schedule. Matt was perched on a cushioned bar stool and sweet-talking his lovely date. He felt as if they were floating on a cloud and drifting closer and closer together. Suddenly he was snapped out of his reverie. The bartender had turned up the radio volume.

As vividly as yesterday, Urban remembers the gaiety of the lounge being instantly triggered into shocked silence by the radio bulletin. Conversations stopped.

Silence prevailed. The tense radio voice announced, "Stand by for an urgent report". Soon the solemn radio announcer tersely reported, "Sunday morning, December 7th, at 7:00 AM, Japan attacked Pearl Harbor. The U.S. fleet was heavily damaged and thousands of American casualties resulted. All military personnel are ordered back to the base immediately! Repeat: All passes are canceled. Return to your outfits!"

The radio message continued. However, it was now drowned out by the clamor of the crowd. Spasmodic cries of shock were blurred by murmurs of dismay. "Unbelievable! It can't be!" People embraced. Shocked expressions now softened. People were seeing each other as close friends.

As never before, the dance band burst into a medley of military songs. "Over There", "Anchors Aweigh", The Marine Hymn --- "From the Halls of Montezuma" --- a hundred voices joined in. Emotions were building with pride and fierce determination. An exceptional inspiration and awareness moved everyone. Throughout the nation people experienced the intensity of this moment. It would live in their memories forever.

MC FADYEN'S POND

This was the site for training army troops how to land on unfriendly shores. Mock-ups and a landing net platform were built. Bewildered G.I.s found this type of warfare training required a skill with much practice. Falling in the water was easy. The 60th Combat Team emerged as victors in eighteen events on Army Day, 1942. One requirement was swimming with full equipment.

URBAN TIMING SWIMMERS

- - - - - - - - -

Troop deployment was now certain. The pressure of combat training was greatly intensified at Fort Bragg. Rigorous field problems were devised. On April 10th, 1942, orders from the Ninth Division Headquarters assigned 2nd Lieutenant Matt Urban and Lieutenant Bill Goodman to another special duty mission. Matt became Chief Swimming Instructor for the Regiment. He and Goodman were responsible to train 4,500 men for waterborne invasion of hostile beaches.

First Urban had to determine how his troops 'took to water'. Each man had to be able to 'get along' in the water. They had only this summer to learn. Later they would be coming ashore carrying packs, weapons, and ammunition, while being under fire from enemy land fortifications. McFadyen's Pond at Fort Bragg was equipped with a platform and landing-net. This became the setting for undertaking the critically important aquatic training.

Most men passed the swim test: swimming, sidestroking or paddling the required sixty feet. Hundreds of others in the 'learn to swim group' were first-time swimmers. Many of the young men had

On May 22, 1942, Secretary of War Stimson visited the 9th Division. He viewed amphibious landing demonstrations at much used McFadyen's Pond. He wrote to Major General R.E.D. Hoyle, "It was a source of gratification to me to see the excellent condition of your men and their training, and to see how much progress they have made since my last inspection of Fort Bragg over a year ago."

never been in deep water. A few were totally obsessed by the fear of drowning.

Mutual rewards resulted when the few remaining reached the 'not frightened of water' stage. Proudly these men were able to paddle five to ten yards to reach the shallow depth of the pond. Urban's knowledge of individual ability became more accurate as the reality of combat neared. The amphibious training saved many lives during beachhead invasions that followed.

Army Day in 1942 was celebrated with a competitive tournament in amphibious exhibitions. The 60th emerged victorious in the eighteen-event contest. One event included swimming with full equipment. Urban recognized that much of the credit for the excellent progress was due to the efforts of Lieutenant Goodman. In their summer months working together, Urban discovered this young Lieutenant possessed a rare combination of ability and character. Lt. Matt Urban admired those essential qualities of leadership.

As their assignment neared completion, Urban noticed that Goodman seemed to be burdened by a personal problem. One evening at the Officers' Club Urban inquired about it.

"Well, Lieutenant, I do have a problem. I'd like to talk about it, and get it off my chest."

"Goodman, I'm here to help if I can," Urban volunteered.

"I'm from Portland, Oregon, and back home there's this girl..."

Urban was sympathetic. Hundreds of military men faced the same dilemma. Each person had the same thought, "What if I don't come back at all?"

"Her name is Betty Cummins. She is my childhood sweetheart and lives next door to my parents. We have been together as long as I can remember. I feel as if I deserted her. When I enlisted, she cried like a baby. She begged me to marry her and bring her along, even if only for a few days."

"How old is she?"

"She's eighteen."

"What do you want to do?"

"I want to marry her. But I've got nothing to offer her -
- no certain future. (The sincerity in Lt. Goodman's
plea touched Urban). I don't want to face death
before I've even had a chance to live life. I love this
girl. It's so hard to know what to do, but I don't know
what's going to happen to me!"

"She's probably considered that." Urban responded.
"You are both adults. Do what you want to do."

"Yeah! That's what I hoped you would say."
Goodman was already on his way to the wall phone.
"Thanks, Urban!"

A few days later Urban drove Goodman and his
bride-to-be to the Justice of the Peace in Dillon,
South Carolina. The ceremony was simple. The
kindly judge and his smiling wife seemed to
understand perfectly. He had married many of the
new soldiers since the opening of Fort Bragg. The
happy faces of the newlywed Goodmans was a
pleasure for Urban. He was so proud that he loaned
his new tan convertible to the newlyweds for their
honeymoon.

It was one happy soldier who returned to camp the following Monday! "That's the nicest thing anybody ever did for me, Urban. I'll never forget it."

"Look after him for me," Betty pleaded in tears as she left on the long trip back home to Oregon.

"I will," Matt assured her. He could not have known then the terrible confusion of battle ... or what fate would prove to be.

CHAPTER 4

ATLANTIC CROSSING
"Operation Torch" -- *Eisenhower - Patton*

As Lt. Urban and the Ninth Division prepared to depart Fort Bragg for Norfolk, Virginia ... Hitler's German Field Marshal, Erwin Rommel, and his inspired Afrika Korps were pounding the British Eighth Army in North Africa. Seizing the Suez Canal would give Hitler clear access to the oil fields of Iran, Iraq, and Saudi Arabia. This would enable a link-up of Germany and Japan at Calcutta or Bombay, India. Russia would be encircled and Axis troops positioned at the 'jugulars' of both China and Australia. A combination of unlimited oil reserves, control over most of the world's population on three inter-connected continents, rocket warfare, and the potential of atomic weaponry would make the Axis powers far more dangerous ... perhaps invincible.

President Franklin D. Roosevelt conferred with British Prime Minister, Winston Churchill, in late December

D-DAY ... NORTH AFRICA

"Operation Torch"

The Allied Team

Approximately 107,000 men comprised the invasion forces under Lt. General (General) Dwight D. Eisenhower. They were the

Western Task Force (Major General George S. Patton, Jr.)

    47th and 60th Regimental Combat Teams (Ninth Infantry Division)

    2nd Armored Division (one combat command and one armored battalion)

Central Task Force (Major General Lloyd Fredendall)

    1st Infantry Division

    Combat Command B, 1st Armored Division

    1st Ranger Battalion

    Corps Troops

Eastern Task Force (Major General C. W. Ryder, until after landings)

    39th Regimental Combat Team (Ninth Infantry Division)

    168th Regimental Combat Team (34th Infantry Division)

    1st and 6th Battalions, *Commandos* (American and British troops)

    11th and 36th Regimental Groups (British 78th Infantry Division)

There never was an undertaking such as *Torch* in the manuals or military textbooks of the world. The planning originated with the Combined Chiefs of Staff of America and Britain.

Like every other major battle of World War II, the North African landings were not a victory of any single branch of service; each arm depended upon its comrades in uniform and upon the productive capacity of the home front. Modern warfare is successful only so long as all links in its complex chain are strong. Seldom was the fact evidenced more than by the invasion known as *OperationTorch*.

of 1941. They were anxious to cut off the Mediterranean and the Suez Canal to separate the Atlantic and Pacific wars. Both decided to strike first at North Africa. Originally called Operation Gymnast, this unexpected approach was designed to present a second front. The goal was to stop Rommel's advance and relieve pressure on the British. Attacking the French Foreign Legion stationed in Africa should (they thought) encourage the Vichy 'Free' French to join the Allies and provide fighting experience for the newly-trained American soldiers.

Army Chief of Staff, General George Marshall, finalized plans for American forces to land at Safi, Port Lyautey, and other points along the coast of Africa. The invasion was officially code named 'Operation Torch'. In October 1942, over 107,000 men set sail on 850 ships. The armada made a 3,000 mile zigzag journey across the submarine infested Atlantic.

The 'Torch' invasion force was under the command of General Dwight Eisenhower. The Western Task Force led by General George Patton, Jr., consisted of the 47th and 60th Combat Teams of the 9th Division and the 2nd Armored Division. The Central Task Force led by Major General Lloyd Fredendall

U.S. Army Troop Transport
Typical Below Deck Quarters

and
Topside Deck Space Is Also Crowded

Urban's ship, The Florence Nightingale, was certainly no exception to the need for utilizing every inch of available space.

consisted of the 1st Infantry Division, Combat Command B, 1st Armored Division, 1st Ranger Battalion, and Corps Troops. The Eastern Task Force led by Major General C. W Ryder consisted of the 39th Regimental Combat Team of the 9th Division, 168th Regimental Combat Team of the 34th Infantry Division, 1st and 6th Battalions, Commandos (American and British) and 11th and 36th Regimental Groups of the British 78th Infantry Division.

Orders placing the Ninth Division on alert, made the troops fully appreciate the U.S. Military with persistence in details for their combat preparations. The 9th Division had been brought to a 'razor's edge' sharpness of combat ability. However, personal thoughts and emotions were in turmoil. In these moments, thousands of men hashed over and over:

"Where are we being taken? "

"If it's 'face to face' in war, will I die, will I ever return home?"

- - - - - - - - -

Several ships being boarded from one pier created a mass of organized confusion. In excited farewells

VETERANS' RECOLLECTIONS & DIARY

among the soldiers, Urban was caught in the middle. His job as Coach and Recreation Officer made him well-known and liked by the GI's from many Battalions. He was hailed by his troops marching past him in columns and also by well wishers from other infantry units. Urban was mobbed or slapped on the shoulder by many with comments of affection not customary to military protocol.

Comments by one soldier may not have set well with an Airforce Colonel waiting impatiently while viewing this action from the ship's deck. The heavily laden infantryman passer-by grumbled loudly to Urban, "Where the hell are you going, Lieutenant? You belong with us and not on that crumby old tub with those flyboys!" That comment may have put the final nail in Urban's coffin.

Prematurely, the order was given to raise the gang plank. Matt leaped three feet over water and hung on the edge of the rising walkway. In no way would Urban miss his assigned ship and be left dockside!

- - - - - - - - -

Anchors Aweigh! Under limited secrecy, this was the troops only send off ... No bands, no public 'Bon

Voyage' or well-wishing relatives to spur them on their trip to the unknown --- WAR. Even so, the exciting atmosphere and spirits of the men appeared to be at a somewhat high pitch. After all, for many of the young soldiers it had brought up illusions of their boyhood days of 'cops and robbers' ..... a challenge, an adventure into the unknown.

Their ship, the Florence Nightingale, slipped quietly from its harbor at Hampton Roads, Virginia, into a calm ocean. On that historical day of October 24, 1942, ostensibly headed for Great Britain ....

Not until the next morning were the 'voyagers' able to unwind and to comprehend the reality of their situation as their minds and tongues 'opened up'. Until this moment war had been sort of a dreamy nightmare. It was something to train for. It was something seen in the newsreels or read about in books and local newspapers. Reality had suddenly sunk in.

A loud "Hey, you guys! Do you realize that they are shipping us out to war --- chances are to get killed --- too!" penetrated above the shuffle of the A.M. chow line. The outburst triggered rumors and fears that spread like wildfire. The menaces of the unseen forces of war were now making everyone apprehensive ... to say the least! Anxiety made some of the troops frantic. Anger seemed to create a chaos.

Crowded decks resounded with G.I. complaints: "We are being shuffled about like a herd of 'cattle'. They are taking us to slaughter!" These expressions of worries were typical. They are to be expected under the stress of war.

Many wondered at their unseen commanders, sending them to God knows where!

Complaints and expressions continued ---

"Nobody but nobody seems to know where we are headed! I hope they know what they are doing! Heaven help us!"

On board the troopship, Florence Nightingale, Lt. Urban had his own problems. He inwardly fumed, struggling to keep his composure. On temporary special duty as the regimental boxing coach, Urban had been separated from his combat unit! The sudden mobilization would force him to be transported with remnants of manpower from various branches of the service. These included observers, engineers and supply officers. Air Force maintenance personnel formed the bulk of the troops aboard the transport.

Urban felt at odds not being with his own troops and not with his own 'breed', the Infantry Men! He envisioned this as a ship of outcasts. He was willing to conform 100% in order to rejoin his men. Urban's situation worsened as he ran into problems with the officer in charge. This portly Air Force Colonel took an immediate dislike to Urban.

Matt wondered why he was the target of this newly found dislike by the Colonel. Could it be that his 'boarding delay' had ignited the Colonel's wrath? --- Could it be due to Urban's obvious familiarity with the departing troops?

There was little physical training on board the overcrowded ship. There was no sizable open spot for recreation. Calisthenics were not ample. After three days at sea, Urban marked off a 20' X 20' boxing ring on the deck of the ship's bow. This was an imaginary boxing ring. It was 'roped off' by a front row of squatting G.I. spectators. Unorganized boxing bouts sprang up --- by invitation or by challenge!

A shouted "Who's next?" by the previous winner strictly determined the boxing card. A couple of bouts had challengers, "Stay three rounds in the ring, and you win $100.00!" These scraps were more for honor, even though side bets sparked the competition. After two short bouts with nearly fatal results, "Who's next?" drew no response.

The climax of the bouts was the appearance of the next performer, Al Sebock. He was 170 lbs of tough muscle. As former Chicago bar owner, he had worked as his own bouncer. Al had boxed professionally. He bore a strong resemblance to Rocky Graziano. As if just uncaged, Sebock was hyper, leaping and gesturing at the encircling crowd of GI's shouting, "C'mon, you suckers! One at a time. You yella bellies!"

All onlookers froze, each feared that any slight movement might provoke the 'gorilla', Al, to make him his next victim. No further volunteers were to be had. The wait lengthened. The silence grew unbearable. Onlookers hoped for a declaration of "The show is over". Each felt, "Hey, let me get out of here!" In a flash all settled down in the excitement of a fight plan that was hatched by Sebock himself.

"I want an Officer!" he bellowed. "Let's see what you 'shavetails' are made of!"

Sebock vs. an Officer was a match that the enlisted men would enjoy. Improbable, everyone thought, an enlisted man fighting an officer! Each soldier felt that seeing this match would be worth all the money in the world.

Sebock firmly planted his heels on the deck's surface and braced himself. Looking up defiantly so he could signal the upper front deck of onlooking officers, he pointed directly at Lt. Urban. He bellowed, "Hey! You punk Lieutenant. Yeah, you in the peanut balcony. I dare you. Show us how gutless you officers are!"

Go! Go! Go! came the shouts of GI's. Confronted by this unforeseen crisis, Urban's mind was quickly trying to decide what to do. "Should I brawl with this obsessed enlisted man? Should I go against the creed: An 'Officer and a Gentleman'?"

On the main deck over a thousand milling troops swayed to and fro. They were barking an unbroken chant: "Go! Go! Go! Yeah! Yeah! Yeah! Go! Go! Go!"

The reverberating chants 'got to' Urban. Subconsciously he was forced into unexpected movement. Before he could stop himself, he was heading down the ladder to the deck.

A total silence resulted as Urban, peeling off his shirt, stood eye-to-eye before Sebock. A blast of cheers rocked the arena as the military bout every GI dreams about was soon to begin --- an enlisted man knocking the 'gentleman' out of an Officer!

Urban and Sebock had both stripped to the waist as the military bout of the century began. Sebock ranted out of control in the excitement of this opportunity of a life-time. He plunged in, snarling, "You stinkin' officer; I'll murder you!"

Urban's controlled style puzzled Sebock with his wild round-house, haymaker punches. Sebock had met his equal. Urban had been trained never to back off. In early training days Coach Allie Wolfe put barriers behind Matt to keep him advancing. Matt took some powerful punches. Every Sebock blow was met with Urban's stinging counterpunch as he jabbed back at his over- eager opponent.

URBAN'S ORIGINAL DIARY PAGES

These copies from Urban's original diary, written during the trip from the United States to the invasion of North Africa, confirm the facts of the boxing challenge from an enlisted man (Sebock) to an officer.

MATTY'S
TRIP
OCT. 13 - Nov. 6
1942

FRI. 6 TROOPS HAD
OCT. 30 BOXING BOUTS ON
DECK - I WAS STAND-
ING ON UPPER BRIDGE
WITH THE OFFICERS -
WATCHING THE BOUTS
TOWARDS THE END THEY
STARTED YELLING FOR
ME TO PUT ON A BOUT
WITH SOME ARMY OR
NAVY OFFICER - ALL
REFUSED - SO THEY PUT
A GOLDEN GLOVE HVY -
WEIGHT AGAINST ME
HAD LOT OF FUN - FLOORED
HIM TWICE AND GAVE
HIM A BLACK-EYE -

DID NOT MARK ME - ONLY
HIT ME ONCE IN THE
HEAD - THEN THE 3RD
ROUND I FOUGHT A
LITTLE PROFESSIONAL
FIGHTER - HE WAS
SMALLER THAN I WAS.
(155 LBS) SO I HAD A
LOT OF FUN - MAKING
HIM - MISS ME - AND
JABBING HIM LIGHTLY
AS HIS SWINGS MISSED
ME - MADE A VERY
GOOD IMPRESSION -
STUDIED MY MAPS - AND
READ

For three rounds they slugged it out, neither man giving way. The crowd went wild with every hit. The match ended, both men satisfied, both felt like winners in the exhibition. The decision of a 'draw' was acceptable, pleasing everyone.

Urban and Sebock hugged in mutual admiration. Eye-to-eye, Sebock remarked, "Hey, Lieutenant, you're some guy! You've got my respect!"

Sebock had always openly raved about his obsessive hatred of officers. From that moment, however, he would own up to the fact that maybe there were many good ones after all.

The increased attention and admiration of Urban from troops aboard ship did not set well with Col. Stevens, the Commanding Officer. Combat troops often operated less formally than other branches. Colonel Stevens expected the formality associated with the traditional military hierarchy. Now he seemed determined to state his case by making examples of the two rough and ready soldiers who obviously didn't know their place. Nothing they had done was outside of regulations. Their indomitable confidence seemed to make the Colonel's stomach knot up. They showed no fear of his rank or authority, and that would have to be changed.

"You, Urban, will take over the galley," barked the Colonel. "You and your soldier here are going to do what you are best at. You've been hiding in the recreation branch long enough. I'm on to you and your avoidance of real combat training. When we get to our destination, I will see to it that you face enemy fire immediately."

"Thank you, Colonel, Sir," responded Urban. "I am combat-trained, Sir, and that is where I belong. Appreciate it, Sir."

"What kind of fool do you think I am?" shot back Colonel Stevens. "Your bravado doesn't impress me, Lieutenant. Before you set foot on solid ground again, we will see what makes you tick. Now get below and prepare for the men to chow down. The real men on this ship need food."

As they climbed down the narrow ladders to the galley, Sebock asked quizzically, "Why don't you level him? One punch and his body would be in sick bay for the rest of this trip. I could never stand officers anyway ... no offense, Lieutenant. I suppose spending time in a kitchen is how you win a war, huh? I don't know a pot from a pan. People always did this work for me in Chicago. How did I go from owning night clubs to cooking slop for a bunch of misfits? That's the U.S military for you!" Sebock complained bitterly. "And where are the broads? Listen, Lieutenant, when we get back to Chicago, I'll show you some action like you never saw in any Ivy League College. If this was my turf that turkey of a Colonel would be flat on his back ... unconscious with his 'stuffed-shirt' attitude."

Men were crowded almost shoulder to shoulder on deck. The galley was jammed with disgruntled men peeling potatoes and carrying huge shiny pots to and from the cooking fire. The Florence Nightingale was an old ship. The equipment was insufficient. Urban reorganized work details so 2,500 men on board could chow down in three shifts with two meals per day. It was necessary to start before 0600 to have the first meal ready for the chow line at 0700. By the time the line ended and mess number two was prepared, it was 1400. With completion by 2000 it was a hurried push to wrap up the cleaning and catch a few hours sleep. Then the whole procedure started again.

Although he saw very little of the ocean, Urban was thankful that his duties mostly kept him out of sight of Colonel Stevens. Occasionally the Colonel would come into the kitchen just to give Matt a hard time. Insults seemed to bounce off the determined young lieutenant as the wills of the two men struggled: one to provoke, the other to maintain dignity.

For Lt. Urban it was three seemingly endless weeks (October 18 - November 8) that passed before the armada dropped anchor. The officers were summoned into the stateroom for instructions. Colonel Stevens opened a sealed document inscribed: "To be opened upon reaching destination". Taking a deep breath, the Colonel methodically read: "You are off the coast of North Africa!" The armada had gathered its forces together near Port Lyautey, French Morocco. An assault would be launched on the French-held stronghold tomorrow. The Kasba fortress and inland airfield were the prime objectives. They would be hit by a combined force led by the 60th Infantry.

Urban's heart leapt. His company would be the first to land! Then his demeanor darkened as Colonel Stevens continued: "All personnel aboard this ship will remain on board until the objective has been secured." The Morale and Special Services Officer, Lt. Urban, he said, would be needed later to organize entertainment for the fighting troops.

Urban looked over at Sebock, and a silent agreement passed between them. They came to fight a war, and they would not be stand-bys while their buddies fought and suffered. One way or another they would land the next morning!

CHAPTER 5

INVASION OF AFRICA
It's Kill Or Be Killed -- Battle For Survival

In the annals of war, no military undertaking had ever been mounted on the scale of 'Torch'. The massive armada carried history's largest amphibious strike force. It hit the enemy target across 3000 miles of submarine-infested ocean. The ships successfully delivered its deadly cargo of munitions and military manpower.

Extraordinary secrecy had kept Lt. Matt Urban and other American soldiers from knowing their destination. Secret sailing plans and courses prevented the Axis powers from intercepting the convoy or countering its threat. Based on false rumors, Hitler's Luftwaffe had sent every available plane to airfields in Sicily and southern Italy. False rumors had been purposefully spread that a large troop movement would be occurring through 'bomb alley' in the Mediterranean.

A 450 mile frontal invasion of North Africa was successfully made by the Western, Central and Eastern Task Forces. The Germans had expected the landings to be made at the Mediterranean Island of Malta. Allies had spread that rumor. Goering's Luftwaffe was fooled. He shifted his Air Force to Sicily and Southern Italy and Sardinia, intending to smash the fleet in the narrow Straits between Italy and North Africa. That area was known as "Bomb Alley".

The ships, equipment, and men in that 1942 voyage represented the fruits of a massive United States mobilization effort. Two oceans had afforded America the protection and time to mobilize without direct enemy assault on either coast. Industrial production in the States was finally pulling out of a decade of sluggishness.

We pumped billions of dollars into weapons, supplies and economic aid to accelerate the war production effort.

The armada enroute to Africa was made up of nine columns of troop transports, fuel tankers and cargo vessels. They steamed across hazardous seas with a protective ring of more than forty destroyers to provide close quarters security. Battleships flanked and led this seaborne parade of power. The combined task force including its screening protection blanketed an ocean area of sixty square miles.

Some miles astern were the carriers and their escort vessels. Overhead patrols of carrier-based aircraft flew anti-submarine watch. A steady 14 knots pace was maintained. There was a zigzagging pattern to the movement across the seas. This course and

Operation Torch invasion forces faced the possibility of resistance by an informed enemy and possible annihilation from land-based aircraft. General George C. Marshall, American Chief of Staff summarized the invasion hazards in his report to the Secretary of War:

"The singular relationship existing between the Vichy Government and Berlin, and with the French provinces in North Africa, together with the differences of religion and race and the deep-rooted hatreds of the heterogeneous populations of Algiers and Morocco, imposed a political problem of maximum complexity on General Eisenhower. At the moment his energies and direction had to be concentrated on the successful penetration of an 800-mile coastline and a vast hinterland by a force of but 107,000 men. To further complicate the situation he must be on guard against the possibility of an Axis stroke through Spain to sever our communications through the Straits of Gibraltar and interrupt by aerial bombardment the single railroad line from Casablanca through Fez to Oran."

Operation torch was coded as <u>top secret.</u> Only a select group knew the full plan. The 850 ship convoy, its 107,000 military men, hundreds of thousands of supply items, were assembled in only <u>four</u> months.

pattern was maintained day and night as the armada forged ahead.

A changing course on October 28th suggested to any enemy U-boat that Dakar, Africa would be the likely objective. Fueling took place on October 30th and 31st. On November 2nd a course change was made to the Northeast as though bound for the Straits of Gibralter.

At dawn on November 7th Admiral Hewitt ordered the armada to split up enroute to the target areas. The invasion troops were divided into three ground forces. The Western Task Force (under General Patton); the Center Task Force (under General Fredendall); and the Eastern Task Force (under General Ryder).

The Western Force was to land near Casablanca, Safi, and Port Lyautey; the Center close to Oran, and the Eastern at Algiers.

The Western Force came from the United States, under U.S. naval command (Rear-Admiral Hewitt, U.S.N.); the Center and Eastern from Britain, under the Royal Navy (Commodore Troubridge and Vice-Admiral Burrough, respectively). The entire

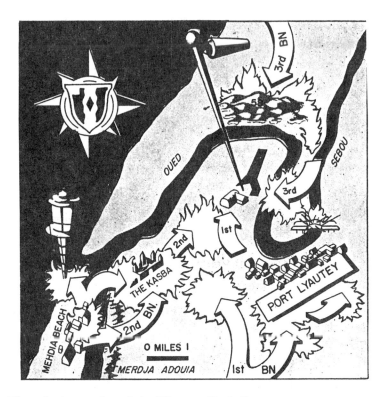

The mission assigned the Western Task Force was:

Attack western Morocco; seize and secure the port of Casablanca as a base for future operations to the north and northeast; eliminate or cripple the enemy air force and secure by dark of D-Day at least one airfield as a base for land-based planes.

To carry out these orders General Patton desired to effect landings and capture three primary objectives -- Safi, Port Lyautey and Fedala.

operation was named 'TORCH' under the Supreme Command of Allied Forces Commander-in-Chief, Lt. General Dwight D. Eisenhower, United States Army.

One prime objective of the Moroccan invasion was the airfield at Port Lyautey. Here was the only all-weather concrete landing strip in northwestern Africa. As the map shows, the airport lies in a loop of the winding Wadi Sebou River - The town lay one and a half miles upstream. At the rivermouth is the small village, Mehdia. Above the village (on high ground) is an old Portuguese fort, the Kasba. A navigation barrier boom had been positioned across the river near this point. The ancient walled citadel was held by the French Foreign Legion. These famous mercenary troops were now in the service of the Vichy French government. Here were battle-wise soldiers of many nationalities. Their reputation of courage and experience made them a dangerous foe.

Prior to sunrise John Ryan of Division Headquarters was given the task of swimming to the landing beach. Matt Urban shares this first-hand account as told to him by John Ryan:

Captain John Ryan, U.S.Army

The University of Iowa swim champions winner played the key role in placing a beaconlight on the North Africa invasion beach. Later Captain Ryan served as an Aide to General Eddy. He participated in eight campaigns of the 9th Division victories leading to surrender of German forces. Ryan received many U.S. Service Awards and the Russian Decoration for Valor at Bitterfeil, Germany. (Photo by Russian Army photographer).

"As a Staff Sergeant I had been a member of the U.S. Military Intelligence headquartered in Belfast, Northern Ireland since January, 1942.

In October, 1942, I was transferred to London and volunteered to take part in our landings in North Africa. I went by boat to Gibraltar, and boarded a British submarine. That took me to the Coast of Morocco. There I boarded a British 'Corvette' in very rough seas. As a member of the University of Iowa swimming team, I was an excellent swimmer and could speak French. For these reasons I was selected to swim ashore towing a beacon to be lighted to identify the invasion landing site. The swim took almost an hour. About fifty feet of line was attached to the beacon and tied to a shoulder harness and headband. This had enabled me to swim the breaststroke from ship to shore. Near the beach I could hear the surf. This pounded me so hard that I became unconscious for a time and did not meet an Anti-Vichy group of Frenchmen waiting to rendezvous with me. Finally I managed to set up the beacon and positioned it so the light would only shine seaward. With the target of the beach clearly identified with the beacon, the landing could now begin. With this mission accomplished, I began a difficult swim to the ships offshore. An L.C.T. finally spotted me and pulled me from the ocean. At that time I was exhausted, cold and in great danger of drowning.

Later I returned to the beach in a L.C.T. which also carried a Colonel Craw and Major Hamilton in a Jeep. They flew a big American flag, a French flag, and a large white flag of neutrality in the center. Despite this neutral approach, French Foreign Legion troops fired directly on the Jeep as it crossed the landing area. Col. Craw and his driver were killed; Major Hamilton wounded.

I was in the following Jeep with Sergeant William Forbes (who had also been at the University of Iowa). We opened fire on the French position with a 50 caliber machine gun mounted on our Jeep."

Meanwhile the full force of the invasion battle erupted. Urban's story continues:

The port area terrain is generally unfavorable for tank warfare. In many places vehicles are confined to roads. In some of the rugged mountain areas, even the Jeeps could not be driven.

Ammunition and supplies would have to be carried on muleback .... Other problems that had to be dealt with: the late fall heavy rains and comparatively cold weather, (averaging 50 to 54 degrees Fahrenheit along the coast) and near-freezing temperatures with snow and frost in the higher country. (Much of mountainous Algeria is between 2,000 and 5,000 feet elevation.)

During the rainy season, dry and almost-dry water courses become raging torrents. In some areas the low-lying country turns into seas of vehicles miring in mud!

The first soldiers climbed down landing nets on the sides of their ships and boarded their landing craft.

To aid identification, each soldier was wearing a small replica of the American flag on the left sleeve of his uniform. It was located just below the official Octofoil insignia of the 9th Division.

At 0430 hours they rapidly headed for shore.

The Mehdia-Port Lyautey Beaches had been targeted as Blue-Green-Red. The First, Second and

L.C.P. (R) Landing Craft, Personnel

U.S. Army troops leave the hinged ramp of the L.C.P. The craft dropped ramps in shallow water, so troops could wade ashore. A few stranded off shore and dropped troops in deep water. Infantrymen had to swim with full packs, drop equipment or drown.

Third Battalions of the 60th Infantry Division plowed through the dark waters to their target.

Hundreds of landing craft formed a silhouette of bumping, grotesquely-camouflaged scows. Each craft had a protective front ramp. These operated much like a drawbridge spanning a castle moat. The landing craft raced toward shore. Each spouted spray over the waves in a seemingly endless line.

From his vantage point aboard the Florence Nightingale, Urban had a panoramic view. He said this flotilla of landing craft making the bizarre frontal attack was envisioned as comparable to the 'Charge of the Light Brigade'. Each landing craft had taken to sea with 'Old Glory' defiantly waving in the breeze. It was proudly mounted on a stern mast of each invasion barge.

Forty or fifty GIs were crouched on the floor of the shallow, water-drenched interior of each bobbing landing barge. Their faces were etched with fear, yet they showed a great determination! They were embarked and bravely moving forward into the unknown. Each wondered what, where and how the action would occur. There was a strange silence which was broken with the battering sounds of water and the flapping sounds from a strong wind. These cold crowded human bodies huddled together. Equipment and men were banging against each other. Each combatant carried two full canteens of water and a one-day ration of food. Armament varied from that of an M-1 rifle or a Springfield rifle to those of Thompson machine guns. The soldiers also carried grenades, ammunition, entrenching tools, combat knives, bayonets, the new M-1 helmets and the ever-present but burdensome gas masks. Most soldiers carried a good-luck charm with personal meaning.

Crowded together like sheep, the soldiers of the 60th Regiment recoiled from thinking of the hideous possibilities lurking on shore. At this state they felt like warfare robots programmed for the attack. They were powered by patriotism, their belief in America, her people, and by their temporary loss of peace and dignity. Winning the invasion battle and survival were the top priorities for each soldier of Operation 'Torch', the name to identify the invasion of the African Seacoast.

Franco-Vichy relationships were in limbo. Briefings had brought our troops little comfort ... one day informed that the French are allies ... the next day, the enemy! Americans were bewildered by the deadly order facing them: "Hold your fire until you're fired upon." No one knew what to expect .... until 'they' fired the first shot! Resulting casualties for the U.S. forces would be a bitter result from this vexing order.

French searchlights picked up one of the boats. A red warning flare burst over the shoreline, revealing the mouth of the Oued Sebou and the adjacent lighthouse. Beyond that, barely visible to the tense GI's, the Kasba, a massive French fort, protruded over the landscape. To the north, less than four miles above the City of Port Lyautey, lay the airfield. Capturing this airport was the main objective for this 60th Regiment American assault force.

A series of open, rolling sand dunes leading to the well-defended Kasba presented the biggest obstacle. Success of the entire operation hinged on the fall of the old citadel. Although neophytes in battle, the 'Go-Devils' plunged enmasse into what seemed the jaws of hell. A devastating baptism of firepower burst all around the invasion force.

A sinister, luminous galaxy --- a blanket of fire, erupted overhead as the thundering roar of the coastal batteries cut loose on the warships. Within moments the destroyer, Roe, and the Battleship, Texas, opened up with their cannon shells blasting back. The long-range French artillery was soon silenced. Urban was astonished at the power and noise of the big guns. It sounded as if the entire battleship had been flung into the air. The other warships joined in with a systematic barrage on the shoreline, creating a constant din of horrible percussion.

To the novice soldiers, shivering in fear, the tumult was their first mind-shattering taste of mighty naval gunfire. The blast of each shot fired sent tremors through their bodies. Some men puked, and everyone thought they would lose their minds. Urban felt powerless. What could one insignificant man among thousands do against such a force? Lt. Urban knew he would have to try.

Many of the landing boats were having trouble with the currents offshore. Several were forced to run aground some distance from the appointed area. A large number of men had to scramble ashore as far as a mile away before they could assault the Kasba.

The first man to hit the beach at the target area was Major John H. Dilley of the 2nd Battalion. He arrived at 0540 hour. For a brief time there was no resistance. Then a French plane appeared 'out of nowhere', swooping low over the beach. It began to strafe our precarious beach-head positions.

Several men were hit immediately. The pilot circled around to dive-bomb our exposed troops. Months of combat training were pent up in these men who had never fired their rifles at a live target. Hundreds of M-1's and Thompson submachine guns pointed toward the sky as frustrated GI's vented their feelings in the direction of the airplane.

A volley of shots hit the plane. Hundreds of husky voices whooped and hollered as the aircraft careened out of control into the sea. The first plane was downed! Wow Whee! Like a bunch of kids they yelled as if they had won the war right then. The crash of the plane into the water acted as a 'shot in the arm' instantly building up the confidence of our embattled GI's.

Beach-heads soon were exposed to a tremendous cacophony of sounds, a thousand angry thunderstorms, unleashed from out of the predawn

URBAN & SEBOCK JUMP SHIP
Col. Stevens raged over the ship's rail: "Lt. Urban, I will see that you are court-martialled."
"But Colonel, Sir, I belong with my troops," shouted Urban in reply.

darkness. Explosions rocked the invasion areas. Sand and water flew in every direction from the impact of the French artillery shell explosions. Men scattered; the first of the attackers vanished into the dim light to carry out their orders.

- - - - - - - -

Sounds of heavy guns and the clatter of small arms fire could be heard clearly below the decks; Urban and Sebock chafed in agitation. Reports kept arriving that enemy resistance was fierce and American casualties were high. Finally the two men could bear it no longer. They grabbed their rifles and draping themselves bandoleer fashion with ammunition and grenades, Urban and Sebock scrambled down nets on the side of the ship to a raft which they had prepared.

As the raft was lowered into choppy water, they heard shouts above them. The men on board the Florence Nightingale had just realized what was happening. Sebock began to row. Urban glanced up through the early morning light just in time to see Colonel Stevens lean over the rail. The Colonel's face distorted with rage, screaming, "Lt. Urban, where the hell do you think you're going?"

"I belong with my troops, Colonel, Sir," Urban yelled.

"Your orders are to stay aboard ship. Get back, God damn it ... or I'll see that you're court-martialled!"

Urban waved. He and Sebock paddled for shore. Enemy artillery and mortar fire thundered down on U.S. soldiers trying to land. One big shell hit the water about 400 yards away, spewing a thin geyser of white water over two hundred feet in the air. Shrapnel gouged the sea surface at 300 yard intervals. Urban breathed a sigh of relief when the explosion died down. Smaller fountains of water signaled each impact of artillory shell explosions that laced through the landing party, and capsizing Higgins landing barges panicked Navy navigators and troops aboard.

As they neared the beach Urban saw the bodies of American soldiers sprawled in the water. Mangled corpses were scattered grotesquely on the sand's edge. A number of frightened and injured men were clinging to the particles of debris that had once been a landing craft. Others unable to jettison their packs and heavy equipment were being swept away from the beach in a strong ocean undertow ... and drowning.

Twenty to thirty of the men had already drowned. Many more were in imminent danger. Inexperienced coxswains reacted in stark terror to the enemy shellfire. They prematurely threw open ramp doors in the bow of landing craft as soon as they felt an offshore sandbar touch the bottom of the craft. Many of the soldiers dropped off the edge of a sandbar into deep water too far from shore.

Together Urban and Sebock began rescue operations. Shells exploded around them. One by one they carried the floundering GI's onto the beach placing them in shallow indentations in the sand. There was no time to give mouth-to-mouth resuscitation or first aid. Too many men needed help!

Urban and Sebock continued rescue work, oblivious to the shelling. As men needing immediate help were pulled from the water, Urban and his partner noticed the disarray and devastation around them. The 'heat' of the fighting had shifted inland a few hundred yards. Urban could see men he recognized pinned down behind sand dunes. The men were scattered around the base of massive walls of the old Kasba French fortress.

Ravaging explosions rocked the waters and unloading areas of the landing craft. It became apparent that shore guns were being directed by an observation team. They were located in a lighthouse point high above the inlet to the river waterway. The gun crews of the battleship Texas, positioned less than a mile off shore, zeroed in on the lighthouse. A direct hit from their 16 inch guns obliterated the lighthouse. Signals no longer existed from that vantage point; thus providing some respite for our 60th Regiment attack force.

When full daybreak appeared French coastal batteries began pounding the fleet again. Tho American ships were forced to pull back out of range to the open sea. Their movement left the 2nd Battalion without naval gun support to counter the enemy artillery which was hammering the approaching troops. French 75's cannons and Renault tanks were causing numerous casualties. They were also making it impossible to land our tanks and howitzers needed to assault the Kasba.

Having done all he could for the men on the beach, Urban left Sebock and began climbing the series of mounds leading to the Kasba. He ran apelike, upward to the rocky ground on the backside of the

Kasba. Matt dove for cover as enemy sniper fire began to find his range. Bullets came whirring savagely over Urban's head. Vicious shells from enemy cannons 'whanged' into the sand all round him.

Heaving and panting, Urban crouched behind a clump of rocks. He fought back the rising fear in his chest. He measured the distance to the next cover. Matt knew it would be suicide to stand up. It would be futile to try moving against the steady stream of bullets pouring toward him from the bunker. Men around him were attacking, but with little aggression in their movements. There were no heroic charges under the reality of enemy bullets. Only grim excitement mixed with fear and determination registered on the faces of these men. Urban couldn't tell what was happening. There was so much confusion all around.

Further up the hill --- by luck or fate --- Urban stumbled onto the men of his own Battalion. The first infantryman he reached was down on his knees, petrified with terror, as he stared down at the torn-up body of his fellow soldier. Trying to settle his own shock, Lt. Urban intervened. He jerked PFC Walter Grabski to his feet, repeatedly howling: "Come on!

Come on! Let's get the Hell out of here!" The other men around took heed. They followed their officer to rejoin the remainder of the platoon. Together they were criss-crossing for clumps of cover, moving inland from the open beach.

They ran Indian-style. Just as they were about to reach shallow cover, a shell detonated, throwing a swash of piercing fragments into their midst. Men fell, screaming for help.

Urban moved, trying to avoid an object which rolled against his foot. He looked --- it couldn't be! A human head!!!

Momentarily stricken, hesitating, uncontrolled courage drove him to pick up the severed head. In a glance Urban recognized the face on the decapitated head of Lt. Bill Goodman.

"No!!! " shrieked Urban. He refused to believe that it was the head of his buddy! Delirious, he nestled the head to him. Raging in passion he shrilled, "You're alive! You're alive! Bill, you're alive!!" A gleam in the eyes, his usual expression, was still there on the muddy face.

Urban frantically tried to reattach the head to its neck as thoughts of Bill's wife asking him to take care of him for her flashed through his mind. The body was warm, quivering in its last reflexive movements. Unable to accept it, Urban tried to make himself believe that his friend was alive. But he was dead!

Rage flooded his entire being like a white hot flame. He grasped Goodman's M-1 in his bloodied hands and leaped up, overwhelmed with anger. Despair bubbled over inside of him.

Urban exploded. Avenge! Revenge! Kill or be killed! The horror of war hit him. If he didn't kill, he would not survive!

Responding instinctively, Urban felt the adrenaline flush through his body. Hostility and terror gripped him simultaneously. Yelling like a madman, he tracked straight forward up the slope into open enemy fire, possessed with but one mania — destroy the enemy who was killing his men. Put an end to the slaughter!

He crouched low and sprinted past the perimeter of entrenched Americans, fearless now, after his baptism of fire. His 'hyped' movement carried him

VETERANS' RECOLLECTIONS & DIARY

into range of the perimeter defenses. As he approached the first objective his senses returned and the long months of training took effect. Do or die! Urban had become a 'war man'!

Maneuvering forward, he flung a grenade into the bunker directly ahead of him. Urban followed it with rifle fire as men behind him rose up. With one accord they followed him toward the fortress. Another of the outposts crumbled, and then another. As GI's fell, wounded and dying, the men of the 60th Infantry pressed forward toward the deadly battlement. Only complete victory would end the carnage.

Word arrived that the lighthouse area on the landpoint on the waterway flowing past the Kasba had been secured. The last of the defenders in the lighthouse area surrendered when four GI's stormed that position through barbed wire and heavy fire. Hearing their volleys of fire, troops from E and F Companies charged up the incline in support. They were met by emergence of 12 prisoners, securely in the charge of 2nd Lt. Charles Dushane, Corp. Frank Czar, PFC Theodore Bratkowitz and another private from E Company.

With the blast-damaged lighthouse captured, the Americans were able to reorganize. Now they could focus more of their frontal attack on the Kasba. They battered against its parapet. Without heavy guns and tanks it was impossible to penetrate the massive walls of the well-armed old Kasba fortress.

The only movement ahead --- was time --- Morning melded into afternoon. A hot African sun glared down on soldiers fighting and dying for a small piece of ocean frontage. Ironically, this battle area had served as a French beach resort before the war. During a pause in the frantic forward fighting, Urban gazed up into the brilliant blue sky overhead. As if waking from a nightmare, he felt the wind on his face and could see the beautiful sandy beach sloping to the sea. He was momentarily aware of the natural world, beauty coexistent with this horrible war. Urban thought: "This is the wrong place to be fighting a battle!" Matt's contemplative reverie was short-lived!

Suddenly the main gate of the Kasba swung open on its rusty hinges. The French forces counterattacked. Urban saw the now-open gates of the fort, and a Renault tank, accompanied by infantrymen, rush out. They appeared to be an invincible force. A second tank followed, and then a third. Without tanks or artillery to retaliate, the Americans were dug in, held together only by discipline of training, individual courage and brave determination.

A captured anti-tank gun was minus its breech, but that deficiency did not stop Corporal (Acting First Sergeant) Frank Czar and one of his buddies. These two 'Go-Devils' activated the anti-tank gun by slamming shells into it one at a time. Frank Czar then aimed the gun at the advancing French Renault tanks. He was aided by Lt. Charles Dushane. The shells were triggered by firing at the base of each projectile with his Tommy gun. These inventive American fighting men knocked out the first enemy tank and two that followed. This action suddenly stalled the attack. Corporal Czar miraculously survived this attack without injury. Unfortunately, Lt. Dushane died while firing the final volley from the tank gun.

Urban was aware of trenches which connected the strong points at the Kasba. He knew these had to be cleared. Matt leaped over a trench barricade shouting, "Let's go," while firing on the run. His troops advanced with him. They swept through the trench area. The French forces turned and fled to the

LT. COL. STEVEN SPRINDIS, Danbury, Conn.

Served as a Private in the Army and was stationed at Pearl Harbor during the December 7 Japanese Attack. He transferred to the Ninth Infantry Division in the invasion of North Africa.

Sprindis and Urban were known as two soldiers who would volunteer for any duty anytime no matter how hazardous. Sprindis has the distinction of receiving four Silver Stars plus many other awards as he rose through the ranks by combat promotions from Private to Lieutenant Colonel.

Urban and Lt. Col. Sprindis are shown in this 1945 photograph reviewing memoirs of their exploits with the campaigns of the Ninth Infantry Division.

protection of the Kasba fortress, leaving their dead and wounded behind.

The frenzied Americans dashed across open terrain under fire and began scaling the stone walls. Several men fell. Two GI's succeeded in reaching the top. From the ramparts, they began firing automatic weapons into the French Legionnaires.

Before the gigantic doors of the Kasba Fortress could be swung completely closed, a handful of 'E' Company's troops made a rapid attack. They were led by Lt. Steve Sprindis and included Private First Class Clarence Mohler and Private First Class John Fisher. They sprinted through the narrow opening of the door which had not completely closed. They drove the defending forces from the courtyard of the Kasba. When the enemy fire became too heavy, Sprindis and his men retreated from the fort. However, they were able to take several captured French soldiers with them as they completed their daring mission.

The veteran French defenders had sensed the will and felt the ferocity of these inexperienced Americans. The French Foreign Legionnaires were now clustered together behind their walls with a vain hope that reinforcements would arrive.

Shellfire was nearly continuous throughout the day. Americans struggled to consolidate their positions. Shock and exhaustion began to wear down both sides. Daylight ended, darkness descended.

The weary 'Go-Devils' formed their line of defense and 'dug in' for the night. Only then was Urban able to enjoy respite from what seemed to be the longest, most fiendish day of his life. He removed his heavy helmet, laid aside his canteen, and webbed ammunition belt. Numbly, rummaging through his pack, he found his knife and used it as a can opener. Urban was keenly aware of an urgent need to restore his energy. He tried to replenish himself with his first bit of food, a cold tasteless can of C rations --- 'hash'!

Urban was exhausted and drifted into sleep. He was still wearing most of his equipment. The C rations were uneaten. In his sleepy nightmare conflicting images churned in his mind: The look of his dear friend's face when he had been fatally injured, his mother and father praying at the church, voices of his hardened old drill sergeants, hazy thoughts of crumpled, crushed bodies spilling blood into the sandy earth, intrepid expressions on the faces of captured French Foreign Legionnaires, the feeling of rough water beneath his troop ship, (the Florence Nightingale), the angry Air Force Colonel. Finally a merciful blackness of deep sleep induced from physical and mental exhaustion engulfed him and temporarily blotted out the horrors of this war.

- - - - - - - - - - -

During the pitch of battle by Urban's Battalion, to the south another invasion force of Doughboys was led by Major Percy McCarley, Jr. of the First Battalion. They were occupying the low ground west of the lagoon. By noon they had an assortment of light tanks, motorcycles and cavalry for the attack by Company A. Thus began a day of tank sorties and clashes with the French Foreign Legion Cavalry. These attacks from the French were beaten back with 37MM tank guns, grenades, bazookas and a steady hail of lead from the guns of Company D.

The 692nd anti-aircraft battalion shot down two of the four French planes. This forced the remaining two to head away from the beach-head and return to their air base a few miles away.

Major McCarley's First Battalion waged a fierce and victorious battle with the First Moroccan Regiment. Through swift action and deception, they captured many truck-loads of prisoners. This led to the surrender of Port Lyautey.

To summarize the situation at the end of the first invasion day, the report would have to indicate that the day was not completely successful. It had been difficult to land supplies, because the tides were too low. Communications were inadequate, many invasion boats became beached in the heavy surf. There were high sand-dunes and scrub growth between the lagoon and the beach where the First Battalion landed. This terrain delayed the entry of light tanks and full-tracks into battle. Thus the armor of 'Goalpost' could not disembark until Monday, the 9th.

Battle notes from the French forces stated:

"Mobile groups were formed during the eight French counter-attacks which we mounted for the purpose of confining the invasion troops and reducing their beachheads. The Americans were pushed back in the Port Lyautey area and held within the limits of Mehdya. The opening bombardments and the first air battles had put 50% of our French defending aviation units out of combat."

So ended the D-Day African Invasion on November 8, 1942.

CHAPTER 6

VICTORY IN NORTH AFRICA
Heroic Actions By: Navy - Army - Air Corps

News of the invasion force 'Torch' swept across the world like wildfire. The balance of power in Africa had immediately shifted from Hitler's Nazi German grasp. Previously the only obstacle to Hitler's capture of the Suez had been the ANZACS (Australians and New Zealanders), Scotsmen, Englishmen, and British WACs holding at El Alamein. Refitted with American-supplied tanks and guns, they now held their ground. On the offensive as the 'Desert Rats', led by General Montgomery, they struck with full force against German Field Marshall Erwin Rommel. They beat back Rommel's weakened Afrika Korps, which had been forced to divert troops to resist the American invasion on November 8, 1942.

Landings at Casablanca and Oran met little resistance. American forces seized most of their

VETERANS' RECOLLECTIONS & DIARY

objectives on the first day. The feisty French Legion-naires had no love of Hitler. Nevertheless, they were determined to resist any encroachment on French sovereignty. Diplomatic efforts were initiated by General Mark Clark with Admiral F. Darlan, Commander-in-Chief of French Armed Forces in Africa, to end the fighting and create an alignment against their common enemy --- Nazi Germany. When that diplomacy failed, the 9th Division was then assigned the responsibility for a military victory.

Matt Urban and his comrades had been civilians only a few months ago. Now they were sailing ships, firing artillery, shooting machine guns, and fighting it out hand-to-hand with the French Foreign Legion! They were already demonstrating a bravery and determination that became the trademark of the Ninth Division.

November 9, 1942, dawned through 'new eyes'. Combat proven soldiers of the Ninth Infantry Division began their predawn assault preparations for another attack against the ancient Kasba Fortress.

'Foxholes' were dug among the dead to avoid a steely death. Incoming shellfire filled the air with explosives that blasted shrapnel among the American troops on the beach-head.

Staying alive seemed to be all that mattered. Everything Urban knew about normal life had disappeared. War had its own rules, but each soldier soon learned 'You had to do .... what had to be done .... in a different kind of world .... a world of terror, destruction and death.'

Through the debris of burning equipment and human bodies, the 2nd Battalion charged ahead relentlessly. Time and time again they were thrown back by firepower blasting from muzzles of French guns Failure to breach the massive Kasba Fortress walls caused American casualties to be extremely high. 'E' Company lost five of its six officers in this deadly attack.

In desperation and with great valor, Navy Commander, Robert J. Brodie, age 22, took a great risk. Nine miles up the Oubed River (past a curvature in the lagoon) was the airfield. It was the ultimate objective in this sector. Brodie's U.S. destroyer escort, Dallam, approached the rivermouth beaches carrying elements of 'I' Company. Putting his naval career on the line, Commander Brodie took the ultimate gamble. He steered his transport into the mouth of the Oubed River! Through waters so shallow that the muddy bottom 'sucked at her hull'. He brazenly maneuvered past the Kasba Fortress toward the airfield beyond. He knew the repercussions --- they could be annihilated if their ship grounded in the shallow river. They would then be 'sitting ducks' for the towering Kasba guns. Betting on the high tides, he steamed upriver. Miraculously they safely navigated the shallow Oubed. High respect for the Navy by the infantrymen resulted from this aggressive action. Brodie's daring move won instant acclaim.

French Forces in the Kasba Fortress were so busy defending, that they scarcely noticed the slow moving Navy ship steam past. This example of a courageous advance by the Navy Officer gave impetus to 'I' Company to strike the airfield with a fury. Joined by flanking attacks from the other 3rd Battalion units, they seized their objective. Only the Kasba remained unconquered.

All day long costly American assaults continued on the citadel. Local legend had proclaimed it invincible.

The complexity of troop movement and battle attacks was almost overwhelming. Hundreds of 'private' wars raged. Each man faced a different battle. There was no way to communicate happenings from one area to another. Fatigue wore at the armies.

During battle, nights are not made for sleeping. Indeed this was true as the cursed rain beat on the helmets of exhausted GI's with a steady ping ... ping ... ping. The Go-Devils were running out of supplies, and their equipment needed repair. The Battalion soldiers were cold, wet and unshaven. This miserable battle would soon end due to their continuing drive.

When many American weapons failed to operate during action, the soldiers of the 60th were instructed by Second Lt. William J. Voller how to operate captured enemy rifles. Through this action many 9th Division units could continue to fight.

At the end of the second day, the required strategy was clearly evident to Colonel de Rohan's 60th C.T.:

They would continue total effort toward capture of the Kasba fortress and then move on the airport. It was evident that the Americans had become battle-wise, and the French did not know where the American drive would strike next.

- - - - - - - - -

On the morning of November 10 the sunrise signaled an all-out attack on the stubborn fort. Most of its perimeter defenses were destroyed early in the advance. Much credit for this success must go to the blasts from two 105 Howitzers. These heavy guns were self-propelled and provided the additional fire-power the Second Battalion needed to ultimately overrun the Kasba. However, the inner fortress still held firm against the American drive.

Lt. Sprindis and Sergeant Milt Westfall took a united action. Together they carried a bazooka and ammunition to a windmill behind the Kasba on slightly higher ground. A rectangular concrete wall enclosed the windmill at about waist height. Inside the area were several dead Legionnaires. Their rotting corpses were strewn among some remains of mutilated sheep. Darkness forced Sprindis and Westfall to spend the night behind the protective wall.

Sprindis took action to discourage the possibility of their position being overtaken. He and his Sergeant moved up and down the concrete wall firing their Bazooka at the fortress doors. This created the illusion that heavy weapons were blasting from the American position. Noise of the exploding Bazooka shells made a tremendous racket as they bounced off the heavy iron doors. The ruse worked! No one attempted to assault their position.

As zero hour approached, Sprindis lobbed a shell high. He dropped it into a machine gun nest which had been set up to guard the rear entrance of the fort. He crept closer to the gate and saw that his shelling had knocked it ajar. On an impulse he dashed through the door. He fully expected a hail of bullets; fortunately, none came!

The French Legionnaires were preoccupied with action at the front gates of their fortress. They didn't notice the single American soldier enter the fort through the unfastened rear gate. Sprindis' rush carried him into the labyrinth of the Kasba. There he hid behind a rain barrel.

Suddenly bullets started flying, smashing into the rain barrel and spraying water over Lt. Sprindis. He wisely dashed out of the fort safely escaping in the hailstorm of bullets.

Outside the gate he assembled men for a concentrated attack. Their action was met by fierce resistance. A direct blast from his Bazooka broke an opening into the fortress. The American attackers ran through like a swarm of locusts, firing guns, heaving grenades while seeking any protective cover available.

The first two men through the gates were instantly knocked down by machine gun fire. Sprindis came next. He hit the ground and put a bullet through the forehead of the French machine-gunner. Within minutes, the invincible Kasba was filled with lethal action. Ninth Division men fought in deadly determination and individual silence while extinguishing the Kasba as a force of destruction.

Simultaneously with Lt. Sprindis' rear gate assault, Urban led his troops in a flanking action. They smashed the two remaining machine gun emplacements adjoining the fort. Pressure on the flanks and the inner fortress placed the Kasba in a double squeeze.

Abruptly it was over. The French dropped their weapons. A white flag was raised over the citadel. The silence was 'deafening'! The killing had stopped!

Urban was flooded with a combination of strange emotions. Exhileration — he was alive! Relief — the danger was past! Grief — a penetrating anguish for men who were dead. "If only the will and power of emotion could bring men back from the dead!" he thought. Matt knew that was only dreaming. Men don't come back from the dead! Guys who were late for reveille, men who had shared good times with him, kids who had never fired a shot at another human being before, were gone forever. They had made the supreme sacrifice for their country. They had paid the ultimate price.

Only now could Urban take in the smoldering ruins around him. His mind echoed the silence of his surroundings.

The destruction was unimaginable. The ancient Kasba lay in ruin. A stench of death filled the air. The beautiful beach area was in shambles.

A couple of days later Urban and Sprindis made contact. Their comaraderie deepened.

"I hear you're a bonafide hero," quipped Urban.

Sprindis laughed, "You know better, Urban. That was a bloody free-for-all. I just did what I had to do, the same as anyone. I did get to meet old 'Blood and Guts' Patton himself. It was quite an honor."

"Is he anything like they say?" asked Urban.

"Pretty much. I'm glad he's on our side! I approached the General saying, 'Second Lieutenant Sprindis reporting Sir,' and he called me a 'damned liar.' General Patton doesn't talk, he growls! As we walked up to the American cemetery, Patton knelt down to pray, just like a Sunday School kid. He said those guys who were killed were lucky, that nothing was as bad as growing old and dying of diabetes or some other disease."

"General Patton's closing comment floored me: '2nd Lieutenant, you are now 1st Lieutenant Sprindis --- a battlefield promotion.' Then, brassily, he decorates me with a Silver Star. Imagine him taking his time with a twerp like me! I was a private in the bombing

GENERAL GEORGE C. PATTON
General Patton led the Western Task Force of Operation Torch in Western Morocco --- The Mission --- to attack and secure Casablanca as a base for future operations --- to cripple the Airforce and by nightfall of D-Day, secure one airfield.

Three primary objectives were Safi to the South, Fedala and Port Lyautey to the North. At Port Lyautey, the airfield was the prime objective.

of Pearl Harbor ... now Patton promotes me and awards the medal right on the damn battlefield! What a soldier ... he is great!"

- - - - - - - - -

Patton's Words About the Invasion Battle:

"The fortress at Port Lyautey (which had held out against American forces for three days) was finally taken through the use of a self-propelled 105mm gun. It blasted breaks in the fort walls. The 2nd Battalion, 60th Infantry, charged through. They assaulted with grenades, rifles and bayonets. This charge was a very tough proposition. The fort had resisted six inch naval fire, trench-mortar fire, and dive-bombers, but this time it yielded to the 2nd Battalion, 60th Infantry troops armed only with the rifles and grenades. I did not go too closely into the question of who survived in the garrison, but doubt whether any of them did. In such a close fight a soldier has no time to change his mind."

General George Patton

Among many stars of movie and the entertainment world that
Matt Urban programmed, was the comedy star, Martha Raye, and
Al Jolson. Troops enjoyed the relief of laughter and ther joy of
being alive.

The Matt Urban Story Continues:

The 60th Infantry was now assigned to guard the Spanish border against possible war involvement by Generalissimo Franco's armies. Their camp was set up in the nearby Mamora Cork Forest overlooking the blue Mediterranean.

Urban was recalled to his duties as Morale Officer. The wisdom of rest and recreation was now being applied. Victorious American invasion forces prepared for USO shows, military parades. 'Proper' use of captured resort facilities was well-deserved --- a needed respite from war. Urban organized sports and entertainment. Troops were on a light schedule that combined training and relaxation. Urban's unit was stationed in Oran for a few days. It was honored with the privilege of representing the American Forces in the impressive daily retreat ceremonies. The 'F' Company honor guard marched in unity with a French honor guard. American and French flags were at half mast. National anthems of France and the United States were played. Amazingly, battle hostilities were now replaced by a unique respect that each side held for the other.

Soldiers with laundered battle uniforms, white leg-gings, web ammo belts and polished boots marched proudly. Clickety clack, clickety clack of military boots echoed down the steep narrow cobblestone street. The picturesque village square spread out below. The sunset's orange glow backlighted a row of palm trees. This and the waterfalls near the Mediterranean Sea created a spectacle of unusual beauty.

Tears flowed on the faces of many watching friends honoring the soldiers who died so far away from home. Solemn, rigid expressions reflected the sense of loss felt by both French and American sides. Hundreds of men had died. For now it was enough that the horrible conflict was ended.

Rest and respite: Urban organized an inspiring show with Martha Raye and Al Jolson. Their travels to entertain American troops was second only to those of Bob Hope. These fighting men as never before appreciated the relief from refreshing laughter, the beautiful visiting performers, and the joy of being alive.

The Mamora Olive-Cork Forest at the cliff's edge was silhouetted against the azure Mediterranean Sea.

The flat bed of a hay wagon became a stage. The 'star' performer was 'Danny Boy' — Al Jolson. But ... wait ...

Yells from a throng of men clustered in a semi-circle brought Urban onto the stage. Matt sang arm-in-arm with Al Jolson in a rousing rendition of "Bell Bottom Trousers — Coats of Navy Blue — Climbing up the riggin' — Like his daddy used to do —." Urban's wit gave balance to the emotions of his men and helped the all-important healing of their spirits.

During their stint on guard duty, the 60th was treated to a surprise visit by the Commander-in-Chief, Franklin Delano Roosevelt! The President had boldly selected Casablanca for a conference with Winston Churchill. Here they helped to plan the next phase of the Allied military strikes. The presence of these two great leaders added inspiration and courage to the American fighting men.

- - - - - - - -

CHAPTER 7

KASSERINE PASS
"A Miraculous 777-Mile Forced March"

Victory in Africa demonstrated the capability of the American fighting forces and the powerful resources of the newly awakened American giant. Realizing the futility of fighting French General Mathenet called for a truce. An armistice was signed. The French forces in Africa then turned their attention to throwing off the Nazi domination and its oppression that dimmed freedom's light. Hitler countered by sending aircraft and amphibious units into Tunisia. Enormous shipments of weapons, and up to 1,500 troops per day, poured into harbors along Tunisian's Mediterranean Coast.

The Vichy government of France had not directly experienced the awesome force of the American invasion. Vichy French forces had cast its lot with the Nazis, even though the free French government despised and feared them. The Vichy leaders

PORT LYAUTEY CITY CENTER

THE CAPTURE OF MOROCCO & ALGERIA
WAS A PRELUDE TOWARD CAPTURE OF TUNISIA

The 9th Infantry Division Combat Teams turned East toward the German troops in Tunisia. They prepared to meet General Von Arnim and Marshal Rommel's vaunted Afrika Korps.

overrode the armistice worked out in North Africa with General Mathenet and his defeated French Kasba troops. Still worse, Marshall Petain encouraged the landing of Axis armies in North Africa. This move unfortunately would cost the Allied forces thousands of lives.

Eisenhower's armies had one victory behind them when they defeated the more experienced and disciplined French Foreign Legion at the Fortress Kasba.

Now they faced an even more menacing confrontation. The Americans were to encounter the first wave of Hitler's elite Panzer Divisions. These Nazi troops were the best armed, best trained, and the most successful fighting force in the history of the war --- to this time.

The American Forces were still 'green' when it came to actual battle experience. They made up for their inexperience with dedication, honor, patriotism, and good old 'Yankee' know-how. The GI's had learned a lot from the well-disciplined, very experienced French Foreign Legion who now fought with them. They were to learn even more from Hitler's Panzer

KASSERINE PASS

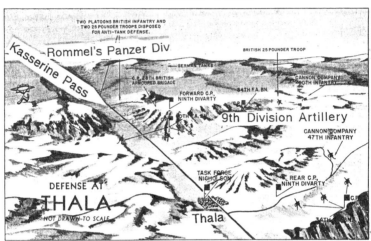

In the closing hours of Feb. 21, 1943, the 9th Infantry Division Artillery completed the 777 mile forced march from Tlemcen, Algeria in bitter weather and almost impassable mountain roads.

On the night of 21 Feb., 1943, without prior reconnaissance or adequate maps, harassed by enemy fire and through congested narrow roads, they occupied battle positions. Communications were set up, obervation posts were established, and they were ready to deliver fire by daylight. German forces were entrenched only 2500 yards distant.

Rommel's Panzer attack to break through the Kasserine Pass toward Thala began at 7:00 A.M. on Feb. 22. It was stopped in its tracks by the flat trajectory blasts from the 9th Division Artillery cannonfire.

The gallant action and heroism of the 9th Division Artillery defeated Rommel's Panzer Division by Feb. 25th; the Germans disengaged from their American pursuers as they fled east.

Divisions under the direction of Field Marshal Erwin Rommel.

An added problem developed when British General Montgomery had stopped to rest and replenish his 'Desert Rats'. Rommel's forces were, therefore, able to capture and hold Kasserine Pass — for six days.

General Eddy and his staff were examining every bit of intelligence to determine the most efficient way to proceed. Small units of French, American, and British troops held passes in Tunisia. They were already being attacked by Rommel's Panzers.

By February 14, 1943, the Afrika Korps flanked the Anglo-American troops and prepared to drive them back into Algeria. Orders were received on February 17 to move the Ninth Division to the Tunisian front, where Rommel had broken through.

The front extended for fifty-two miles and this greatly affected the Ninth Division's lines of communication. The Ninth Signal Company and the Ninth Reconnaissance Troops performed distinguished service on this long line of defense and prevented serious gaps in the communication line. These two units met the difficult task. For example, signalmen

VETERANS' RECOLLECTIONS & DIARY

covered an area which would normally have required ten times the available equipment and personnel. Reconnaissance troops patrolled the entire sector as far south as Gafsa. They kept contact with a rapidly moving enemy while displaying thoroughness of effort and speed.

General Patton assumed command of the II Corps in early March. He determined an alternate strategy that would use the infantry to open a path through the enemy lines. Then Patton's mobile armor of tanks and artillery could race through. The American forces in Tunisia consisted of the 34th Infantry Division, which was in the north where the Ninth and First Infantry Divisions were aiding the British. The First Armored Division and special units were to the south of that area.

Once again the Ninth Division troops forced themselves to extremes. Their artillery units moved over dangerous mountain roads to reinforce the British at Thala.

This necessary American movement became a historic 'forced march' of almost physically impossible accomplishment. The Ninth Division Artillery transported: 411 vehicles, 138 officers, and

KASSERINE PASS AND DEFENSE OF THALA

The road to Thala was maddening. It was winding, narrow, slippery, and jammed with traffic of all kinds, through which . . . drivers had literally to fight their way . . . It was learned later what General Irwin's orders had been. He was to command a mixed group of British and American Artillery in supporting 'some elements of the British 26th Rifle Brigade' in holding the Thala defile "at all costs!"
—*Combat Report (60th F.A. Bn.)*

Distinguished Unit Citation

. . . *9th Infantry Division Artillery,* is cited for conspicuous gallantry and heroism in battle on 21, 22, and 23 February 1943, in repelling an attack by vastly superior forces, which were attempting to break through the Allied lines in the vicinity of Thala, Tunisia . . . *9th Infantry Division Artillery,* completed a 100-hour forced march from Tlemcen, Algeria, covering a distance of 735 miles in bitter weather over tortuous and almost impassable mountain roads on the night of 21 February 1943. Without prior reconnaissance or adequate maps, harassed by enemy fire, and forced to maneuver through a congested narrow road, nevertheless . . . occupied battle positions, set up communications, established observation posts, and was ready to deliver fire by daylight. Although enemy forces were entrenched only 2,500 yards distant and there were only three platoons of friendly infantry in front of the artillery, the unit maintained constant and steady fire with such deadly effect that enemy tank units were dispersed and driven back. The cool and determined manner in which . . . *9th Division Artillery* entered into battle, after an almost incredible forced march contributed in great measure to the defeat of the enemy's attempt to break through the Thala defile. The gallant entry into battle and the heroism with which the volume of fire was maintained, despite terrific enemy fire, are in keeping with the highest traditions of the American military service.

2,032 enlisted men over more than 777 miles of narrow, treacherous, winding gravel mountainous roads. Transit time totalled only three days!! Throughout daylight and dark they pressed on without rest. Heavy guns repeatedly slid off trails made slippery by continuous sleet, rain and mud. Some of the 'big guns' were lost over the edges of sheer cliffs. Miraculously, the Ninth Division artillery and troops arrived on schedule! They set up their weapons and began shelling columns of armored enemy troops as they exited the narrow Kasserine pass.

Skillful training in marksmanship and teamwork of the American Ninth Division paid off! The Desert Fox, Field Marshal Rommel, was flung back from Kasserine Pass by the amazing display of Allied firepower delivered from the 9th Division Artillery reinforcements. Then highly effective B-17 bombers delivered air bombardment. This provided the support power needed in 'shagging out' the Desert Fox and Field Marshal Rommel's Panzer Tanks.

The Ninth Division Artillery, led by General Leroy Irwin, received a Distinguished Presidential Unit Citation for stopping Rommel. This Allied victory prevented the Axis from expanding its earlier tactical

COL. WILLIAM   C. WESTMORELAND
This 34th Field Artillery Commander is being awarded the French Legion of Honor, Grade of Chevalier,   from French General Koeltz.

Westmoreland later became General William C. Westmoreland, Chief of Staff.

triumph into a strategic success. A remarkable young Lieutenant Colonel named William Westmoreland of the 34th Field Artillery filled an important role in this historic American victory.

- - - - - - - - -

On January 30, 1943, the 2nd Battalion boarded aged narrow-gauge railroad box cars --- destination: Oran. The men despaired at the thought of being crammed into every stinking nook and cranny of box cars, which had been used to transport livestock. They were complaining good-naturedly, until their Sergeant's words cut through their restlessness.

"All aboard the African Donkey Express! Nothing is too good for the French mules and American GI's!" The words, uttered in a deep southern drawl, drew laughter which raised spirits.

"Git aboard! Ya'all hear me?" Despite the putrid odors which gave evidence of the previous occupants, the men cheerfully found places to sit in the piles of fresh straw. Thousands of soldiers filed through the cow chutes of the dilapidated train yard.

URBAN'S 2ND BATTALION DONKEY EXPRESS
Destination Oran! Good-natured complaining stopped abruptly when their Sergeant called, "All aboard the African Donkey Express." The second order was blunt and in street slang, *"Git aboard! Ya'all hear me!"*

"So this is a mule train," Urban chuckled. "Hauling asses is nothing new to these African engineers." His men who huddled together on the floor had to laugh at the antics of their leader.

The chugging steam engines could barely pull the boxcars full of men and weapons up the gradual inclines. Going over the mountains, GI's had to get out and 'personally' push the doggone train up the steep rises ... Then they ran like hell to catch up and jump aboard as the train started rolling down the other side! Complaints continued, but not one preferred the alternative of hiking through those mountains. Urban was acclimated to Africa by now. His adaptability was beginning to thrive on change. He took these unusual 'Bohemian' transport conditions in stride. Even the cold, rainy weather and muddy bivouacs did not dampen his spirits.

Urban's troops were assigned to hold the Germans from getting around behind the British. They were assisted by an American gunnery crew, who reached a position at the base of a steep hill. German Mark IV tanks appeared suddenly, cutting off the only avenue for gunnery crew retreat. Lt. John Allen clearly remembers the gunnery Sergeant

GERMAN TANK ADVANCE
Lt. John Allen and his Gunnery Sergeant had this view of the cannon coming their way. They improvised with their 155 Howitzer buttressed against the cliff. They blasted a dozen tanks off the cliff.

Allen and his Sergeant blocked the advance of the Panzer tanks by their heroic action in destroying a dozen advancing German Tiger tanks along the narrow road on the edge of the cliff.

ordering his men to buttress their '155' howitzers against the side of a cliff.

"What are you doing?" Allen questioned his Sergeant. He was certain that all of them were about to be killed or captured.

"We're goin' to save our lives," replied the Sergeant, "and yours too!" The field pieces were not intended for a flat trajectory. The gun crew aimed the '155' outriggers down. This strategy aimed the short barreled artillery guns into a point blank direction of the oncoming tanks.

Only one tank at a time could enter the valley on the narrow road cut into the edge of the cliff. As the first German Tiger tank came into view, the massive muzzle of its 88 millimeter cannon swung toward the entrapped men.

"Fire!" yelled the U.S. Gunnery Sergeant. The American gun roared first. His men gaped in astonishment. The shell blast knocked the turret clear off the body of the roaring German tank.

"Take your time. Count your men and load again," the Sergeant ordered in a calm voice. Firing almost

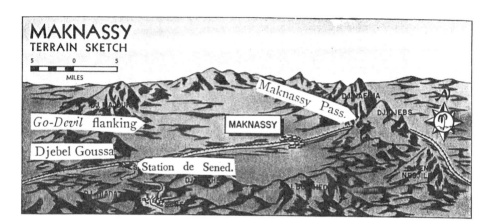

On March 19th, 1943, the 60th Combat Team moved cross-country to Djebel Goussa which dominated the rail line to Sened Station. The Go Devils flanked Goussa -- capturing the objective. On the 20th the strategy was to open Maknassy or El Guettar Passes to force Rommel's retreat or capture. Maknassy Pass was captured on April 9 after some of the heaviest fighting the 60th Combat Team had met.

point blank, they destroyed the second Tiger tank as it rounded the rise --- and then the third. Urban gathered a small contingent of sharpshooters. He set up a defense post to repulse German footsoldiers who swarmed behind the giant Tiger tanks.

All German attempts to crash the U.S. positions were stymied. Before the battle ended, a dozen smashed and smoldering tanks littered the valley. These 'dead Tigers' blocked the pathway of the Panzer advance. That innovative Sergeant and his crew knew their equipment. By using their long trajectory artillery as a close range anti-tank cannon, the crew saved the lives of many U.S. infantrymen.

- - - - - - - - - -

General Patton gave word on March 15 to move beyond Thelepte in preparation for an assault on Maknassy. Patton himself would lead this operation.

Strategy called for the Ninth and the First Infantry Divisions to form parts of General Patton's II Corps. They were to attack on the Gafsa-Gabes axis and relieve pressure on General Montgomery's forces to the south. Reaching their objective required a forced march. The punishing pace pushed every soldier to the limits of his endurance.

9TH DIVISION FALCON TROOPS & SWITCHBOARD
Communications switchboards were critical to the success of the
progress made by the combat teams. Rugged mountain terrain
and stifling desert heat and dust were trying conditions for these
troops.

Urban had never known such exhaustion! Mile after mile he plodded, often asleep on his feet. A stuporous trance allowed him to rest in motion, eyes slitted against the hot African sun. He trudged on, nearly oblivious to the weight of his pack and the sores where his equipment rubbed his skin raw. Clinging sweat oozed from every pore in his body, soaking his battle uniform.

"Stealth and Sweat!" Urban reminded himself in his more lucid moments. "Stealth and Sweat, rather than Blood and Death, is the way to win battles!" Those words of General Eddy became softly hypnotic as he repeated them endlessly.

Urban felt his face and neck burning from intense rays of the desert sun. A cruel mirage danced ahead at the edge of sight, teasing Urban's consciousness with its 'cool water' illusion, and nagging hunger knotted Matt's stomach. His lips and mouth were parched. Thousands of tramping feet kicked up a trail of dust. The turbulent stream of earth particles stung their eyes. It caked on sweat-wet uniforms and sunburned skin.

"Keep moving." Forcefully Urban led and pushed his men. "Every minute counts. YOU CAN DO IT!

PUSH ON! PUSH ON!" The repeated charge picked up momentum, buoying emotions and determination that this heroic effort would not fail.

Most infantrymen accepted the impossible pace with stoic resignation. They considered 'Blood and Guts' Patton as one of the greatest Generals in the military. Others were driven to despair by his tactics. A few guys complained bitterly. Endurance, emotions and body were stressed by 'super-human' performance demands. Patton's forward-moving boldness sometimes resulted in many Americans being killed. Most combat men believed more lives were saved by their 'warrior' because of his aggressive attack methods.

Then it was over! Finally Matt's men reached the high ground objective. "Dig in along that ridge," Urban ordered. He knew if they stopped moving, muscles would stiffen up and his infantrymen would lose the remaining bit of their ebbing strength. Like a massive colony of aggressive badgers, the men began digging burrows. Preparing for the attack of the 'Desert Fox' was of urgent necessity. Everyone instinctively knew it.

General George Patton's demanding and fast-driving attack made it possible to reach this prized objective ahead of Rommel's forces. U.S. troops seized the high ridgeline. Their position dominated miles of lower lands on one side. It overlooked a high plateau reaching to the far horizon on the other side. There had been no need for a drawn-out fight for these heights. Seizure had been accomplished by Urban's belief in the 'stealth and sweat' tactics learned long ago from General Eddy. Getting up there before the enemy was the initial target. Matt's men met the test. The objective was secured without any loss of American lives.

From his vantage point Urban surveyed the horizon with binoculars. He was shocked at the sight of an unusual cloud of dust emerging in the remote distance. The dust cloud erupted into an apparent sandstorm. As it neared, he realized that he had spotted onrushing columns of Field Marshal Erwin Rommel. He gave a low whistle. "G-D Damn!" Then Lieutenant Allen took a look. "That's no damned sandstorm out there. Those Nazi fanatics are bringing up their heavy artillery."

"Look at that ordnance," Allen groaned. "As if their damned 88's and those 'lousy' Tiger tanks weren't

GERMAN TANK

This is typical of many Panzer Division tanks used so effectively by the Germans in Tunisia and elsewhere.

U.S. SHERMAN TANK

The Sherman Tank shown is equipped with a 'Long Tom' artillery cannon. This was an advanced piece of military equipment which proved effective and important in many campaigns of the 9th Division.

enough." Lt. Gail Brown ranted, "Those cannon have more than three times the range of our Stuart tanks, twice the range of our Grants, and the sons of bitches throw rocks the rest of the way! The new Shermans can nearly match them, but all of them were delivered to Montgomery's 'Desert Rats'. German-built machine guns fire faster than ours and don't jam as bad! Their 'potato mashers' are more dangerous than our grenades. Then we have to seize the positions the Krauts spent months fortifying!"

"You sure as Hell are a lot of comfort!" shouted Ed Pavlich. Allen's eyes were still glued to the binoculars, "They are bringing up 240mm cannons. We don't have a damned thing that can even reach them!"

As he watched, the German armored column deployed to the left and to the right. This formed their assault line.

"Easy, soldiers," Urban cautioned. "Don't spend it before you earn it! I would guess that General Patton has a few tricks up his sleeve. The last word was that he's positioned nearby with his armored column. We can count on him to advance when and where needed. We'll hold!"

"Wow! This may be the battle of the century. Damn!" exclaimed Lt. Brown. Old 'Blood and Guts' Patton face to face against Field Marshal Rommel, the 'Desert Fox'!"

"I'll second that," added Lt. Irving Shuttleworth. "I've been told that those two trained together in armored tactics before the war."

"They say each can read the other's mind. Each knows what to expect from the other," 1st Sgt. Miller added. "But which one of them will first be aware of the other and gamble on a countercharge?"

Sergeant Carl Hull said, "I'm betting on Patton!" The four observers drew back to their original field positions.

Rommel's potential strength had been weakened in spite of a string of victories in the past months. Rommel's requests for necessary support in replenishing his manpower and supplies in Africa had fallen on deaf ears. The strengthened Allies had him outnumbered. However, the elusive 'Fox' felt confident that his superior armament, well trained tank troops and familiarity with African terrain would again allow him to conquer.

As the advancing German units cleared the distant slopes, they appeared to veer to the south. Urban's emotions allowed slight relaxation. He thought Rommel's strategy may be to storm through the unlikely southern edge of the defensive ridgeline.

General George Patton was not to allow his prize adversary to escape. In a brilliant counterstroke, he positioned the Ninth Division with artillery and Patton's 'baby tanks' (as Rommel had labeled them), to cut off that possibility. In no way was Patton to allow the hungry 'Fox' to feed on 'Blood and Guts'.

Rommel placed his heavy propellant armament behind a distant ridge directly in front of 'F' Company's position. He planned to annihilate the entrenched American defenses.

Rommel's attack was swift and brutal.

First came the artillery. Sheets of orange light belched in the distance followed by the steady roar of continuous cannon fire. Urban felt as if his eardrums would burst from the explosive blast shocks. Hell 'rained down' hour after endless hour, and his flesh 'crawled' in revulsion. His ears rang. Thick, rancid dust and smoke clogged Urban's nostrils. H e feared that he would smother in the choking sand and dust. His parched throat craved water. Any kind of freshness would be welcome. How long could he and his men survive in such an atmosphere of hellfire?

Night and day the long, drawn-out whine of overhead shells was followed by death and destruction. A deafening roar filled their ears. "There was not a single minute for three days that a shell wasn't falling," Urban recalls. From over a mile away they could hear the explosion and began to flinch, awaiting the shell impact, explosion and shock. The sound got louder and louder as each cannonshell approached. It changed to a screech as it neared impact. Every closely exploding shell caused the infantrymen unbearable tension. Muscles tensed involuntarily, as each man waited, wondering if the next one had *HIS NAME ON IT!* Unable to sleep, the infantrymen cringed in bleak terror. Agony was etched on every face.

The few available medics were kept in constant service. As casualties mounted, it seemed that there were cries coming from every foxhole. In the noise of battle, an undercurrent of swearing, babbling men could be heard begging for help. The handful of medics with dwindling supplies were forced to treat the wounded and dying soldiers as best they could. Even men who escaped being hit were sick and dazed.

Occasionally a man would crack under the battle pressure. His comrades would pull him down and hold him until the stark raving madness passed. A nineteen year old soldier, shuddering in an epileptic-type fit, began banging his head deliriously on the edge of his foxhole. Blood poured from his ears. Thick foam, like discolored shaving cream flowed from his mouth, collecting in a clump like a foul slag. Guttural sounds without meaning could be heard in the brief seconds between shells. Battle-tested soldiers seemed on the verge of collapse. The incredible shelling continued for three days. Everyone felt as if his eardrums would burst from the pounding and that their brains were about to 'gush out'.

Armored attacks slugged at the southern end of the ridgeline. Menacing German Tiger tanks drove against the precarious position. Their grinding clash interspersed with the cannon roars of the mighty 88's. Swarms of running, screaming German soldiers provided infantry support.

VETERANS' RECOLLECTIONS & DIARY

A devastating barrage by Patton's tanks threw Rommel's assault line into disarray. Panzer tanks were disabled one by one. For every American who fell, another rose up to take his place. Rommel's attack stalled. It then retreated. Next the firestorm of shelling intensified! After the long enemy barrages (designed to soften resistance), the courageous Ninth Division stubbornly held its ground. Every rush by the terrifying tank brigades was stopped cold. Blistering fire from mortars, bazookas, and anti-tank guns of this heroic Ninth Division was insurmountable.

Respite finally came .... only after the infantry guys had sustained one of the longest non-stop artillery barrage battles in military history. Although suffering a lot of casualties, American troops were formidable in perseverance. They held that strategic high ground which shook and trembled during 72 hours of endless explosions from Rommel's big guns.

The sudden silence was 'eerie'. Urban clambered out of his foxhole. He focused his binoculars on the column of German armor retreating in the distance. The area between was covered with burning vehicles and mangled corpses. Over 10,000 Allied soldiers died in the entire sector. Only 2,000 Axis troops were lost, but they constituted the major part of Rommel's force.

"They're pulling back!" Urban's voice sounded strange in the stillness of the battle area. A metallic taste filled Matt's mouth. He bellowed, "We did it!"

"Lord, I pray I never have to live through another hell like this one," shouted Staff Sergeant Ted Preston as he emerged from the ground, brushing dust from his uniform. "There will be hell to pay for this!"

"We survived," 1st Sgt. Miller stated flatly. "Tomorrow is another day."

Sergeant Kerans added, "If we live that long! They know we're still coming!"

The next few days were spent evacuating the wounded and replenishing supplies. Urban noticed that those young men who had survived seemed to show an 'inner aging'. The gauntlet of fire in Africa had stolen their youthful appearance and exuberance.

Matt led his troops to a recovery area along a ridgeline below the leeward side of a tall cliff. The wall of the djebel (cliff) was 2,000 feet high. It 'reached out' for endless miles from north to south, with a wadi (dry creek bed) along the edge. This dry 'winding canal' had solid ten-foot-high walls of densely packed sand. A natural barrier was created that provided a welcome protection from enemy fire. The only passageway to the vast plateau above, was a single track dirt road that climbed at a 45-degree angle up from the desert floor. Matt's 'F' Company felt they would be safe there.

After personally observing the outposts, Urban settled in with his men for some chow. The inevitable army 'C' rations! Minutes into his meal, Jim Panzone's voice over the field telephone interrupted his feast, "We have enemy activity!"

"Damn the Bastards!" exclaimed Sgt. Preston. "If they can't shoot us, they'll starve us to death!"

Open cans of C rations were discarded in favor of automatic rifles, as men scrambled up the road to the front line foxholes.

"It looks like a raiding party or a sneak attack," reported Bert Skins from the forward machine gun nest. "The grass is high, so I can't see how many there are -- or who they are." Panic registered in the sentry's tone.

"Sit tight," Urban ordered. "I'll get a rifle squad up there pronto."

Minutes later Matt was 'on line' with an assigned squad. Peering out into the open field, they could see no motion. All at once a flurry of movement caught their attention. A band of Arab bandits had been crawling on their bellies like snakes through the grass. Rising to their feet, they rushed the supply dump, snatching anything that was loose. Timed like clockwork, they ran one at a time, scurrying tho loot twenty yards almost like moles. Grabbing cans of C rations, equipment and clothing, they turned and fled for the protection of the tall grass.

The raiders were scary looking. Robes covered their bodies. They were armed with old rifles and large blade knives. Without hesitation the Americans opened fire. Cries of anguish rang out as the intruders who were hit went down.

"Hold your fire," Urban commanded. "They aren't going to do us any harm." They continued to watch as the last of the limping, injured bandits disappeared.

"Where did they start crawling?" Elton Harrell wondered aloud. "They must have started about two miles back. It's a wonder the guard ever saw them!"

"Fear does wonders for your eyesight!" Sgt. Joe Boylan commented with a grin.

"Let's get back to chow!" Sergeant Skertich called out.

"These Arabs are good for throat-cutting and grave-robbing! They won't bother us in broad daylight." Moments later the men were back to their rations. The incident was deeply imbedded in their thoughts of the day.

Lt. Urban spent the next couple of hours reconnoitering his sector. Responsibility of leadership rested heavily on Matt this day. Satisfied that they had a good protective emplacement, he settled in for a richly deserved rest. It seemed that he had just closed his eyes when the telephone crackled once more.

"Civilians approaching," reported the point man, Tom Saunders.

It was already morning. A murky dawn greeted the awakening Lieutenant. A woman from the nearby village had come seeking medical help for the Arabs who were wounded earlier. Her son had been one of the interlopers. "What to do," Urban pondered. There were no guidelines in his officers' training to cover this one.

Her plea was sincere. The thought of wounded men left untreated was too much. Taking a volunteer medic, Frank Carrol, and Staff Sergeant Campbell, Urban accompanied her back to the village.

"What have I gotten us into," he wondered as they walked some distance into the Arab enclave. "What kind of people are these? We could be walking into an ambush."

"Sir, I can't decide if we are brave, compassionate, or just naive for taking this assignment," Campbell said looking puzzled. "I sure have some mixed emotions about walking into that village. It could be a death trap."

"It's a good day to die," their medic laughed nervously, adding, "But I would just as soon live. At least they won't kill us until I have patched up their men. Unless they just want this morphine and bandages."

"We'll be okay," Urban said hoping he sounded confident. Deep down, like the others, he SUS-PECTED EVERYTHING!

Approaching the village, a group of filthy, naked children and barking dogs greeted them. Mud huts lined a narrow alleyway littered with garbage and animal dung. The odor of raw sewage wafted through the early morning air. Eyes gazed out from the open doorways of straw-roofed dwellings. Hostile eyes? Urban couldn't tell.

"Look at those savages. These people live like animals," said Sgt. Campbell.

"They sure smell like animals!" agreed Carrol.

Closing ranks, they followed their guide. Urban was well aware that every step could be their last. Images of tribesmen harboring vengeance and armed with ancient rifles seemed to loom behind

every hut. They continued along the dirt path that
served as a street. Finally they stopped at a hut in
which one of the wounded men was housed. They
were too late to do him any good. He died shortly
before their arrival. Low moans were coming from an
old dark-skinned woman who was sitting on the floor
in a corner. She was rocking back and forth like a
sorrowful child. Her teeth were gnashing, and
whimpering sounds came from her nasal passages.
She reminded Urban of a pitiful injured dog.
Apparently the dead man had been her husband.

Moving on to the next hut, Sgt. Campbell touched
Urban's shoulder, "Did you see that? Did you hear
her? Her wailing twisted my guts!"

Each hut brought a different scenario. Most of the
others had superficial wounds. Their people
slouched on the verge of revenge. Urban and his
medics had been expecting to be clawed at or spit
on. The natives were actually showing a mixed
appreciation, totally unfit under these critical
circumstances.

The mission climaxed with the last hut. Here was a
man who was mortally injured, feverish, barely
conscious and with a bullet in his chest. His wife and

mother were hysterical. Children gathered at the door, watching with wide eyes.

"Nothing I can do for him," the young medic said sadly. He was accustomed to blood and gore, but this time he looked as if he were about to be sick. "Nothing anybody could do for him," was the final verdict.

Walking out of the village, Urban and his men were keenly aware of their backs exposed to any concealed hostility. The final twenty yards seemed to take forever. Only when they were out of sight of the village did they begin to breathe easily.

"My God! Those kids really got to me. War is one thing, but women and kids ... living in this hellfire!"

"You did all you could do." Urban's attempt to comfort the young medic fell on deaf ears.

"I thought I could take anything. Lord help me. If there is good or justice on the earth, let me see it. I just hit bottom," was the medic's response.

Carrol was silent.

No sooner were they settled in with the troops, than Tom Saunders, the point man, radioed in for the third time. "Vehicle approaching, Sir. We seem to be a real popular attraction!"

Down the dusty, winding road Urban could see a jeep carrying an unusual cargo. The driver and the two men in the back seat were armed and wearing military uniforms. A tall majestic figure in flaming red robes and wearing an immaculate white turban stood rigid and erect. His hands rested on the top edge of the jeep windshield. As they drew near, Urban saw a huge gold medallion hanging around the man's neck. Ornate bracelets and rings decorated his arms and fingers. The vision was so unexpected and incongruous that Matt Urban felt as if he was seeing a dream image. "The king of the Sultans," he thought.

"Who is in charge?" the knightly Sultan asked in broken English.

"I am, Sir," Lt. Urban replied. "What am I in for now?" he thought to himself. "Have I violated our international relationship?"

"Thank you. You kill bad man! Thieves no good!" The man's face brightened into a wide smile, showing a rack of bright white teeth bridged with shiny gold.

With that, the jeep made a wide U-turn and drove away without so much as a backward glance from the visitors.

Men emerged from cover and converged on their bewildered leader. The entire group was laughing and imitating the Arab official.

CHAPTER 8

THE NORTHERN TUNISIAN CAMPAIGN
"You Cannot Do This --- It's Against the Geneva Treaty!"

On April 13 the Ninth began the tedious overland trek to northern Tunisia. Again, by secretive deception the 'Old Reliables' had moved from southern Tunisia to the extreme northern flank bordering the Mediterranean to relieve a British Division! Assigned to them were four Tabours of Goums, grisly, stalwart, warriors in pigtails who fought alongside their American, British, and French comrades in the Corps D'Afrique.

'Goum', a word these silent Berber tribesmen never used in referring to themselves, is an Arabic term meaning 'irregular soldier'. Their appearance frightened the Arab children, who would run away in terror, shrieking for Allah. Wearing turbans and burnooses along with their 'bathrobes', the Goums fought under French officials. They specialized in

Goums (Berber Tribesmen), Mohammedan by faith, white mountaineers of the Atlas Mountain area, had been hired by the French Foreign Legion as warriors. Goum -- means Clan -- Later it meant irregular soldier. Berbers did not like that expression. They spoke no English, French or German. Their pay was whatever they could loot. A light-fingered touch of the hand on a helmet --- identified if American or French. If not --- a slit throat and looted body often resulted. All worldly goods were carried in the Goum's tent-like robe (djeballah).

phantom-like patrols. Their stalking was a source of terror to the German troops. They were known to slip into a bivouac of sleeping Nazis, slitting their throats and chopping off ears for trophies.

Out of curiosity Urban approached a Clan of Goums who were squatting nearby. A bossy tribesman confronted Urban as he was gaping at their outlandish styles and behavior --- before Urban was able to blurt out: "Kamarade speak-a the English?" The tribesman nodded and mumbled the sound of jargoned English with hand gestures of "What can I do for you?"

Urban, focusing on repetitious words, spoke, "Comrade -- Germans -- How many?" With his moving finger count raised before his eyes, Urban continued, "Lots, lots of Germans?"

The Goum responded with an unending head nodding and arms vibrating indicating positive, "Yes, many."

Urban, "Where? Where? How far?" with his arms encircling the mountain peaks.

Goum: "Come" --- waving his comrade forward --- frantically, with continuous pushing --- face and head fidgeting --- his arm pointed towards a western ridge and then in a ceaseless motion noted --- "follow me."

Urban thought, "Why not grab this opportunity of having the services of a native bushwacker to guide me to the enemy's back door?" Indeed so it was, as their next strategy most likely would require a scouting mission.

In the pre-dawn haze of the following morning, two silhouettes seemed to slide through a chain of curving wadis and burrows out into the far distance. Urban was astonished at his guide's secretive abilities. He had to discipline himself to the 'dragged-out' cautiousness that finally steered them into the enemy's 'backyard'.

It was here they parted. The Goum went on his own, seeking to make his mark on several of the sleeping German troops. Urban maneuvered on to complete his reconnaissance patrol, bellying towards a rise with a view.

Field glasses revealed a cement enclosure in the distance (approximately 8 feet by 12 feet in size) with no roof. Urban climbed down a sand bank into a wadi and crept along for some distance as an indirect approach to the Kraut position.

Progress was excruciatingly slow. His body was in constant motion, but the movement was slow so as to be indistinguishable from the rocks and bushes on which his bare hands rested. He traveled only a few yards per hour.

Compromise entered his mind. Chances were good that he could cover the last stretch unseen. "Stick to procedure," Urban disciplined himself. "Survival depends on it." Paying attention to that inner voice had kept him alive. He listened to it now!

He was aware of the sun's arc through the sky and of the distance he had to traverse before nightfall. Crawling silently from one bit of cover to another he eventually gained access to a clump of rocks less than 100 yards from his objective. Urban's cautious reconnaissance had taken the better part of the day.

From where Matt crouched behind a boulder he could see wires, intercoms, and advanced radio and telephone equipment. He stared in amazement. This had to be Rommel's communication center for that entire sector. His thoughts raced as he considered his next move. In the peak of excitement, he sensed: "Holy Toledo! This is a gift!" Heart pounding, he knew what he had to do.

The enemy defenses were lax. In their rear position the Germans were over a mile from their own front lines. It was dusk of a seemingly drawn-out dreary day. Low stormy clouds added to the dismal atmosphere. The weather conditions were a God-send from Urban's perspective. It would be a shame to waste this advantage.

The enemy platoon assigned to guarding the only possible route of attack was scattered about their stations as if war were the furthest thing from their thoughts. They were providing minimum security, grabbing the opportunity to 'dog-it' in the absence of their commanding officer.

Two operators were in the cement structure manning the switch boards. Everyone else seemed to be on break.

Crawling and scrambling over the rocky ground Urban pulled the pin on his first grenade. One ... two

... he flung the 'pineapple' directly into the cement building. Loud explosions ripped the air.

Urban rushed the entrance. Firing his .45 caliber pistol, he dropped the two equipment operators as they dove for their rifles. His second grenade ripped through the small enclosure, tearing wires and destroying delicate equipment.

Startled cries from the encircling outposts alerted Urban of the danger he faced. He leveled several shots into the midst of the onrushing defenders before he dashed for cover. A 'potato masher' grenade exploded beside him. He felt the white hot shrapnel penetrate the flesh of his right hand. He was knocked to the ground by the force of the explosion. Scrambling to his feet, he hit the ground running. His only chance was to gain distance.

Urban sprinted for cover amidst a hail of bullets. No athletic event ever motivated him like this! Fear stabbed the pit of his stomach. He ran for his life. Behind him he could hear the sounds of the chase punctuated by intermittent gun fire. He experienced the fright of the prey.

In a long minute he was out of sight of his pursuers.

Easing up his pace, Urban maneuvered over the rough terrain until he sighted his own lines. About 200 yards from the safety of his own troops, he dropped to the ground to avoid the confrontation of bullets. Urban was being fired on by his own men! He dove into a shallow depression in the earth, breathless, his sides heaving in exhaustion. He crawled closer, waving a white handkerchief.

"Who goes there?" challenged Corporal Herb Brasington (later Captain).

"It's Urban, you jerks. Look where you're shooting," shouted Adam Drust

Upon realizing that it was Matt, the men erupted in laughter. Soon he was surrounded by comrades, eager to hear about his 'scouting mission'. "That must have been the fastest three miles you ever ran," quipped Brasington.

YOU DID WHAT?!!! bellowed Captain Kriz when Urban reported the results of his patrol. "Damn, Lieutenant, I don't know whether to court martial you or decorate you. Leading this company is tough enough without you grandstanding!"

"Yes, Sir. You are right, Captain," Urban assured his Company Commander, Robert Kriz, that he would follow military operating procedures from now on.

"You probably saved a lot of lives," Captain Kriz snapped. "Get the hell out of here while I'm in a good mood --- and Urban, get some medical attention for that hand."

"By the way, congratulations, Lieutenant," Kriz added as Urban turned to leave --- "and that is strictly off the records."

- - - - - - - - -

Principal handicaps in the African Campaign were the shortage of adequate maps and the unavailability of communications in the vast and rugged terrain. Supply needs always created a big hardship. Three hundred mules were obtained from the French. The regiments were forced to rely solely on pack animals for supply, transportation, and evacuation over the terrain of steep 2000 to 3000 foot djebels which ran in unbroken ridges from Maknassy to El Guettar.

General Eddy realized the futility of attempting a frontal attack on the Green-Bald Hill position. He, therefore, decided to deploy the bulk of the Division in a wide flanking movement. This was through almost impassable terrain. The intent was to circle behind enemy strongholds and cut their lines of north and northeast communications.

Lt. Matt Urban was in charge of 'F' Company. It was his job to lead the assault on the massive mountain. It had three steep sides merging into a series of ridges on the fourth side. German defenses were ringed with stone emplacements and elite troops on the mountain crest. They effectively covered every conceivable approach to the stronghold. Hundreds of British troops had been lost in a frontal assault to the mountain fortress.

Strategy called for an attack through a most impossible avenue. 'F' Company was to serve as the spearhead in an extremely hazardous maneuver. This required that a large column move single file through impassable jungle terrain to hit the position from behind.

Regimental battalion followed battalion. They were moving along in the African tribesman style, like a giant snake winding through the hills and jungles of Africa. After several hours of slow progress the jungle growth became increasingly dense. The task seemed to be insurmountable! Insects swarmed. Time came to a standstill! Darkness pervaded as lush green vegetation nearly blocked out the sun. Ever so slowly, the column inched along.

Urban struggled alongside his men against the dense wall of creeping vines. Unbearable heat and humidity drove them to despair. Responsibility for the mission weighed heavily on Urban's mind.

One man dropped off into the brush. "I can't go any further," he groaned.

Sgt. Miller dragged him to his feet. "I'll put this gun to your head!" he threatened. "Take my arm," h e offered as the man struggled to his feet.

The GI on point position hacked away at the jungle until he was exhausted. The big flat blade was then passed to the next man in line. One after another the men spent sweat and strength to tear a hole through the relentless underbrush. Finally the effort came to an end, as the lead men overcome with despair, fell exhausted. They could not edge ahead any further.

"I wish you could see just one of the ineradicable pictures I have in my mind today.   A narrow path comes like a ribbon over a hill miles away, down a long slope, across a creek, up a slope and over another hill - - - -

All along a length of this ribbon, there is now a thin line of men. For numberless days and nights they have fought hard, eaten little, washed none, and slept hardly at all., Their nights have been sleepless and miserable with the crash of artillery.
- - - -
The line moves on, but it never ends. All afternoon men keep coming around the hill and vanishing eventually over the horizon. It is one long, tired line of ant-like men."

By Ernie Pyle

Urban wormed his way along the file of overwrought men to take over the lead. His lungs burned and his limbs were leaden. With energy born of desperation he took the machete and began to slash away at the dense foliage. After about 150 yards the jungle slowly thinned out!

By luck or 'Hand of God' the attackers had penetrated onto the foothills where the vegetation diminished as they reached the edge of the slope. There was enough cover for concealment, yet the ground allowed for maneuverability. By late afternoon the exhausted troops reached a jump-off point. They rested in seclusion at the edge of the jungle.

Here they shed canteens. They secured bayonets on their M-1 rifles. A tense and total silence accompanied last minute preparations. The faint sound of laughter drifted over the rise. The German troops were completely unaware of the impending attack. "These guys aren't even looking," Urban thought to himself. "They are goofing off." Fear and excitement marked the faces of the men around him.

The soldiers of the Ninth were in position below the enemy force that had held out against British

Commandos for months on end. Lt. Urban moved up and down the jump-off point. He was double checking to see that all equipment was secured, so no metal would clank nor any sun reflective surface would signal their approach. All communication was reduced to hand signals. Dirt was rubbed onto sweaty faces. The attack force was ready for its 'Big Jump'.

With a flare gun in one hand and a .45 in the other, Urban crept a few yards in front. He fired the flare along a flat trajectory. This dropped the torch-like shell smack in the middle of a German machine gun nest. Men scattered in every direction. Some enemy soldiers gaped in frozen amazement as the next volley of burning phosphorus exploded. It showered the perimeter of the machine gun nest with streaks of dreaded luminous red fire. Urban lobbed another cartridge with his innovative 'miniature flame thrower', if only to demoralize the enemy.

At Urban's signal the troops of the 60th Infantry moved forward and burst over the stone gun emplacements before the bewildered German defenders realized what was happening.

A world of hell broke loose! Urban vaulted over a stone wall, firing his .45 caliber pistol and screaming orders over the noise of the uprising!

"Spread out! Keep moving! Don't let 'em recoup!"

Confused, bewildered faces turned to greet 'F' Company. The shaken professional enemy soldiers spun around to meet the attack on their rear. Mounted machine guns and mortars were pointing uselessly down the hill in the expected, but oppposite, direction of attack. German soldiers were grabbing desperately for their rifles and machine pistols, many falling before they could make use of their weapons.

Hand-to-hand combat ensued. Enemy troops flung themselves on the ground to escape the devastating barrage of bullets and thrusting bayonets. Others fought bitterly. Men fell throughout the bloodbath of the fierce hand-to-hand struggle.

Staff Sergeants Earnest Stamey and Lester Boswald fell early in the firefight. Shortly thereafter Staff Sgt. Joe Boylan was killed. Always heroic, these platoon Sergeants had led the fierce attack and were cut down. With this costly loss of his great soldiers (his right-hand leaders), Urban's emotions drove him beyond the edge of his normal fighting instincts. Again he knew the smell, the sound, and tone of combat. Death seemed very close at hand .... almost inevitable.

A German soldier rose up to oppose Urban and instantly reeled back. He was stunned by a blow from Urban's pistol butt. In the terrible noise of battle Urban was still keenly aware of death. His awareness and reactions were instantaneous, as if in slow motion. He was aware of events throughout the compounds as his attention absorbed more and more of the fast-moving struggle.

Most of the defenders were driven out of the stone bunkers. Unable to stem the tide of the sudden attack they fled down the face of the djebel. Immediately soldiers of 'F' Company jumped into the machine gun emplacements and opened fire on the fleeing figures.

At the edge of the crest Urban saw Allied prisoners whom the Germans had captured in an earlier attack against their position. Matt watched in horror. The fleeing Germans opened fire on them! The helpless

Allied prisoners were defenseless. Many died. Others were needing medical help.

One Platoon Sergeant who had been shot in the face was squirming on the ground, screeching and trying to claw his way out of the 'bamboo-like' thicket into which he had fallen. A German soldier emptied his gun into the man. Urban raged! He poured a steady stream of bullets into the offender.

A wounded, boyish looking American soldier who was trussed, looked up pathetically. He was gunned down by a retreating German officer. It was the first time Urban saw prisoners being executed. The surrendering Germans' inhumane slaughter of the American prisoners and of the helpless wounded men ignited Urban's passion for vengeance. It took all of Urban's willpower to hold his fire.

Quickly he shouted for the German prisoners to be lined up. In retaliation he made preparations to have them executed. Suddenly he regained his self-control and decided against the shooting. However, seething emotions needed to be satisfied, so he continued actions which the Germans assumed meant their certain death.

URBAN THREATENS RETRIBUTION
Urban's passion for vengeance against the German prisoners
was ignited by their execution of American prisoners.   Will power
prevailed, and Urban held his fire.

"YOU CANNOT DO THIS! IT'S AGAINST THE
GENEVA TREATY!"

These shrieking words rang out over mountain top
and into the jungle valley below. The shrieking was
by a short and cocky Prussian. He was a scholarly
looking Major with high boots and spectacles. He
was trying to uphold his 'status' by prancing up and
down the line of German prisoners.

The elite Nazi troopers, now POWs, were all six
footers. The troopers were trying to maintain their
German composure of stern rigidness –- models of
the Wehrmacht.

The Major, goose-stepped his way to affront Urban.
He gave an arrogant Nazi salute, "Heil Hitler!"
Lieutenant Urban looked down at him, unimpressed.
The man's nose paralleled Urban's chin, and the
Major shrieked again:

"YOU CANNOT DO THIS! IT'S AGAINST
THE GENEVA TREATY!'

That must have been the limit of his English. Urban
fought an urge to 'break his face' --- or worse!

Actions and movements of the American soldiers were complicated and different because of the problems imposed by the burden of so many German prisoners. A few of Matt's men were questioning whether to shoot or keep the Nazi's as prisoners. Arguing and shouting, they seemed uncertain about 'how they wanted to go'. Their behavior rattled the Nazis.

"Shoot the Bastards!" shouted Fred Herrin.

"You saw what they did," cried Lorenzo Filetti. The American soldiers were enraged! One GI spit in the face of an inhumane Hitlerite

Signs of weakening and expressions of fear began showing on hardened faces of the gritty, murdering Nazi Germans. In turn, their captors relished the emotional terror that they were imposing on the enemy. They spontaneously continued to 'pour on' their deathly threats.

Whether play-acting or real, they continued their harassment to the extreme. They prolonged the ultimatum, furthering their torments as they surged toward them, with shouts of of "Shoot 'Em! Burn 'em all! Look how they butchered our guys!" Several enraged GIs had to be physically restrained. Rifle shots were fired aimlessly but effectively adding to the harassment.

This scene of threatened massacre continued for about a half-hour. It must have served its purpose. In consternation the Nazi troopers began babbling in German, apparently trying to plead for mercy. The 'goose-step' was gone. Shoulders began to droop with the thought of impending death. They were escorted by gun barrel jabs as they were marched down the slope. Their passing was marked by the major's loud echoes ringing off the canyon walls:

"YOU CANNOT DO THIS --- IT'S AGAINST THE GENEVA TREATY!"

Eventually the captives were shuttled back on the narrow path which the 60th Infantry had laboriously slashed through the jungle. They were passed along from troop to troop to a POW holding area away from the battlefront.

- - - - - - - - -

ERNEST (ERNIE) PYLE   1900-1945
American war correspondent, Ernie Pyle, was stationed in London during the blitz of 1941.   He moved with the troops to cover the Invasion of North Africa with the 9th Division and continued with them through Sicily, Italy and France.   He transferred to the Pacific and accompanied assaults on Iwo Jima and Okinawa. On April 18th, 1945, he was killed by a Japanese sniper on the Island of Ie Shima.   Ernie Pyle's eye-witness accounts centered on the battle experiences of the ordinary soldier. He won many awards including the Pulitzer Prize for Journalism.

Stars and Stripes Army Publication:

"The Ninth has the kind of leadership and spirit that make a fighting outfit. They showed it by their brilliant envelopment of Green-Bald Hills in the Sedjenane Valley Campaign which led to the fall of Bizerte. They showed it in one of the bitterest battles of North Africa when they forced marched some 900 miles to help stem the Rommel thrust at Maknassy and the Kasserine Pass. When they proved themselves by their innovative tactical maneuver on the Green-Bald positions which the British had assaulted unsuccessfully for months --- the 60th Infantry massacred a German counter-attacking force."

- - - - - - - -

Ernie Pyle Reports on the U.S. Infantrymen:

"Now the Infantry, the 'God-damned Infantry', as they like to call themselves.

I love the Infantry because they are the underdogs. They are the mud-rain-frost-and wind boys. They have no comforts and they even learn to live without the necessities. And in the end they are the guys that wars can't be won without.

I wish you could see just one of the ineradicable pictures I have in my mind today. In this particular picture I am sitting among clumps of sword grass on a steep and rocky hillside that we have just taken. We are looking out over a vast rolling country to the rear. A narrow path comes like a ribbon over a hill miles away, down a long slope, across a creek, up a slope and over another hill.

All along a length of this ribbon there is now a thin line of men. For numberless days and nights they have fought hard, eaten little, washed none, and slept hardly at all. Their nights have been sleepless and miserable with the crash of artillery.

The men are walking. They are 20 feet apart, for dispersal, their walk is slow, for they are dead weary, as you can tell even when you look at them from behind. Every line and sag of their bodies speaks their inhuman exhaustion.

On their shoulders and backs they carry heavy steel tripods, machine gun barrels, leaden boxes of ammunition. Their feet seem to sink into the ground from the overload they are bearing.

They don't slouch. It is the terrible deliberation of each step that spells out their appalling tiredness. Their faces are black and unshaven. They are young men, but the grime and whiskers and exhaustion make them look middle aged.

In their eyes, as they pass is not hatred, not excitement, not despair, not the tonic of their victory -- there is just the simple expression of being here as though they had been here doing this forever and nothing else.

The line moves on, but it never ends. All afternoon men keep coming around the hill and vanishing eventually over the horizon. It is one long, tired line of ant-like men.

There is an agony in your heart and you are almost ashamed to look at them. They are just guys from Broadway and Main Street, but you wouldn't remember them; they are too far away now. They are too tired. Their world can never be known to you, but if you could see them just once, just for an instant, you would know that no matter how hard people work back home they are not keeping pace with these combat infantrymen. "

By Ernie Pyle

CHAPTER 9

THE 'DESERT FOX' ON THE RUN
General Erwin Rommel

An Easter Sunday --- In A World Of Hell

In the bloody battlefields of North Africa, American GI's were reinventing war. American ingenuity and daring disrupted the traditional methods of the German armies. They didn't charge into fortifications like the British. Their attacks were not accompanied by music like the Scots. There were no vodka-inspired, human-wave attacks as those of the Russians. They lacked the noble battle cries of the French. Quietly, methodically, they approached each objective as a unique problem to solve. Their silent efficiency was unnerving to a Nazi military machine that was accustomed to having its way. They just kept coming ... with a power and performance that proved to be unbeatable.

THROUGH THE
SEDJENANE

In this Northeastern Area of Tunisia, Urban and his 'F' Company endured some of the most difficult conditions (heat, dust, mountains, combined with strong German resistance), which were almost intolerable , but did not stop 'F' Company.

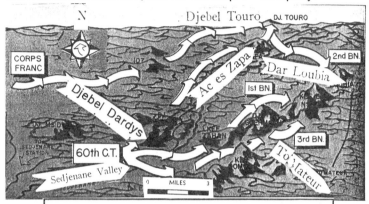

Distinguished Unit Citation

The *2d Battalion, 60th Infantry,* is cited for extraordinary heroism in the face of the enemy during the period 23 and 24 April 1943. This battalion formed the spearhead of an attack on 23 April against the Germans in the vicinity of the Sedjenane Valley, taking its first objective, Djebel Mrata, in an advance over densely wooded mountainous terrain, sooner than anticipated. Upon occupation of Djebel Mrata it became obvious that this position was of temporary importance because it was dominated by Djebel Dardys (sic), a higher ridge overlooking all terrain features in the vicinity. The battalion organized, pushed forward, and took the second position. On the morning of 24 April the Germans counterattacked with a force estimated at two battalions of infantry supported by artillery. The position defended was of considerable size and more than would normally be allotted for defense to a battalion. The attack lasted from 0800 to 1200, during which time the enemy made assaults from practically every direction. Fierce resistance and local counterattacks after the enemy had penetrated the position prevented him from gaining a foothold, and he retired leaving 116 dead, 48 wounded, and prisoners within the position. In this action the *2d Battalion* lost 21 dead and 111 wounded. The gallant and intrepid conduct of this entire battalion afforded a great tactical advantage in seizing and holding dominating terrain and assisted the advance of our forces culminating in the defeat of German arms in North Africa.

General Eddy's stealth and General Patton's speed shocked the Nazi war machine. Their heroic approach, using 'sweat and stealth' instead of 'blood' epitomized the modern approach to war. American servicemen were considered to be a most valuable, trained, and precious commodity. Applied intelligence replaced 'bravado', and 'strategy' replaced raw force. Here was a new form of warfare for the German military forces to digest. The lessons were costly! In only twelve days, the highly touted Afrika Korps and its reinforcements were routed! Southern Tunisia was in Allied hands. Rommel, the celebrated 'Desert Fox', was on the run!

Urban's 'F' Company maneuvered over difficult terrain to the final northeastern mountain range of Tunisia. The final objective was Hill #409. This formidable German position was perched on a controlling peak at the edge of the mountains. Beyond lay the desert and access to Bizerte. Yonder to the north was the Mediterranean Sea. Southeast lay the Mareth Line, the desert, and the 'Fox'.

General Rommel was finally about to be flushed out into the open. This was the beginning of the end of the war in Africa.

Lt. Matt Urban's weary, sweaty troops pushed their way onto an adjoining ridge in view of Djebel Cheniti. This was the last piece of dominating high ground overlooking Rommel's flight to the sea. Movement was difficult. They had marched a long distance over mountains and ridges that were considered impassable. They moved by mule train, carrying whatever heavy weapons could be packed by men or animals. By day they concealed their whereabouts in the sparse vegetation. Night travel was used whenever possible.

Days were hot under the blistering sun, and nights were freezing. To survive the wet, cold nights, the men were forced to sleep in piles, stacked one on top of another in foxholes to preserve precious body heat. Urban shared his blanket with Miller (who was a giant of a man) and Panzon, nicknamed 'Pinnochio' because of his slight frame. They slept in 'shifts', each man taking a turn in the middle. There warmth was optimal and weight was minimal. Despite the cold and intense discomfort, they had to snicker when it came time for Panzon to sleep on the bottom of the heap.

Chances for rest were rare. Most of the march was conducted in days of pain and bone-tired weariness.

Matt Urban felt that no one could ever visualize or realize what his men were going through. There was no way to describe this animalistic existence. No words Lt. Urban had ever heard could communicate this agony. IT WAS HELL!

When it seemed that they could not push ahead any longer, Urban ordered a rest. He mounted one of the stronger looking mules. Matt planned to ride ahead to the crest of the hill and reconnoiter. The mule was a pack animal. It was not accustomed to passengers, especially not to this energetic Urban. The tired, obstinate mule wanted to stay with the pack. It first bucked and kicked. Then the stubborn beast balked with all four feet planted firmly on the ground. That mule wasn't going to move, even with a fire beneath him. Eventually, the more stubborn of the two won out ... and Matt Urban rode off to scout the situation ahead.

From his vantage point on the highest ridge he could see the entrenched enemy. They appeared to be of regimental size. Another mobile regiment was staged in reserve a few miles away.

The final objective for Urban's troops was a heavily fortified ridge, Kef Domous, held by the German

VETERANS' RECOLLECTIONS & DIARY

army. They had successfully withstood months of pounding by the British.

Once more, silence, concealment, and their unexpected presence gave the American troops an advantage over the superior enemy force. They were poised for the attack, unnoticed, and right under the nose of the superior German military strength.

Urban's troops rested briefly to prepare for the attack. An imposing figure, the tall 2nd Lieutenant John Allen, stood up and emptied his can of cold beans on the ground. He bore a striking resemblance to the actor, Jimmie Stewart. He had the same precise accent and mannerisms. "C'mon, Urbie," he drawled. "There's not as many of us as the British lost altogether on this hill, so what have we got to lose?"

"We licked 'em so far, and we can lick 'em again!" Miller joining in, exclaimed. "Let's get to it!"

The German troops had scheduled time for mess. This was followed by 'siesta-time'. This African custom was scheduled from 1200 noon - 1400 PM to avoid the burning heat of the desert sun. Consequently, only a minimal crew manned the mighty fortifications. Enemy troops felt secure in a belief that they were far from the scene of battle. The time for a surprise attack was ripe.

Urban and the men of 'F' Company were positioning themselves for attack. The Germans were 'changing the guard' in a relaxed fashion and moving most of their guard troops to the rear. At the moment of maximum opportunity, Urban's men struck.

Fortifications were seized suddenly. American soldiers swarmed over the area. They rapidly occupied empty enemy machine gun emplacements. They cut loose a hail of machine gun fire on the defenders with captured German weapons. The rout was over before the defenders had time to regain military discipline.

As the German troops ran for cover, 'F' Company was consolidating its gains. They were forming a protective, dug-in double line staggered throughout the sturdy buttress. Sgt. John Miller, Staff Sergeant Joseph Boylan, and Pfc. William Nichols positioned themselves near the end of the defense line. They planned to bolster the right flank against any counter-attack.

None too soon! The first wave of a counter-attack struck within minutes. Enemy flanking forces showered them with heavy machine-gun fire. Sgt. Miller, standing upright, shuffled forward. Firing his Thompson submachine gun with deadly accuracy into an advancing German machine gun squad, Miller seized their gun. He fired it from the hip into a winding line of German troopers attacking up the slope. There he remained, fully exposed to enemy fire, withstanding repeated waves of attackers throughout the day. He was later awarded the 'Silver Star' for gallantry in this courageous action.

American soldiers of 'F' Company were vastly outnumbered, yet they had seized the winning initiative by bold action. Now they were assisted by the firepower of the captured enemy machine weapons. The German-built guns had a faster firing rate, and they were loaded with tracers. This line of lightning-white fire spewing death was terrifying.

The attacking Germans were having to face their own diabolical defenses! To overpower the thin, heavily gunned skirmish line of American troops, they had to cross a wide open slope. There they could be fired on effectively without being able to return fire. Next was a labyrinth of barbed-wire fences constructed so it was impossible to crawl under them. Defying all odds, these Hitlerite fanatics were about to plunge into the 'jaws of death'.

As the first wave of men reached the obstacles, they were swept away by a blaze of automatic weapons fire. The entire regiment must have been coming up the hill. The troops in front were being forced ahead by the press of men behind them. Casualties were enormous. Bodies fell, twisted in bizarre contortions, limbs bent, as if they had been dropped there. Dead and wounded piled up around the fences. The German attackers had to climb over bodies of their dead comrades to move ahead, becoming bodies themselves in the process. The hideous screams of the wounded and dying could barely be heard above the noise of the heavy caliber guns.

The suicide attack nearly worked, as the fanatical Nazi troopers made it within a few feet of the defenses. Clusters of hand grenades tore holes in their ranks. The desperate Americans beat back this horrible onslaught. In a wave of hellfire, Rommel's elite rear guard was pushed back and off the mountain. The few determined American defenders again earned battle success by grit, perseverance, ingenuity and daring initiative.

For a moment Urban reflected on the dangerous situation they were in. He felt the desperation of their predicament. He needed reinforcements ... at least an acknowledgment of the whereabouts from his adjoining units, if there were any! Matt needed to know that others were aware that 'F' Company had taken the dominant objective in miraculously quick time.

Suddenly the table top of the ridge erupted with earth shattering explosions. It seemed as if the world was coming to an end. The retreating Germans had turned their heavy artillery around. An enormous concentration of shellfire burst all around the perimeter. It was turning the entire area into an inferno! There was nothing to do but hold and wait. Urban knew their chances of survival were slim. Then came the sound of men screaming in the distance. Another Nazi attack wave was upon them.

Mercifully, there was no time to think or feel anything. Survival was the only consideration. German burp guns, machine pistols, and potato mashers were counteracted by 'F' Company's M-1's, machine guns and hand grenades in a horrifying confrontation. Again, the headlong rush was crushed temporarily by the murderous barrage of the American defenders.

A loud cheer burst forth from the besieged American troops. They had repulsed a second major attack! Casualties were mounting, yet nothing could dislodge them from their hard-won victory. They were 'boxed in' and endured direct fire from the heavy stuff that was being thrown in around the clock. 'F' Company was surrounded! If there was to be any food, medical supplies, or ammunition, it would have to be airdropped.

Night followed day. Through its light fog and mist, moans and cries of the wounded could be heard throughout the long night. A single dead GI stood upright in full view of his comrades. His body had become jammed against a rock. A single bullet hole was showing through his helmet.

This is an emotional phenomenon known only to those who have endured combat and seen the battlefield deaths. Every man agonizes for them. They realize the pain and suffering of their buddies. There were no doctors and few medical supplies for the marooned Americans of Urban's 'F' Company.

The two medics performed wonders on many shattered American bodies. They could do little or nothing for the pleading screams of pain. A heavy-set young private was shot through the leg. No bones were broken, and he seemed to be fine. "You have a million dollar wound," the medic told him. "You've got your ticket home." But he died suddenly in the night from complications arising from shock and injury trauma.

By far the most unbearable injuries were to those infantrymen whose faces were torn apart. One man had his nose and part of the surface of both cheeks blasted away. His agitated thrashing evidenced his agony. Another was left with only a dripping, bloody stub where his lower jaw, mouth, and bottom teeth should have been. With indescribable pain, he was slipping in and out of consciousness, driving fellow infantrymen close to the limit of their emotional endurance.

Pitiful moaning became more eerie with the passing night. The men's yelps and pathetic pleas tore at Urban's insides.

In a delirium of pain, the soldier cradled in Urban's arms cried out begging, "Captain! Shoot me! Shoot!

Let me die!" In vain attempts, Urban could only force himself to bring his .45-caliber barrel inches in front of the man's imploring eyes. Then he placed the gun barrel to the back of the suffering soldier's head, but Urban's trigger finger would not move!

Matt's shoulders drooped, heavily laden with inner thoughts spinning. "Did I renege on my responsibility?" An unsolved dilemma flooded the Captain's thoughts: "Why the turn-about in mercy. How come I forsook my soldier in his plea to be put out of his misery?"

Urban made his way past several of his onlooking soldiers. They glared motionless, tensely awaiting the climax! The watching men released their breath, reflecting a sigh of relief. Their response eased Urban's pent-up emotional trauma.

His compassion and brotherhood was with his men. With the sound of their release of breath, relief engulfed Urban. By far this was the most dreadful moment; the most incredible night of his life! He had just faced the worst nightmare imaginable. He now knew that he could deal with anything. Urban's agony gave way to a sense of tranquility.

EASTER SUNDAY!

Oh, to be at home! Every man preciously reminisced of home and family even though the air was full of death.

The men of the Ninth Division expressed their Easter feelings right there in the middle of a world of hell! They mentally fabricated the mood of going to church, the blessing of food in Easter baskets, and of Fifth Avenue --- that Easter parade song: "Put on your Easter bonnet, with all the frills upon it ...."

Vividly they recalled family dinners, Easter egg hunts in green backyards, the gardens blooming with multi-colored flowers. Treasured scenes of hometowns, villages, family --- there were so many pleasant things to remember. The stark reality of their surroundings cast a cloud over beloved memories during the few early morning hours before pandemonium erupted!

The American troops --- eyes closed in reverie --- basked in the sun of the area's serene background, yet they were so close to death. All conversations were of peace and home; not of hatred, not of killing, but of LOVE.

They took turns comforting the two whose faces were half blown off. Holding the warm, quivering body of a person you loved like a brother, with no face, was unbearable!!! It was a horrible experience to try to comfort a fellowman in such dire agony and to look at an oozing, bloody, coagulating mass of flesh, the lower half of the nose, lips, teeth in shreds.

Urban said this description may sound exaggerated, because it is difficult to conceive the way it was. Every impression is essential to express the way it was on that bloody mountain top.

To look at them, to hold them, to console them, to try to talk to them -- what words can you attempt? What tone of voice, if any, would help?

You shoot dogs! You shoot horses!

What to do? What can you do?

"Maybe someday I will understand," thought Urban. "I will try to understand! I hope and pray --I will --- someday."

The Battle Rages On:

"Here they come," shouted Preston. The GI's settled back into the cruel warfare, and survival became first and foremost for each infantryman. After two more long days of battle and shelling were endured, they still held their position! Late on the third day, medical supplies were airdropped to Matt's area. Urban thought, "Thank you, Lord, for this miracle from heaven!" Packages of sulfa and morphine were grabbed up quickly. Urgently needed ammunition and food supplies were also air dropped that day.

On the last day they engaged in a particularly bitter fight with the Germans. A foggy, misty dawn surfaced with an enemy on an all-out attack.

Urban was awakened by his men stampeding past him in full retreat. He tried to stem the rush, yelling and holding up his hands, bumping into several with shouted orders: "Return to your foxholes; hold your positions!"

Mass confusion had erupted. Everything was made more difficult by the fog-shrouded visibility of just a few feet. Urban pushed his way up to the ridge crest

FROM THE STARS & STRIPES WEEKLY
Saturday, October 2, 1943

"Former star boxer ... grappled with a Heinie ..."
The 60th Regiment of the 9th Division goes by the name of "The Go Devils". They acquired fame for their wide flanking movements through terrain the enemy regarded as impassable in the Green and Bald hill area. With the French Goums, they constructed a thirty-four mile road through the wilderness to bring up their heavy artillery. It was so rugged that supplies sometimes had to be dropped by plane. At times the mules could not make it.

The battalion was commanded by Lt. Col. Michael B. Kauffman of Laramie, Wyoming. His battalion received a special citation in beating off a German counterattack in the Sedjenane Valley. In that counterattack, Captain Matty L. Urbanowitz (Urban), a former star boxer for Cornell University, grappled with a Heinie, grabbed his machine pistol and turned it on the advancing German squad.

where he heard what appeared to be one of his troops in perfect English loudly commanding, *"F Company, fall back!"* His men had picked it up ... and followed the order.

Urban worked his way up to the source. A German paratroop Captain waving a 'Burp' gun was yelling in clear English for Urban's men to fall back! Urban jumped on the man's back, stuck a trench knife into his windpipe, slitting his throat, and grabbed the German 'Burp' gun.

Urban instantly put the German's gun to good use. He reported: "It was like shooting ducks off a pond." Matt opened fire on German troops as they emerged in clusters from the fog.

The first wave of men dropped like dominoes as Urban fired at close range. Another cluster followed. Urban leveled them as they came into view. The only gun firing for a few moments was the German-made machine gun. Its much faster firing rate made a different sound than the American made 'Tommy Gun'.

The 'Jerries' pressed towards the sound, thinking that it was one of their own men firing on the Americans.

Urban began yelling for his men to heave grenades into the area. "Get back to your positions," he roared. Almost immediately his men now realized the ruse of the German paratrooper order for "Company F fallback". Men of Company 'F' now dug in for battle! It was the most determined counterattack of the three days. Once again the stubborn Company 'F' defenders repulsed Rommel's zealous, fanatic troops and held onto their defensive position.

As full daylight cleared the fog, a white flag preceded a German request to collect their wounded. German medics moved in to pick up injured men who had fallen in the last attack. 1st Sgt. John 'Whip' Miller counted 116 dead Nazis.

The wary Americans watched carefully. Too many comrades had fallen following German deception in similar circumstances. In this case, however, the mangled, bloody enemy troops were removed without incident.

The next objective of II Corps was Bizerte, "The Last Stop".

On May 8 the 894th and Company A of the 751st Tank Battalion and Lt. (Captain) Orion Shockley and several forward observers of the 47th Cannon Company were the first to enter the city.

Urban's 'F' Company, with a few of Patton's tanks, were the first infantrymen to enter the historic city. British troops entered Tunis approximately the same time. The two victories signalled the collapse of the Nazi and Axis power in Africa.

The American liberators posted guards outside the city limits of Bizerte. Headquarters had issued strict orders that no one be allowed to enter the city without authorization.

A two-star General approached the city in a Jeep and was unable to provide the proper authorization signature approved by commanding General Omar Bradley. He was refused entry. He fumed at the obstinate sentry: "You know who I am? I give orders around here." He commanded his driver to proceed.

THE 47TH CANNON COMPANY
AND THE 2ND BATTALION

On May 8th Lt. Shockley's 47th Cannon Company and Lt. Col. Johnston's 2nd Battalion entered Bizerte.   Urban's F Company followed the first tank into the city.   For political reasons a Battalion of Corps Franc were taken from reserve and placed to the left of the 47th.   Although the Americans entered Bizerte first, the combat team was withdrawn. The French were allowed to mop up remaining resistance. This gesture allowed France a major step toward liberation of its homeland.

"I wouldn't do that if I were you, Sir," growled the sentry, lowering his carbine. "My orders are clear: *Shoot anyone who tries to enter!*"

The enraged General ordered his driver to turn around, and they departed.

Foot soldiers commandeered the plush hotel that had housed the German High Command. The enlisted men raided its food and champagne. They felt like kings for three days. The velvety (Nazi officers') cocktail bar was turned into an enlisted men's haven. Officers and Non-Coms were permitted as honored guests. Together they reaped the relaxation that they had earned after enduring a long, strenuous battle campaign.

1st Sgt. 'Whip' Miller, as always, lived up to his name of 'Whip'. He set up a strict regimented schedule. He intervened with his challenge to high living. The duty order was as follows: The first four hours required being stationed to assigned roadblock posts. The next four hours were for 'happy hour' at the plush 'Whip's Whippin' cocktail lounge.

This routine was followed by eight hours of heavenly bliss in the hotel's fluffy beds, only to be awakened to

GERMAN AND ITALIAN FORCES SURRENDER
On May 9, 1943, the enemy surrendered in the II Corps Zone, and only scattered Axis units remained to offer resistance.

Soon there were thousands of P.O.W.s in the massive II Corps cages, including General Jurgin von Arnim, the German supreme commander. An arrogant enemy army was getting a taste of its own medicine!

the 'disaster-call' of Whip's volcanic wake-up voice! "Up and at 'em, you no good GI's". Startled men almost scrambled over one another running down the stairways to report before their beloved 1st Sgt, 'The Whip'. They appeared on time, and in order.

The outings ended all too soon. Shortly, the Ninth Division Infantrymen reported to a regimental assembly area outside the city. Uniforms and equipment were replenished.

Once more they were pressed into service. This time they were to guard thousands of Axis prisoners crowded together on several acres on a nearby plain. Over 150,000 German and Italian prisoners were captured. Very few had escaped capture, because British ships in the Mediterranean sunk or burned nearly every escape vessel.

On May 13, 1943, the Tunisian Campaign ended with the surrender of all Axis forces under General Von Armin. A total of 238,240 German and Italian prisoners were taken.

The American troops now began procedures for an amphibious assault, destination unknown. Wherever it was, the Americans would be ready!

CHAPTER 10

THE SILENT MARCH - SICILY
One of the Greatest Strategic Maneuvers in World War II History

On May 11, 1943, Churchill arrived in Washington for the Trident meetings to discuss strategy for the next move by the Allies.

Captain Urban's men of the Ninth Division were busy replenishing supplies, healing wounds, and training replacements. The U.S. intelligence community meanwhile allowed fake messages to be found by the Spanish. These suggested that the next attack would be launched through Greece and Sardinia. Sicily was identified as a 'cover operation'. The German high command believed the messages to be genuine. They planned accordingly. On June 1, American bombers pommeled into submission a strong Luftwaffe base on Pantellarea Island.

MESSAGES TO THE 9TH INFANTRY DIVISION

. . . . The ability of the Division to push forward, in some cases over rough terrain where roads were non-existent, hurried the final results.

—Lt. General (General) Omar N. Bradley

18 August 1943

TO: All Troops, 9th Infantry Division

With the campaign in Sicily drawing to a close, I can tell you that once AGAIN you have brilliantly justified my confidence and pride in you as a courageous, efficient, fighting organization.

The mountainous terrain over which you so successfully attacked must have been a challenge to your spirit and stamina—a challenge, I want to say, you met in the highest tradition of the United States Army. The problems you were forced to solve in supply alone would have stopped a less determined division. You have accomplished almost impossible feats of engineering, communication, and evacuation. The lessons you learned in Tunisia have served you well in Sicily.

In every branch you have well earned in the minds of your commanders, your country, AND YOUR ENEMIES, the title of "the VETERAN Ninth Division."

You have all witnessed the wretchedness, the suffering, and the want that war brings to the people of the land in which the war is fought. God forbid that our loved ones at home will have to experience what the peoples of Sicily, Italy, and Germany are now experiencing. It is up to everyone of us to see that this war is brought to a quick and successful conclusion. This can be brought about only by determination for vigorous action in that direction by every individual of this command.

—Major General Manton S. Eddy.

On July 9, 1943, American forces made an amphibious landing on Sicily. This surprise move was to gain a 'springboard' for an assault on Italy. The weakened government of Benito Mussolini was a prime target for takeover. A sweeping air attack preceded the landing. Most of the German airfields and aircraft on the island were utterly destroyed. A terrible onslaught of Allied naval batteries saturated the beaches. The combined pre-invasion assault cleared the way for an Allied amphibious landing. On July 10, 160,000 soldiers, 1,000 artillery pieces and 600 tanks were put ashore.

Opposition was sporadic from the demoralized Italian troops. They could see no logic in fighting. Within a single day almost a third of Sicily was conquered. The enemy resistance then stiffened in the rugged mountains around Troina. The First Division (Big Red One) bogged down in difficult terrain against hardened Nazi troops entrenched in fortified mountain strongholds. The Combat Engineers built bridges and roads capable of handling two-and-a-half-ton trucks along sheer cliff edges. Still the tenacious Nazi enemy could not be dislodged.

General Omar Bradley visited General Manton Eddy. Together they conceived an extraordinary tactical

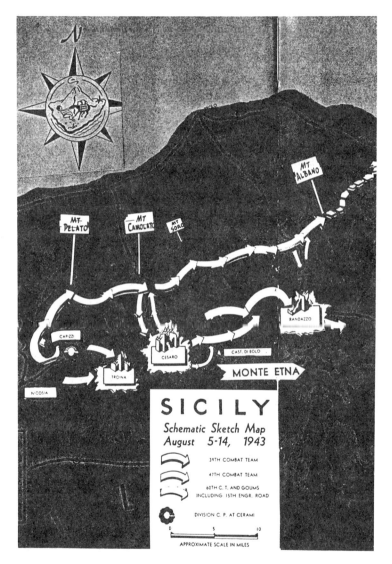

MAP OF CENTRAL SICILY

The strategy of the Silent March began at Capizzi -- to Mount Pelato, Mount Camolato and Mount Albano. All were Northeast from Capizzi. This action caused German retreat from Troina to Randazzo.

234

maneuver. The men of the Ninth Division would carry out a flanking action by secretly crossing the central mountains in total silence.

The 60th Combat Team disembarked from Africa at 1130, July 28, 1943, on the S.S. Orizaba. The food and dry accommodations on board ship were a welcome luxury for these GI's who had been existing for months in muddy foxholes. They arrived in the harbor of Palermo at 2000 on July 31 and spent the night aboard ship. At 0415 they were bombed by German planes. Urban was on deck as usual. An anti-aircraft gunnery crew lost its spotter in the volley of 'Stuka' machine gun fire. Urban jumped into the crewman's position. He grabbed the dying man's binoculars in time to sight the enemy plane swooping in at the 11 o'clock position. A burst from the anti-aircraft gunnery blasted the incoming German aircraft. It went down in flames.

THE SILENT MARCH BEGINS

Not a sound accompanied the eerie marching column. Over 4,000 men stalked silently through the night carrying weapons and supplies. Mules with hoofs wrapped in clumps of cloth gave evidence of

235

Lt. Col. "Mike" Kauffman
C.O. 2nd Battalion
60th Infantry Div.

Nicknamed "Black Mike" by his troops because of heavy black moustache. This highly respected leader was responsible for the 60th Infantry Regiment flanking movement which forced German troop retreat from central Sicily (Troina Area). The key action became known as "The Silent March".

PRESENTATION OF SILVER STAR
FOR GALLANTRY IN ACTION

General Manton S. Eddy, 5 September, 1943, Cefalu, Sicily, presented Lt. Col. 'Mike' Kauffman with the Silver Star for gallantry. On this same day Lt. John Allen and Lt. Matt Urban were also recipients of the Silver Star military award.

the elaborate preparations. Minute attention to detail had gone into suppressing every possible noise.

The Ninth Division Band became the 'mule-skinners'. They were assigned the job of transporting food, medical supplies and ammunition by pack animal. All through the hot days they crouched in the underbrush holding the animals by the bridle to keep them concealed. Their pack-mule service was essential to victory in Sicily.

Division orders called for the 2nd Battalion 60th Infantry led by Lt. Col. Mike Kauffman to spearhead the strategic formation through the heart of Sicily.

'Black' Mike's battalion was a logical choice. His wisdom and control had led to a score of triumphs and two Presidential unit citations. His success was based on recognition and trust in his front line, battle-wise officers.

Even today General Kauffman openly voices recognition to Matt Urban, Steve Sprindis, Bill Voller, Ralph Johnson, John Allen, Robert Kriz, Willard Barnwell, Max Wolf, Hiram 'Speed' Tye, Roland Nelson, Irving Shuttleworth, Don West, Bob

Patterson, Loyd Tallent, Jack Ames, Kennard, Emmerich, Doxsee, Morton, Higgins and Wilson.

- - - - - - - - - -

Several other 60th Regimental officers who emerged as heroic leaders from the African Campaigns included General Norman Chick Hennen, Joe Scheidel, Karl Ingebretsen, Carey Cox, George Sharra, Wyett Coclasure, Harold Smith, Irving Scott, Otto Koch, John Brooks, Arden Brill, Jesse Hayes, John Whitmore, Robert Herzog, Al Bruchac, Pat Williamson, Keene 'Slick' Wilson, Lt. Quentin 'Hardtack' Hardage.

Actions beyond the call of duty have been earned by such enlisted men and non-commissioned officers as Jim Etue, Robert Rucker, Ed English, Nic Moraza, Ollie Clapp, John McChesney, Ed Kerans, Jim Rodgers, Bob Kerr and many others. They structured themselves into a team of 'brotherhood' based on superior performance.

The swarthy, robe-draped Goums had accompanied them from Africa. They provided valuable scouting assistance. The 1st Battalion of the 60th Infantry Regiment served as a decoy by walking nonchalantly

Regiment served as a decoy by walking nonchalantly through the streets of Capizzi, giving the enemy an impression that this was to be the route of assault.

Stealth required rigid discipline. The use of silent flanking maneuvers was becoming a standard method of operation for Urban and his 'F' Company. His unit was delegated to take the lead point on several of the forced night movements over the Sicilian terrain and 'washboard' rough gravel roads.

At the outset of this 'silent' march, timed nightly from 2100 to 0500, all were indoctrinated with the belief in the need for extra precautions. All orders were in low whispers. Their methods had to be 'like mountain goats', marching single file over narrow animal trails along ledges circling mountain peaks. This was necessary to avoid the roads and certain detection.

On the Silent March, Captain Urban's Company 'F' consisting of 150 men, led off on the march with full packs. Slipping silently through sparsely inhabited alpine country without being seen or heard was a trying challenge. Otherwise, rumors would be carried to the enemy, their whereabouts discovered, and the mission reduced to defeat!

PRESENTATION OF SILVER STARS
FOR GALLANTRY IN ACTION
General Manton S. Eddy, 5 September, 1943, Cefalu, Sicily, presented the Silver Star awarded for gallantry to several of the troops of the 60th Regiment. 2nd Lt. John Allen (second from the right) and Lt. Matt Urban (3rd from the right) were recipients of the Silver Star that day.

Cattle could not even be disturbed. German scouts were known to wear cowbells as a way to remain undetected in these hilly pastures. Frequently the soldiers of the Ninth Division found themselves crouching in the underbrush, waiting for a herd of scrubby dairy cows to pass. Even the singing of birds and the routines of wildlife had to be undisturbed. It was imperative to avoid giving any signal of the whereabouts of the elusive American Ninth.

Most difficult of all were the necessary halts during twelve hours of daylight. Infantrymen, already cramped by the penetrating cold of the mountain altitude, had to crouch in awkward positions, squeezed together, almost motionless. They were forced to endure long, drawn-out days. Areas infested with biting insects made their flesh twitch and suffer painful stings.

Adding to their distress, a comforting warmth from the morning sun grew glaringly hot by mid-day. It was sapping away some of 'F' Company's shreds of stamina as they tried to hang on. They opened 'C' rations and with fingers attempted to eat 'C' rations, hash, and beans. Like robots they kept moving in methodical silence.

CAPTAIN MATT URBAN LEADS F COMPANY
ON THE SILENT MARCH
The olive drab army blanket draped over the head for warmth gave Urban and his troops a silhouette which a herdsman mistook for ghosts. He accepted this as a delusion brought on by having guzzled too much wine.

Captain Urban was leading his 'F' Company by a few yards. To combat the near-freezing night cold on the mountain, Urban had draped an olive drab army blanket over his head for warmth, and his troops had done the same. A 'copper' moon shining through thin cloud cover gave the shrouded Urban and his men an eerie silhouette.

It was reported by a herdsman that a strange line of men was led by a 'GHOST'. Fortunately, the wine guzzling Sicilian accepted this as one more of his delusions!

On the following 'pitchblack night' Urban moved ahead cautiously in measured steps, careful not to knock loose a stone ... or to step into the abyss ... off the cliff edge where there WAS NO STEP.

Late on the third night Urban stumbled into danger. Legs weakened, eyes weary, mind hazy, his next step had no end. Off he fell into the darkness below the trail. His voice caught in his throat, paralyzed in the attempt to withhold the gasping shriek that was bursting to get out. He felt himself slipping down the precipitous edge of the cliff in sudden shock. "Heaven help me!" was his instant thought.

ROCKY TERRAIN TYPICAL OF SILENT MARCH
This view shows the hazardous   mountainous trail on the route of
the Silent March. It was dark, and from this narrow trail Urban
slipped over the precipitous edge of the cliff.

Another miracle! Matt's arms were outstretched with his body sliding down the mountainside. Abruptly his hands clamped onto a knobby, firmly grounded root. Urban held his grip at the edge of eternity. With his grasp weakening, Matt felt aching fingers slipping a bit each minute.

Matt wondered if there was any hope, any chance of rescue ... and if anyone knew that he was gone. He knew they were following at spaced intervals. In his mind Matt kept repeating to himself: "Surely they know that I fell. Will they realize that by the grace of God, my big drop was stopped only 30 feet below them?" He prayed they didn't assume that he lay dead some 1,000 feet below.

He thought in desperation, "To hell with the stringent silence. Being this far distant in this dark of night, I will yell to live! But, no, I cannot. Not even a whimper!"

Fortunately, Urban's men had missed him and were looking for him. Pausing and groping towards the edge, they had faith in the slight possibility that their Captain was still alive somewhere 'down there'.

Suddenly, hope and action were aroused. Sgt. Skertich made out what he thought was a slight sound down below. Aided by Corporal Clark, he collected belts and other materials to hook and tie together with length and strength to save Matt's life. The rescue was incredible. The ledge trail was less than two feet wide with crumbling edges. There was only enough for a single man. To haul Matt up to the rescuers, required some careful maneuvering. Then suddenly he was safe ... and standing proudly with his faithful troops.

There was great mutual excitement. Voices wanted to shout, "We did it; we brought our Captain back!" This was no time, and not a safe place for vocal celebration. An unspoken sense of joy and great pride engulfed all of them. They continued their steady march with greater inspiration and determination.

The remaining penetration of Axis lines was completed methodically. This secretive flanking maneuver caught the Axis forces off guard. By the time the enemy discovered the presence of the American military men, resistance had become futile. Urban and his men were inside the villages before anyone suspected their presence. Large numbers of Italian troops were taken prisoner.

The German troops, deeply entrenched at Troina, were alerted by the early action. They abandoned their fortifications, dismantled artillery, and retreated to their next line of defense. This result otherwise would have taken many days and cost hundreds of American lives. A direct battle was averted by 'stealth and sweat'. Again the strategies of General Eddy and General Bradley prevailed with dramatic success.

Sicily capitulated on August 17, when American troops stormed into Messina. General Eisenhower declared the island liberated on August 20. A major victory rested with the Allies. An enemy force of 405,000 troops had been routed from their mountain fortress in only thirty-eight days. Despite the rugged enemy-held terrain, blown bridges, minefields, and other factors, this victory was a recognized logistical miracle.

For years Hitler's evil regime had its way conquering and dominating the countries of Europe. With this Allied victory, people of that continent received their first intimation that Hitler's Nazi terror might be coming to an end.

- - - - - -

Urban and his 'F' Company bivouacked near an Italian village. Captain Urban was treated as a dignitary at a three-hour lunch. Fine wines and many courses of the best Sicilian food were the 'order of the day'. The village's Padre, the Mayor, Lieutenant Brown, and 'Commandant' Urban were treated by a local businessman to celebrate the end of the war in Sicily. Conversation was spirited and noisy, as Lt. Brown attempted to bring across his 'off-the-cuff' comment:

"We fought the French for the Kasba, and now they are our allies. Hitler is buddies with Mussolini, but the Italian people hate them both. Communist Russia is fighting Nazi Germany as our ally, but they were working together with the Germans a little while ago. The puppet government of Norway has joined with Germany, while the Norwegian 'underground' is fighting for us. Does anyone understand this?"

With all this going on, Urban still was able to personally observe the deep gratitude of these Sicilian people. They were 'free' at last from the domination of the Nazi-Fascist machine. The threat and terror of war was now greatly diminished --- or already gone!

A BRIEF R & R ODYSSEY

That afternoon Urban joined Ben (Bomber) Murell, George Albert and Charlie LiBretto for a trip into town. Along the way they passed an isolated stone farmhouse with a tiled roof. It was set off by out buildings, grape fields and olive trees. The mountains added a protective background to the picturesque scene. The farmer and his four daughters were working together in the field. The youngest girl looked to be about seventeen. For these GI's, the sight of these olive skinned girls was refreshingly exciting.

Sicilian families tended to be very strict. During the German occupation the young women had been hidden in the mountains. These young ladies returned the gaze of the handsome American men in uniform, who were enjoying the view from a distance. The young men of Sicily had been forcibly conscripted into the Fascist armies of Mussolini or shanghaied into Nazi labor camps. Loneliness was one of the lesser casualties of war.

The girls were delighted at the attention from American GI's passing by throughout the day. Pa Pa, however, was keeping an eye on them! By a stroke of luck the old man stepped into the barn just as Urban and his men came by. The lovely sisters took advantage of the situation to shyly approach the fence. Ben Murell knew just enough Italian to make himself understood. He boldly approached the fence. In broken Italian he asked, "Will you join us for the afternoon?" He spoke directly to the oldest sister.

"We cannot. Our Pa Pa is very strict!" Her voice carried a hint of interest.

"You are very beautiful. And your sisters are lovely. Perhaps you will meet us tomorrow night."

Their conversation continued, erupting into laughter as the others looked on.

"What are they saying?" Urban asked.

"They can't come with us because of their father," Murell replied.

At that moment Pa Pa emerged from the barn carrying a pitchfork. He was a swarthy man with a bushy dark mustache. Under his stern glare, the girls scurried back to their work.

"That's just my luck," grumped Albert. "Too bad."

"Maybe not. They are going to try to slip out tomorrow night. They want to see us again," replied Murell.

"Manana! Manana! Hey Paison. We have hit the jackpot!" chuckled LiBretto as the GI's moved on down the road.

"More likely we'll meet up with a shotgun if their father catches on," Urban joked. "This is more dangerous than the war."

Murell agreed, "If they get caught, their old man is apt to beat the daylights out of them, or insist on a shotgun wedding."

Albert laughed and exclaimed excitedly, "Did you see the bodies on them? If I have to die, let it be for something so good! I haven't seen a woman in months. They are the answer to my prayers!"

A SICILIAN R & R REMINISCENCE
(A Composite Photo)
George Albert, Charley LiBretto, Ben (Bomber) Murell and Matt
Urban reminisced at a 9th Division Reunion. These good friends
enjoyed again recounting the fact and fantasies of their dates in
Sicily ..... We still aren't sure that 'Bomber' Murell really can sing!

The night was black. The lights in the little house flickered out early. Behind a pile of hay, four GI's waited with anticipation, hearts pounding excitedly.

Finally a door opened. Four beautiful young ladies appeared. The girls were dressed in long peasant skirts with low cut blouses that did little to hide their obvious charms. Thick black hair was combed back. As they approached they smelled fresh and clean. Obviously they had planned carefully for this rendezvous.

Not a word was spoken. Each girl had determined her choice in advance. They took the hands of their chosen partner.

Soon they were out of earshot range from the house. 'Bomber' Murell explained that they had to avoid town because the girls couldn't afford to be seen.

That was okay with Urban. His feelings were charged, and so were the emotions of his date. 'Maria' she said softly, pointing to herself. Her large, brown eyes held his gaze.

'Matt', he replied. The rest of the conversation was unspoken. Eyes spelled out what the mind imagined. Hands eloquently carried the message. They playfully explored each fascinating sensation, both new to the expression of love, both living as if there were no tomorrow. Emotions were caught up in the grip of an overpowering force....

Down along the river bank, a sturdy male voice resounded, singing words that seemed to be made for the moment. Laughter welled up from the depths of Urban's being. He didn't know that 'BOMBER' could sing!

"O Sole Mio. When life is nigh, there's no tomorrow, there's just tonight."

CHAPTER 11

MILITARY BUILD-UP
WARTIME ENGLAND -- BRIDGE TO INVASION

E.T.O. Boxing Championships -- Joe Louis

Over two thousand weary footsloggers were crowded onto the decks of a ship designed to carry less than half that number! The destination was unknown, but rumors were that they were bound for Merry Old England and a respite from the fighting.

The troop carrier was in dire confusion. Crowded decks and noisy chatter left no spot to meditate, relax or engage in physical recreation. Crowded conditions brought apprehension to everyone. There were doubts in each mind, thoughts of "rightfully, we should be sent back home ... we earned it!" But the possibility hung heavy over the ship that they were going to be pushed back into the hell of war.

The shortage of combat-experienced soldiers may force the high command to turn to their 'ace-in-a-hole' and shove soldiers who were 'belly-full' of combat into yet another war --- the European invasion. This dreaded feeling festered into the highest peak of frustratlon.

The first days of heavy seas added misery to the calamity. On the third evening the voyage finally settled down. Restlessness appeared to ease a bit. The bright moon above lit a huddle of men busy at shooting dice.

Captain Urban, peering over their crouched shoulders, noticed that a soldier was winning every pot. The losers were beginning to become suspicious. Accusations began to fly. Tempers woro chort and anything could happen in such a potentially explosive environment. Urban moved in quickly, grabbed the man's cupped hands and yelled, "Let me take a look at those 'dominoes'." The shooter revealed the cubes of chance; however, a quick body search exposed a pair of loaded dice stashed in a stocking attached to the open bottom of his inside right pocket. The thirty or so guys crowding around, pressed in. Cries of anger erupted. "That son-of-a-bitch, let's throw him overboard! Give him to us, Captain!"

Stark terror registered on the man's face at the thought of his doom. Although Matt shared the anger of his men, he also was responsible for the well-being of all the troops. He picked the small-statured culprit up by the collar and the seat of his pants, raised him over his head, and strode purposefully toward the edge of the deck. The man was screaming, "No, No, have mercy!" There was no reversing the mob psychology of the lynch-hungry crowd.

At the edge of the deck, Matt flung the man over the ship's rail, but held onto his trousers at the beltline. Suspended in mid-air over the edge of the ship, the man screamed for his life. For a long time the crowd yelled and demanded their revenge. Rancor finally subsided when they saw that the offender had experienced fear sufficient to 'pay his dues'. Matt dragged the man unceremoniously back onto the deck and spoke in low tones to the crowd, "Okay, it's over. Now every man take from the pot what belongs to him. This joker is off limits to any more gambling."

The rest of the ocean journey to England was relatively uneventful. Urban tells us that there were many quiet thoughts of the anticipated peaceful times at the next base to which they were being ordered. He said that everyone aboard ship had fervent prayers for returning home safely at the earliest possible time.

Temperatures dropped as the ship entered the northern climates. Through the foggy, windy, Irish Sea and into the mouth of the Mersey River they sailed. Finally they docked at the wharfs of Liverpool. The sea part of the voyage was over. They were soon loaded onto trains. Urban and 'F' Company were shown to their barracks that evening in Winchester, England.

They were overwhelmed by the relative luxury of their surroundings. After months spent sleeping in wet trenches and bitter cold weather, their new barracks at Camp Bushfield were like a second home. The 60th Rifles of the British army formerly were stationed at Camp Bushfield. The British made much of this coincidence of mutual numerical identity.

Hitler had failed to conquer the determined Britons, but American soldiers soon conquered the hearts and minds of these warm-hearted, generous people. The happy, carefree 'Yanks' were well received. The 'chemistry' of mutual interest between the cultures and customs created a positive and friendly atmosphere. This feeling was to live forever in the hearts and minds of those American and English friends.

Passes and furloughs were quickly arranged for Urban's grateful infantry men. London, with its Picadilly Circus, was the most popular spot to visit. A pass to that city was considered a great treasure.

Even by British standards the winter of 1943 was an extraordinary time in England. They had withstood years of being pounded by the Axis forces and still held out in the most heroic fashion. The country was now rearmed and teeming with thousands of Allied soldiers. Britons welcomed the military men with open arms. They both had a common enemy and a tremendous unity among the predominantly Caucasian populations and English-speaking armies.

Similar cultures and mutual interests bonded the formal Britons with the brash young Americans. The horror of war and the personal losses that were felt so deeply brought about a mutual respect based on a shared goal ... DEFEAT HITLER!

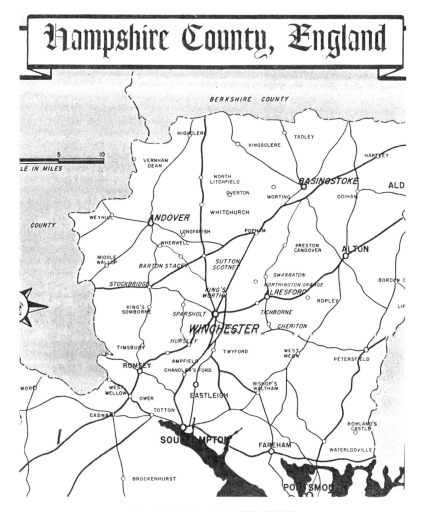

𝕳ampshire County, England

BACK TO CIVILIZATION

England was a welcome home away from home for the 9th Division. Everyone enjoyed hearing and speaking the English language. These soldiers had spent a year or more in substandard living conditions, devoid of normal pleasures and without seeing those tourist attractions that appeared on travel posters. They looked forward to movies, girls, dancing, better drinks, furloughs, quicker mail service and regular bathing facilities! Everyone enjoyed regular meals and PX supplies. Winchester was ten miles north of the English Channel and the Port of Southampton. It was approximately forty-five miles southwest of London.

England had already lost more than a million of her young men. The women of the British Isles were particularly interested in this influx of so many American men. A spirit of 'nothing to lose' combined with impending danger and the glamour of uniforms. The military atmosphere created an emotional tinder box. The British men had three regular comments about the American soldiers: 'overpaid, oversexed, and over here!'

Despite this, the British-American cultures were distinctly harmonious. The Americans had great admiration for their hosts and a sincere appreciation for their British environment. Men from around the world converged in Britain to form the greatest strike force ever assembled in the history of mankind.

Winchester, ancient capitol of England, became the host to American troops and was a second home to the 9th Division forces. This historic city welcomed Yanks during the first World War when thousands of them were stationed on a high ridge beyond the city.

World War II brought many troops to this city. The most popular were the 9th Division American troops. Battle-hardened veterans of the African and Sicilian Campaigns almost became a part of the 1,200-year-

15-E PHOTO

DISTINGUISHED UNIT CITATION PRESENTED
General Omar Bradley formally presented the 2nd Battalion of the 60th Infantry with a Distinguished Unit Citation. This special ceremony on the 2nd of December, 1943, was held on the Quadrangle at Winchester Barracks. The action cited was for extraordinary heroism in the face of enemy action in the vicinity of the Sedjenane Valley in Tunisia.

old community with its city of five castles in a thirty-five mile radius from the city center. Men of the 9th Division enjoyed seven months of unforgettable friendships in this area and surrounding towns. Unquestionably, they felt this was 'Merrie Olde England' at its best. There were strange and memorable first sights in this new land. Some seemed odd to the Americans; others reminded the Division of home. Above all, here was a land where English could be spoken and understood. This was a welcome respite from a hard year of war in 'foreign' lands. Each day was enjoyed to the fullest.

Although he was bound to a heavy training schedule with the boxing team, Urban occasionally found time for the lighter side of life. One evening in Picadilly Circus he met a beautiful lady, Marie Brown, who had been Miss England a few years earlier. She was an attractive and shapely brunette. Her wit charmed Urban, bringing forth feelings he had deeply buried in himself during the nightmare of carnage he had witnessed in Africa.

As the evening progressed, their companions parted. Marie and Matt were together sharing a drink. This seemed to Urban like a scene that could only have come out of a movie. He was taken by the soothing tones of her voice. The distinct British accent and Marie's relaxed, confident manner attracted Matt. He enjoyed the quiet happiness. Matt was glad to be alive!

As a gentleman should, Urban escorted her home, even though that required a twenty-mile ride by train into the suburbs. At the doorstep he gave her a lingering kiss. Reluctantly he made ready to leave. Smiling, she reminded him that it was after one o'clock in the morning .... also, that no trains were running. There was simply no way for Matt to get back to his barracks. "So," she said, "why don't you stay over?"

Urban had no choice but to spend the night in her elegant English Colonial brick home with pillars and balconies. Its setting was in a beautiful rolling hill countryside.

Although Urban expected to be sleeping on a couch, chair, or possibly on the floor of the living room, he was escorted to a guest room. Matt was shown to a very elaborate bed with a white lace canopy. Textured fabric walls adorned with French windows created a clean, elegant picture. Leaded glass doors opened to a spacious balcony with comfortable wicker furniture.

Urban was a soldier who had not seen any luxury in over a year. He had never seen anything as beautiful as this. Urban was spellbound by these elegant surroundings. His rough hands seemed leathery. His simple military attire stood out in stark contrast to the soft materials and lovely smells. Matt's quick thought: "Perhaps he HAD DIED after all, and this was HEAVEN!"

Urban bathed and climbed between the fresh cotton sheets, savoring the luxury. Moments before he dropped off to sleep, he felt a rustle, then movement on the bed as Marie joined him, her warmth and fragrance exhilarating.

"I was a perfect gentleman," remembers Urban, "and each person will have to interpret that for himself. She was a gracious person. Our friendship was very meaningful to me."

A knock on the door, sunlight in his eyes, and what he thought was a 'rise and shine' call, awakened Urban. Like a shot, he was halfway over the bed about to leap for cover. His battlefield instincts were alert to any danger! Pictures flashed through Urban's mind of a father with a shotgun or an irate husband. Marie had told him she wasn't married! With heart racing, his imagination caused him more instant fear than he experienced in battle!

A lovely lady entered the room. Matt thought this must be Marie's sister. At least he was hoping it was her sister! "Good morning", she said, and Marie responded, "Good morning ... Mother."

Again Urban felt the urge to run. His route of escape would be a dash and a leap out the window of the nearest balcony. He didn't know how things were in England, but he knew he had been caught in bed with the daughter! He must be in big trouble! Instead, he noticed a breakfast tray in the mother's hands. Matt sat transfixed as this incredibly friendly lady brought the tray over and served them breakfast in bed!

Fresh eggs, muffins, and preserves were served. The mother sat on the edge of the bed. She had a warm smile on her face. Matt's instant panic of a moment earlier turned to serenity as he experienced the incredible roller coaster emotions so typical of all his war years.

Urban was only one of many soldiers who came to know the English girls. At the train stations he often saw GI's closely hugging British girls, both within the cover of a single large army overcoat. Soft movement, and the expressions on their faces were the only indications of what was occurring invisibly ... but in a public place.

Urban recalls, "It was a time and place like no other. Men and women living at the edge of war respond differently. People treated one another with great respect. For a world at war it was simultaneously a time of intense personal friendships and uninhibited trust.

In one hilarious episode the men crowded about a narrow window to watch as a newly arrived officer was led by the hand into the barracks by an attractive English lassie who knew exactly what she wanted. A naive Second Lieutenant, a 'ninety-day wonder', fresh from Officer's Training School in Fort Benning, Georgia, was a source of entertainment for the worldly soldiers. Those men were veterans of more than just the battlefield.

As each pushed and shoved for the best view, they began to snicker as the couple neared the adjoining barracks. First the lady's hat and gloves were shed, followed by her jacket, each step choreographed while neatly keeping her charge in tow. Chuckles turned into loud guffaws as her shoes were dropped and scooped up in a single motion. Buttons began to pop free. The men howled with delight as she cleared the steps. Her skirt was falling away, revealing a tantalizing glance of shapely buttocks disappearing through the doorway. The shy lieutenant was being dragged reluctantly to his initiation.

At reveille the next morning the Lieutenant came running up to the formation a few seconds late, trying to straighten his tie and tuck in his khaki shirt, his face flushed with embarrassment. The bugle blew, the flag waved, and as all lines were facing forward, a barracks door opened to their immediate front side. With every eye looking straight ahead, out stepped the gorgeous young lady with curly hair and typical British attire. She was wearing a tight skirt with a vest and high heels. Her hose were rolled down to her ankles, as if she couldn't be bothered to pull them up. She was buttoning her blouse, straightening her skirt as she bounced, unconcerned, down the five-tiered steps.

Not a single eye blinked, yet, not a single motion escaped the attention of the men, standing at rigid attention. At the foot of the steps, she made a direct left face, traversed 1,000 yards along the frontal asphalt parade ground roadway on her jaunty way to exit. She was putting finishing touches on her attire in full parade review of the 1,000 GI's. The clack, clack, clack of her high heels resounded in the early morning silence, calling the eyeballs of these well-disciplined soldiers to 'dress left' in protocol and respect to the lady. The silent mirth of each man made it a reveille and a dress parade long to be remembered.

- - - - - - - - - -

The respite from battle action took other forms as the military undertook the job of training soldiers. They were also seeing to their need for recreation. Matt Urban was only twenty-three at the time, but he had the responsibility for directing the boxing program for the VII Corps. Urban was setting up schedules for championship boxing bouts in the entire European Theatre of Operations.

Joe Louis, boxing's heavy-weight world champion, made his first overseas appearance at Urban's VII

Joe Acts as Middleman

U.S. Army Signal Corps Photo

With world champion Joe Louis refereeing, Pfc Pete Morelli of Stockton, Cal., took the Ground Force heavyweight crown from Pvt. George Albert, of Waynesburg, Pa. Here, however, Albert is landing a stiff right to Morelli's stomach.

**WORLD HEAVY-WEIGHT BOXING CHAMPION
JOE (THE BROWN BOMBER) LOUIS**

One of the high points for Urban was arranging for the first overseas appearance of Champion Boxer Joe Louis when he appeared in an exhibition bout at the VII Corps Boxing Tournament.

Corps Boxing Tournament. The eight team bouts were to range from fly-weight to the final heavy-weight scrap. To accommodate the large crowd, the boxing arena was located outdoors in a picturesque valley. The event was timed to make best use of the afternoon sunshine and warmth of the early June day.

As show-time approached, Urban recommended two options to the Captain representing Joe Louis. It was a choice of spotting Joe's exhibition bout in the middle of the eight-team match, or as the grand finale, when Joe's exhibition would have impact as a closing attraction. Urban thought the champ would prefer to be on the program where the interest would peak.

The visiting Captain insisted that Joe open the show early, sparring only with one of his own road crew. His firm decision, expressed openly and loudly, was that 'Joe Louis should not be subjected to catching a cold if it became unexpectedly breezier in late afternoon'.

Captain Urban quickly and sharply countered with: "And how about my guys? They have just come out of a year of foxholes, ditches, mud, rain, and sleet! Does that make them immune?"

Louis' Captain stomped out, threatening that the whole deal was off.

The bouts progressed with Urban worrying. He knew his men were looking forward to seeing Joe Louis' exhibition fight. The mid-point of the program was completed. Matt was wondering, "Will they sit through a 15-minute break? Will Joe Louis appear?" Urban's worry ended when a roar blasted from the crowd! Joe Louis, the Heavy-Weight King, World Champion, was prancing toward the ring, waving, throwing kisses to his excited audience of admiring soldiers.

That evening the boxing entourage was treated to sandwiches and beverages in the club room of the town hall. There Urban first met Louis personally. They hugged as Urban tried to explain to Joe about the switch in scheduling. The 'Brown Bomber' responded: "What change in bouts! It was never discussed with me. Man, I would fight anywhere, anytime for these heroic, real guys!" In Urban's mind, that was the mark of a real champ!

Boxing brought many rewards. Urban was delighted to be reunited with the Ninth Division Boxing Team and his old friends from Bragg. Benny 'Bomber' Murrel, George Albert, Al Sebock, Tom O'Mara and Earl Evans were reunited thousands of miles from where they had met. Once again his team emerged victorious in almost every fight. The excitement and inspiration generated by their coach was contagious! Urban was on the sidelines of every bout, shouting and screaming encouragement for every man to exert his last bit of energy and fight as if his 'life depended on it'.

In one particular bout, Ben 'Bomber' Murell was fighting a seasoned pro. Ben was faring badly. After the second round, Murell came back to his corner literally 'out on his feet'. "I'm all done, Captain. I can't go on. I gave it all I had."

"No! Benny ... Benny ... listen to me," Matt begged. Ben! You've got a lot 'inside'. "Use your left! You've banged him some good ones! He's worried! Just finish! FINISH THE JOB FOR ME PLEASE, BEN!"

As Urban gently shook Murell's shoulders and gave a pat of confidence, the 'Bomber' became obsessed

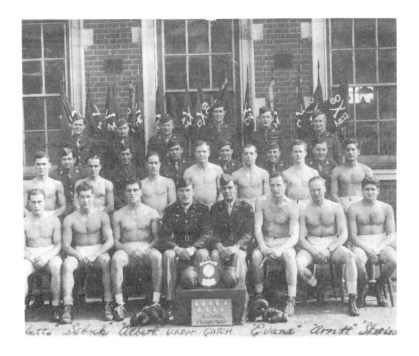

CAPTAIN 9TH DIVISION BOXING TEAM

As morale officer, Captain Urban organized team sports. His 9th Division Boxing Team became champions of the European theater of war.

Front row left to right: Tebetts, Sebock, Albert, Urban, Gatch, Evans, Arndt, Skopinsky.

with winning this bout. From somewhere within he found the reserve of power to continue.

As the bell rang, Murell sprang across the ring. His opponent had barely risen to his feet. Murell bombarded his opponent with an unstoppable fury, knocking him flat on his back. Abruptly the bout was over! To this day, Ben Murell claims, "Matt Urban made each one of us BELIEVE we could do anything!"

The men who made up the boxing team of the Ninth Division remembered their activities as 'the best of times'. Urban's determined persuasiveness on behalf of his boxing team was effective. It resulted in a 'training stable' of boxers being created. This was exceptional considering the war times.

The team members recall their special treatment in becoming an effective military boxing team. They had schedule managers, physical therapists, and they also were billeted in special quarters. All of this had been ordered by Colonel de Rohan, who had a dedication to the belief in the importance of physical training. He also realized the importance of team competitiveness and the recreational value of these sports activities for the entire Division.

The boxing team enjoyed the release from rigorous military training required by the Ninth Division soldiers. Urban, however, scheduled his team for strenuous exercise programs. This included a great deal of road work. These men were relieved from the ghastly war experiences of the immediate past. This interim boxing period brightened the present. It helped to bring out the best ability they had in their favored sport. Their success as a team earned the respect of their fellow infantrymen of the Ninth Division. Scheduled boxing events provided pleasure and necessary relief for their fellow soldiers.

- - - - - - - -

The real reason for the troops being in the United Kingdom was always clear. There was no doubt that the war was in its full fury. Bombs and rockets continued to devastate British cities.

The *United States Journal* and *The Stars and Stripes* kept the GI's informed of global events in World War II fighting. Victory in the Pacific at Guadalcanal boosted the determination and spirits of America's fighting men.

Urban was greatly impressed by the courage of the English people in the face of their deprivation and destruction. After each bombing raid they would stubbornly continue with the best efforts possible. They would proceed with their business or obligations with a dedication that appeared to ignore the disastrous effects of wartime destruction. Highly efficient rescue teams took care of the dead and aided the wounded. Damaged areas of the cities would be cordoned off immediately. Construction teams would promptly begin the work of repair or restoration.

The magnificent churches and cathedrals of England were packed with GI's every Sunday. They joined in worship with thousands of British citizens. Soldiers melded their hearts and devotional prayers with those faithful Britons. In times of stress, disaster and war, all people turn to God in one way or another ... to strengthen faith, confidence, and overcome sorrow or fear.

Christmastime of 1943 was a relatively happy period for Urban. It certainly was a dramatic contrast to the yuletide spent on the freezing mountaintops of Africa! Mail was on time in England. Several of the men regularly received news and gifts from home. Mail call was a most important part of every GI's life. Each eagerly awaited their letters. Urban watched each

SPRING, 1944, RAILROAD STATION
WINCHESTER, ENGLAND
LEFT TO RIGHT: Major General Manton S. Eddy, Commanding General 9th Infantry Division----Prime Minister Winston Churchill---General Dwight D. Eisenhower, Supreme Commander Allied Forces, Europe.

These leaders were enroute to the Winchester Barracks where Prime Minister Churchill addressed the First and Second Battalion, 60th Infantry Regiment, 9th Division.

time that the mail Jeep arrived. Matt jotted down the names of those who received no mail. Sometime within the next few hours Urban would 'bump into them' for a little chat. Always the conversation was the same.

"Did you hear anything from home?" Matt would ask. Although Urban already knew the answer, it was important to allow each soldier to vent his frustration. Matt would then counter with reassurance that the man was cared for also, that his people were thinking of him, and 'damn the army mail system' for failing to bring the mail which he was certain had been sent. These sessions strengthened the appreciation for their C.O. It made the tough job of 'soldiering' a bit more tolerable.

As the drab winter melted into spring, military training intensified in preparation for the all-out D-Day invasion of the European continent. Scale models of the Normandy countryside were faithfully reproduced from aerial photos. Every action plan of the coming invasion was practiced and memorized by those responsible for success.

The invasion was certain --- no one could prevent it. On the surface the GI's appeared to lead routine lives. They always lived with fear and uncertainty of the unknown. Some days were good; others were bad, each soldier wondering when he would be thrust back into the hell of war. The majority of GI's who waited on the beautiful isle had never fired a weapon in battle. They tried to stay close to the experienced veterans. They were hoping to gain knowledge, reassurance and confidence.

The 899th Tank Destroyer Battalion was officially attached to the Ninth Division during this pre-invasion training period. They were the outfit which had used their M-10 destroyers, three-inch guns, Bazookas, and 'guts', to stop Rommel's Panzers in Africa. The presence of these experienced troops was a morale-booster to all of the others.

INVASION ALERT!

At 0600 on May 27, 1944, the 9th Division received an urgent six-hour alert. Events began to unfold quickly. Talk of D-Day flowed through every camp. All conversations with civilians were prohibited. Everyone rushed to complete the loading of necessary equipment. Each man was concerned about his personal belongings. Once again, the GIs experienced the old familiar 'hurry-up --- and wait!'

There was little chance for any prolonged goodby or last minute business. Once again, 'this was it' --- the journey into the unknown. Throughout the Division preparations were rushed to completion. Necessary clothing and equipment were set out. The remainder was tossed into barracks bags, duffle bags, boxes and foot-lockers --- to be seen again or maybe not. There seemed to be a million things to do that could be done now; many were tasks which had waited too long. Most of those things had to wait except for personal letter-writing and preparations for sailing.

Meanwhile, many preliminaries had been completed. There was a muffled tension of veterans who knew what to expect. Unit Commanders issued last-minute instructions, and old timers cautioned rookies. A few wisecracks were made about unimportant things to help keep up any sagging spirits.

- - - - - - - - -

On June 5 at 2230 hours the Regiment was ordered to pack and be ready to move out! Urban's battalion moved to Boscome, England, in the suburbs of Bournemouth. By 0600 the next day, all equipment was loaded, and the battalion began its march to the loading docks. Urban observed swarms of planes

WINSTON CHURCHILL AND GENERAL EISENHOWER
Prime Minister Churchill reviewed the honor guard from F
Company, 60th Infantry Regiment, at Winchester, England,
when he addressed the troops there in the spring of 1944 just
prior to the D Day Invasion of Europe.

winging their way back to home base from missions over Europe.

At 0930 confirmation that American, British, and Canadian invasion forces had landed on the coast of Normany spread like wildfire through the dockside troops. Now the 9th Division had boarded ships for France. Their long-anticipated battle on the European continent was about to begin.

Urban was acutely aware of everything in his surroundings. As he looked down into the waters of the English Channel, he sensed his heart beating faster than normal. His reactions caused the skin on his face to feel hot while his hands were cold. From the moment of departure, he existed completely in the action of the moment.

During the stretched-out time of crossing the English Channel, GI's were emotionally writing personal letters home. Others were quietly conversing, and some talked in groups with hyperactive conversations.

One soldier told Matt: "If I blow it for any reason, I want you to shoot me! I have to look at myself in the mirror every morning, and I'll never be able to do it if I let you guys down."

Another rookie boasted of his fearlessness and bragged of what he would do under fire. The words rang hollow with the Ninth Division veterans, but there was no correction or put-down of the bravado. Who could really know what would happen under fire?

The 'old' veterans were actually young! Most were between 18 and 23 years old. They had developed a self-controlled discipline that distinguished them from the replacements. As they joined together on the transport decks they conversed in low tones, planned how to put affairs in order, and were speaking their minds about the coming battle, with comments such as: "No matter what you think of Hitler and his rotten government, these German guys know how to fight. We are up against the best. They are military smart and courageous, and their entire army performs in an excellent manner. We are in for the fight of our lives."

CHAPTER 12

THE NORMANDY INVASION ---
OPERATION OVERLORD
General Omar Bradley's 1st Army,
"The Finest Army in the World"

Operation Overlord was planned by General Eisenhower and the Allied Chiefs of Staff who met a few miles from London in the former game preserves of Henry VIII. General Omar Bradley was called to England to unite the American divisions into the First Army, later considered by military experts 'the finest army in the world'.

Hitler felt confident that his combat-tested armies could repulse any onslaught. The Ninth Division was one of only two participating American Divisions with previous invasion combat experience (North Africa and Sicily). The second division was the First Infantry Division (Big Red One, the old partners of the Ninth Division in the invasion of Sicily).

Paratroopers from the 82nd and 101st Division took off for Normandy, France, on June 5 just before midnight and the impending invasion. The 4th Infantry Division under General Barton landed on the UTAH Invasion Beachhead. They took the first of the German defensive fire. Later, the 4th Infantry joined up with the 82nd Airborne Division and the 101st Airborne troops who had been fighting German positions to the south. The airborne divisions had been clearing river and marsh areas near the point of advance of the 4th Infantry Division.

During the initial invasion on the beachhead of UTAH, the Army enginoors woro forced to combine their various construction duties with those of infantry soldiers. The engineers quickly alternated between construction equipment, shovels, and automatic rifles ... as the situation required.

The German troops opposing the assaults consisted of the hardened SS troopers and the highly experienced German Third Parachute Division. They were supported by several motorized Panzer Divisions. These Panzer Divisions were Hitler's 'ace in the hole', which he had held in reserve. The Germans (Hitler believed) were now deployed to seize the initiative and drive the Allies back into the sea. These enemy troops rarely submitted to capture. Often they were under Hitler's orders to fight to the death.

General Norman 'Chick' Hennen, reflecting on the landing of his 60th Infantry Regiment, reported that the intensity of the German counterattack had made the battlefield conditions hotter than they were on the D-Day invasion.

Just three days after the June 6 forces of operation OVERLORD invaded the beaches of Normandy, Matt Urban and his battalion received their orders to join the battle in France.

On June 9, 1944, at 1730 hours, Urban and the men of his battalion boarded the S.S. Empire Battleaxe, an American-built troop transport, which was sailing under the British flag. They departed at 1900 hours, leaving the friendly shores of England. Urban spent a restless night aboard the ship. It anchored off the coast of France near UTAH Beach at 0600 hours the following morning.

All that day the troops remained aboard ship. They were bored, yet anxious and agitated by frustration while waiting for the inevitable fighting soon to come.

NORMANDY BEACHES 'D' DAY OPERATION

GENERALS PATTON AND EDDY INSPECT
DESTROYED GERMAN GUNNERY 'PILLBOX'

At 2200 hours, the ship hoisted anchor and sailed around the French Coast to UTAH Beach, where the 2nd Battalion was to disembark.

On June 11, 1944, at 0830 hours off-loading of the troop ship began. Men climbed down net ladders into the Higgins landing boats. These dependable wood landing craft had been developed for amphibious landings. At 0930 hours the first Higgins boat reached the floating breakwater emergency pier. It had been built by engineers in England and towed across the channel. It provided a sheltered landing pierhead. After being flooded with seawater, it rested solidly on the ocean bottom at the beachhead.

A wall of masonry paralleled the UTAH beachhead for nearly 10,000 yards. The Germans armed the wall with revolving tank turrets set on concrete bases. These 'Tobruk Tips', as they were called, were further supported by intricate mine fields and machine gun emplacements. Behind these fortifications parallel to the ocean was the beach road. This roadway carried troops to Ste. Mere-Eglise, Quineville, Montebourg, Valognes, and on into the famous Bocage (hedgerow) country of France.

HEDGEROW FIGHTING

The hedgerow enclosures of farm fields formed natural defenses of stone foundations in rectangular patterns. These were topped by bushes or trees. The German troops had the advantage over the Allied Invasion Forces. The hedgerows were effective tank and troop barriers. The 9th Division spearheaded an important drive along the St. Lo-Periers Road.

Every field in the Bocage country was an individual battlefield. Each was separated by solid earth and stones which rose from three to seven feet high (similar to dikes). They were then capped with a four- to five-foot-high hedge. These natural barriers were three feet thick and covered with brush, vines, briar, and barbed wire. Hedgerows enclosed each one of the farm fields. They were cut only by tow paths which were openings between the fields. Urban now led his battalion into this vegetated, rolling countryside with its 628 stone and hedge-enclosed cubicals dividing the fields and pastures. Their fight was to be against the Panzer-Lehr.

The enemy had been entrenched here for months. American progress was difficult because German tanks could remain hidden while American tanks were forced to halt until openings could be blasted through the hedgerow walls. Both sides used these hedgerows for cover. This created a deadly 'game' of hide-and-seek for the combating forces.

Urban's 'F' Company advanced single file across the beaches on a marked path through mine fields and artillery shelling. After regrouping they met the enemy resistance head-on in the 'checkerboard' of hedgerow enclosures. A terrifying clacking of

German Panzer Lehr tanks approaching pierced the sounds of thunderous enemy fire power. The Germans halted Urban's 'F' Company advance, and suddenly retaliated with a concentrated counterattack. Where the invulnerable Panzer Division expected the invaders to retreat, Urban's infantrymen dug in and stood fire. Direct, continuous tank and machine gun fire kept coming at Company 'F' from very close range.

The enemy's counter-offensive was inflicting heavy losses on Urban's 'F' Company. Urban took decisive action. He side-glanced to his Bazooka gunner as the man folded, grasping a gut wound. Urban hastened to a shell-shocked ammo carrier who was standing still. Matt, 'patting' a hard shove on his back, yelled, "Let's go!" The GI ammunition carrier had a sack over his shoulder, similar to that of a newspaper delivery boy; except, the ammo bearer's sack contained a load of shells for the Bazooka!

Machine-gun fire ripped up the ground around Urban and the 'ammo' bearer. Terrified, both glared at the oncoming steel monsters of Panzers. As the lead tank was about to run over them, Urban loaded his Bazooka and fired. The tank exploded in flames.

Urban reached for another shell. Then the following tank zeroed in on Urban. His sense of urgency did not allow Urban time to run for cover. Matt loaded the Bazooka, sighted in, and fired! Meanwhile the 2nd Battalion was pinned down by heavy machine-gun fire.

The second tank erupted in smoke from Matt's frontal, off-the-ground, bulls-eye Bazooka shot. Off to his right, Urban heard the throaty yells of his troops. They burst from cover and ran up the incline firing into German positions.

Further away, a third Panzer Lehr tank emerged from an adjoining hedgerow-enclosed field. The ground shook as the tank advanced, firing its guns. It appeared as if Urban's 'F' Company advance would be stopped dead. Matt attempted to sight his Bazooka on the tank. Suddenly the tank stopped. Its turret was turning. The big turret muzzle gun exploded, firing directly toward Urban. Matt dropped his Bazooka and leaped for cover quicker than the turret muzzle gun could be accurately aimed.

There was a roar from the shell explosion. An almost instantaneous concussion hit Urban as he was scrambling for protection of a hedgerow. The shell

293

exploded only a few feet away. The concussion hurled Urban clear back to the American's side of the hedgerow. Shrapnel ripped into the back of Urban's leg. It missed the knee, but took a chunk out of the calf muscle. The explosion covered him with rocks and debris. Lights went off in his skull, and the blackout of unconsciousness began to close in. Somehow Matt did remain conscious. He was determined to survive this 'nightmare'! Within minutes a medic had pulled Urban from the debris, and put a tourniquet on his bleeding leg.

The battle raged. There was no time for compresses or morphine. The medic yelled for help to carry Urban. "Ship the Captain back. He is out of it for now."

"The hell I am!" Urban yelled. "I'm not going back! I'm staying with you guys until we take our objective!" Urban had been ordered to take the junction of the road. He intended to stay until the mission was completed.

His troops finally relented to his determined and all-too-stubborn will. They arranged a portable pallet. With a man on each corner of the litter, Matt Urban was hand-carried from one position to another as the battle ensued.

As twilight came, Matt's battalion was on the move and pressing the attack. They were consolidating as much ground as possible before enemy reinforcements could be brought up to counter the unexpected effectiveness of the 2nd Battalion forces.

Major Norm Weinberg (M.D.) was a close friend and fellow officer of Urban during Fort Bragg days. Upon hearing of the dilemma that Urban's medics faced by their Captain's insistence against being evacuated from his troops, Weinberg took immediate action. He hurried to the front lines. He stood over the stretched-out Urban and directed: "Matt, as your battalion physician, I 'prescribe' that you be rushed back to the field hospital --- in preference to my pulling rank by the order of a Major to a Captain."

Urban thought and questioned himself: "The 'Doc' has good common sense?" He also knew he should only question decisions of higher rank, if they were way off base. Urban said, "You're right in a 'mean' way, Norm ... Yes, Sir! Major! Evacuate it is." Matt said sadly, "See you guys .... I'll be back."

FIELD HOSPITAL SURGICAL TENT
On orders of Major Norm Weinberg (M.D.) Urban was ordered evacuated to the field hospital surgical tent. Here he received surgery on his injured leg. The operation was done by lantern light under local anesthetic.

A few miles behind the front lines, doctors in a field tent and by lantern light administered only a local anesthetic. They sliced all of the burned and dead flesh from Matt's leg. The two doctors seemed to know exactly what to say to keep Urban's spirits high and boost his confidence. One doctor gathered up the burned flesh and brought it to the head of an elevated cot, which served as the operating table. In a gory joke he asked, "Wouldn't this make a beautiful hamburger?"

The humor was appropriate to relieve stress and caused Urban to grin at the doctor's joke. He had deep respect for the ability of the people who had been brought together to serve in the United States Army Medical Corps.

"When can I go back to the front, Doc?" asked Urban.

"You're not going back, Captain! This is more serious than you know. From here, we are shipping you to a hospital in England."

"But Sir, I aim to be with my troops!"

"Captain, if you don't stay off that leg, you will never walk again, and you will be no help to anyone," responded the doctor. So it was that Captain Urban was placed in another troop carrier and again crossed the English Channel. This was a ship filled with injured and dying men. Matt was impressed by the positive spirits and extraordinary bravery of all these wounded soldiers.

- - - - - - - - -

In a red brick hospital, Urban was placed in a real bed! Matt felt himself to be in the 'lap of luxury'! He spent every possible waking moment laboring to walk again. He questioned every man who came in from the front lines. He got word that the 60th Regiment was taking the brunt of the battle and had sustained serious losses.

Meanwhile, the embattled Ninth Division completed its rout of the Germans from Cherbourg Peninsula. They crushed all resistance from the heavily fortified Hill 173 to Hill 176, which was the dominant ground overlooking Ste. Croix, Hague. On June 30 the city of Beaumont, Hague, fell to Captain Stephen Sprindis and his 'E' Company.

Captain Sprindis cleared a heavy mine field by using a cane and feeling with his bare hands as h e cautiously moved forward. His group crossed this seemingly impossible barrier and took Beaumont. They resolutely moved on to their final objective, Joburg, at the tip of the Cap De La Hague Peninsula.

By 1900 hour, June 26, it was all over. Prisoners by the hundreds poured into the POW enclosure. German soldiers surrendered in such great numbers that it was nearly impossible to keep an accurate count.

Ernie Pyle, the famed war correspondent, visited the Ninth Division during the Cherbourg campaign. He wanted to see Urban and Sprindis, as he had heard of their battle exploits. But Urban was in the hospital wounded, and Sprindis, having just completed an all-night scouting mission, was asleep when Pyle arrived.

Captain Lindsey Nelson (who was later to become the famed announcer for the New York Mets), was available to meet with Pyle and answer his questions. It was the first publicity for the heroic 9th Division, which in secrecy had fought so well throughout Africa and Sicily. As Pyle and Nelson conversed, a loud noise rang through trees in a nearby grove. Nelson and Pyle instantly exchanged glances. "No need to worry," Pyle assured Nelson. "That was just a harmless rotating band."

"Yeah, that's what it was." Nelson agreed. Just for the heck of it, they decided to explore further. They were shocked when they came across an unexploded 240mm German cannon shell!

In his newspaper report Pyle wrote: "For some reason which we have never fathomed, the 9th Infantry Division wasn't released from secrecy and censorship as early as it should have been, while the other Divisions were."

— Ernie Pyle

With each passing day, Urban felt more and more as if imprisoned. He became increasingly restless. Matt began suggesting ways to get across the Channel, but he was blocked by determined, concerned doctors at every point.

One of Urban's greatest blows was news that his good friend, Lt. John Butts from Buffalo, N.Y., had died in action. Butts had sustained several wounds over a period of days, and had continued fighting. In attacking a well-fortified hill held by the Germans, he rose up to rally his men. He was cut down by a burst of machine-gun fire. Writhing in pain, he struggled to his feet. Despite his severe stomach wounds, he ordered his men to flank the German machine-gun nest. Holding his stomach together with one hand, he then made a lone frontal assault to draw fire upon himself. He moved to within ten yards of the enemy lines before he finally went down under heavy machine-gun fire. His bravery enabled his men to easily capture the position. Lt. John Butts was posthumously awarded the Congressional Medal of Honor in recognition of his loyalty and bravery in action.

Another sadness came to Urban when he read the communique that the respected Commander of the 39th Regiment had been hit by sniper fire and mortally wounded. Col. Harry 'Paddy' Flint had been a great leader. He had earned the respect of all of the men of the 9th Division. As a gifted individual whose exploits were legendary, he became a cherished person to his troops. Urban felt a familiar 'hollow' in his chest as he mourned the loss of this heroic leader ... his respected friend, Colonel 'Paddy' Flint.

On July 12 Lieutenant Colonel 'Black Mike' Kauffman was wounded by enemy fire from a Panzer Lehr tank.

A new arrival, Lieutenant Colonel John J. Shinberger, assumed command of the 2nd Battalion. The durable Kauffman had been with his men from the very beginning (the invasion of North Africa). His experience, skill and leadership would be sorely missed.

- - - - - - - - - -

As the month of July wore on, the hospital in England received a sudden influx of casualties from Urban's unit. The 60th CT had completed their advance into the long-remembered Battle of the Hedgerows. The wounded arrived daily with stories of horror and devastation. The 9th Division was now facing the toughest fighting that they had encountered in the entire war. As the infantrymen came in (or were carried in), one of their first requests was to see Captain Urban and talk with him.

The Colonel in charge of the hospital turned a deaf ear to Urban's repeated requests to be discharged. He often told Matt, "There is no way you can go. You could lose that leg!" Urban considered many options. He felt he had to return to the battlefield for his own satisfaction and for the sake of his men. He considered going AWOL. As the days wore on, and his leg became stronger, he discovered another and better possibility.

He was sitting in the courtyard of the hospital one day. Urban noticed an outlandish group of slovenly soldiers march by. He was curious about the dirty, unkempt men. They were marching out of step and making wisecracks at their leader. Upon inquiry, Urban found out that these men were deserters and prisoners from stateside who had been released to the custody of the army. The condition of release was that they would serve in the military campaign.

Forty prisoners (undesirables) had been yanked or 'volunteered' from military stockades. Pre-war deserters, draft dodgers, felons, and near illiterates had been banded together as a unit. They had proved to be incorrigible! No amount of threats, skill, or reasoning could penetrate their resistance to military discipline. They had been shunted from officer to officer. Now they were stationed near the hospital and were considered as a group that was impossible to lead or train.

Urban hit upon a plan to finagle a quick return to the continent! He requested and was granted command and responsibility of these misfits. Matt dubbed them the 'Dirty Forty'. Within an hour Urban was standing in front of the Colonel with military jurisdiction over this unusual detachment. Urban said, "Sir, in the Army I have learned leadership skills. As an experienced boxing coach, I have learned to deal with individuals. Colonel, if you will permit me to train them, they will become productive enough at least to work effectively behind the lines in France."

That evening Urban was standing in an overgrown field near a small cluster of tents. In front of him stood his line of misfits. Matt had never seen such an 'outfit'! The men were a rag-tag group. They wore ovory imaginablo kind of olothing mixod with partc of military uniforms. Their hair was long, skin dirty, many had missing teeth. All smelled as if they had not had a bath in months. As they stood before Urban, their line was crooked. Sneers indicated that they welcomed the challenge to resist discipline from Matt or any officer.

Urban's first impression was, "Impossible! These guys would rather go to hell than war!" During reveille, retreat, or in formation, hanky-panky went on every time a moment of opportunity presented itself: cards, rock-scissor-paper challenges, dice, and continuous horseplay.

In the beginning Captain Urban often had to hold back his own laughter. Some of their typical responses were, "Yah, boss". This was never totally replaced by "Yes, Sir" or "Yes, Captain". They relished the boxing bouts that Urban programmed at the close of the day. With no time limit, no rounds, no headgear and big sixteen-ounce boxing gloves (pillows), they flailed away until exhausted. The combatants slumped into their cots at an early hour. Total peace and quiet reigned until the bugler sounded the 0500 reveille call.

The unusual personalities of this group, their antics and freakish comedy, combined with street lingo, created a setting of ongoing and sometimes outlandish hilarity.

Urban looked upon these men as his return ticket to the battlefront. He had no illusions about their true potential. Urban decided not to go against the misfit pattern of this group. Instead, he relied on his ability to get along with all types of people. He could interact as well to adults, children, or people of any level, race or culture. In this case it seemed wise to adapt himself to this odd outfit. To try to make them 'shape up' to military standards would likely fail. Knowing that Urban was a boxer greatly impressed

THE DIRTY FORTY
This sketch represents the misfits of Urban's 'rag-tag' group. He took them on as a challenge to his ability to create some military discipline and respect. Urban also viewed this group as 'his return ticket' to the battlefront. He was right!

this group. Urban's descriptions of his experiences in battle caught their attention and respect.

Urban did not dress as a Captain 'should' with a tie and officer's cap. He approached his 'misfits' with open shirt, no hat, and no tie. Matt played his part as well as he could. He figured if he could carry out this training charade for two weeks, he would be back at the front in France with his men of the 2nd Battalion!

Urban was right. He and his charges were ordered to European action!

Just prior to shipping out, Matt's new charges were herded (several by force) and restrained in a barracks where half a dozen barbers performed instant shearing jobs amidst yelps and screeching protests. The scene was hilarious. It reminded Urban of an Australian sheep-sheering scene. Some of his charges laughed uproariously as they ganged up to hold down the more resistant fellow members of their group.

MP's were doubled on 'guard duty', and the neighborhood was alerted as the 'Dirty Forty' marched single-file into the daylight, each was sporting a poor imitation of a marine 'white-side' haircut.

The critical move came as the group marched outside the gates of the army barracks. They were becoming hyper in the realization that they were about to face a showdown. The results would soon be known. Urban wondered, "Will they make a break for it and run? Will they obey orders and follow my commands?" Urban was somewhat philosophical when he thought to himself, "Whatever will be, will be".

As this group of rebellious recruits marched, they did follow Urban's orders. However, as they prepared to board the ship for Europe, two of the men scrambled overboard from the gangplank and had to be fished out of the water. One of them yelled, "No way am ah gonna be cannon fodder!" The others of the group roared in laughter. They boarded the ship and followed Urban to the area he designed for them. The ship slowly left the dock and moved out across the English Channel toward the European continent.

The next day after the English Channel crossing, Urban dropped off the 'Dirty Forty' to a waiting officer at the UTAH beach shoreline.

Urban began his lone trek up the narrow path. He was limping slightly on his sore leg and walked with the aid of a cane. Captain Matt Urban moved across the sandy beach up a winding gravel road. He disappeared over the crest of the hill. Now he was out of sight and felt 'out of reach'. Pausing, he looked back thinking, "Safe at last!"

COLONEL HARRY A 'PADDY' FLINT

Col. Flint, upon becoming Commanding Officer of the 39th Infantry Combat Team, said, "From now on, we're all one gang. We're going to work and stick together as a gang and help each other. He painted AAA - O on the side of his helmet (anything, anywhere, anytime, bar nothing). Many of his troops did the same. Flint was a leader of whom it was said that the men of the 39th would follow through HELL without a canteen of water!

CHAPTER 13

ST. LO BREAKTHROUGH ---
OPERATION COBRA

"Greatest Air-Land Assault in the History of War!"

Fate decreed that Urban would arrive at the front lines of the Normany battlefield on the morning of July 25, 1944. On this day 'Operation Cobra' was unleashed. The combined power of the Allied air and ground forces was set to break out of Normandy and smash through to Northern France. The ground offensive was to be coordinated with Air Force saturation bombing runs on enemy fortifications. The attack was postponed several times due to rainy, cloudy weather. Army meteorologists finally gave the 'go ahead'. The morning of the 25th dawned bright and sunny with billowy clouds floating overhead.

The 9th Division had forged its advance across hedgerow country to the St. Lo, France area. They had faced every form of warfare imaginable, from the treachery of enemy soldiers wearing American

VETERANS' RECOLLECTIONS & DIARY

uniforms, to Panzer tanks, to mined roadways which the Germans set up as death traps.

Now the 'Old Reliables' of the 9th Division were issued Field Order #6, OPERATION COBRA. This directive outlined the action they would provide in the St. Lo Breakthrough.

The 9th was to fan out from the St. Lo-Pieres Road with the support of the 4th and 30th Infantry Divisions. They were to strike deep into German-held territory in the heart of France. Over 3,000 planes, pilots and support crews were utilized for the most intense battlefield bombardment ever attempted. It was planned to 'soften up' resistance and pave the way for a successful Allied penetration and breakout through German defenses.

At 1040 hours all units of the 9th Division pulled back approximately one thousand yards from an air bombing safety line. This safety area was marked by standard strips patterned on the ground to signal the precise bomb drop area to overhead planes.

Over thirty battalions of medium and heavy artillery were stationed directly behind 9th Division troops. Artillery gun fire was to provide saturation shelling of

RUINS OF NORMANDY

German positions prior to the American ground attack. All troops were ordered to remain in foxholes or shelters until zero hour to reduce the possibility of error.

At 1140 hours, wave after wave of American and British planes flew in from the northeast. Unfortunately, they unloaded their bombs on a run short of the target area. Many bombs fell among American soldiers of the 35th Division. Over 800 were lost in injury or death, accidentally killed by bombs from Allied Forces planes. Lt. Gen. Leslie McNair, Allied Ground Forces Commander, was among the fatalities that day. Many of the 47th Regiment of the 9th Division became casualties in this same bombing. The remainder of the incoming planes were ordered deeper into enemy territory to unload their payloads on secondary targets.

In this action, American military was pioneering a revolutionary style of warfare. Inevitably, costly errors resulted from disagreements between the various branches of the military service. This failure of agreement was certainly offset by the effectiveness of the Air Corps. The European Theatre of war was definitely shortened.

SAINT-LO

La Cathédrale

RUINS OF ST. LO, FRANCE

Members of the 1st Battalion, 355th Engineers, clean rubble from the streets of St. Lo to permit movement of traffic by road from Omaha and Utah Beach.

The pay-off of this multi-force bombardment and Air Force action saved countless American and Allied lives. Air superiority had been firmly established. It systematically destroyed the Luftwaffe and blasted German transportation in France. It practically destroyed meaningful production in the industrial base of Germany.

From their crouched positions in shallow foxholes, the men of the 9th Division could hear a droning sound. In the distance it was similar to the hum of bees. However, the deep hum became louder ... and louder. It soon filled their ears with a roar that drowned out all other in the battlefield sounds. Waves of bombers streaked across the sky, circling. Then they were peeling off one at a time. First the P-47's struck, dive bombing to mark the target areas with smoke bombs and flares.

Behind the entrenched American troops, the roar of artillery guns burst forth. They were firing shells emitting orange-colored smoke. This artillery fire was aimed to further illuminate enemy positions. Three hundred fifty medium-heavy bombers rapidly dropped their loads of 500-lb. bombs. They were followed by the incredible B-17's letting go their huge payloads.

AMERICAN B-17 BOMBING FLIGHT

Big flight groups consisted of 26 planes <u>each.</u> The lead plane and a half dozen others were equipped with top secret Norden bomb sights. They targeted the area to be hit. The other planes dropped their bomb loads accordingly. Saturation bombing was planned for a thousand-yard strip separating German and American forces. General Leslie McNair, Allied Ground Forces Commander, was accidentally killed in this action on July 25th along the St.Lo-Pierre Road.

Bombs were now raining down along the three-mile stretch in front of the 9th Infantry Division. Early tremors in the ground increased steadily until the heavy concussion of bursting bombs seemed to shake the entire earth. The din of the bombing increased. Orange-white light flashed across the sky. Smoke rose in gigantic columns. The entire area was darkened by a large gray cloud of dust and smoke blanketing the St. Lo Battlefield.

Practically everything above the ground was pulverized by the gigantic bombardment. Still the resourceful German troops rushed forward even as bombs were dropping. They reoccupied positions which the men of the 9th Division had vacated that morning to form the safety zone! Other enemy soldiers dug deep into their foxholes and waited out the terrifying holocaust. The 2nd Battalion of the 60th Infantry moved to attack at 1100. It had to recapture the ground which they had held earlier (the safety zone), which now was occupied by German troops.

Despite the magnitude of the bombing, enemy resistance was fierce. It took many American lives and determined action just to regain that lost safety zone. Then the attack stalled. From here the Americans were to clear high ground on the western side of Marigny, France. This ridge was positioned in a north-to-south direction. It was required to enable armored equipment to enter Marigny and to secure it as a jumping-off point for General Patton's tanks to drive through the hedgerow country and on to Paris, Belgium and Germany. Vigorous enemy resistance stopped the forward movement of American troops. They dug in to hold their position. They were unable to gather enough power to advance against the German forces.

- - - - - - - - - -

Very early on that morning of July 25, Urban had deposited his outlandish converts at the UTAH beachhead. He then hobbled across the beach and on the road to a tent hospital area. There he tried to commandeer an ambulance ('meat wagon') to drive him to the front lines. His first effort failed. The driver refused to budge. Next, Urban selected a n ambulance operated by a new recruit. After much pleading he was successful in convincing the assistant ambulance driver to give him a lift when he shouted, "This is war!" Having finally talked the driver into transporting him, they headed off for the front line.

As his chauffeured 'meat wagon' rumbled down a country road past lines of American artillery, Matt and his driver were impressed by the overflight of thousands of bombers. They filled the sky to the horizon. The tight flying formations nearly blocked out the sun. The airplanes gave Urban the impression of a swarm of mechanical locusts. Urban was overwhelmed by such an incredible concentration of firepower. He was thankful for the American workers who were doing their part by producing beyond all normal expectations.

Matt's 'adopted' ambulance driver carried Urban well into the front lines where American troops were stalemated. Their positions were pinned down; troops seemed frozen in foxholes and roadside ditches. By now German artillery zeroed in and was tearing up the road and surrounding areas. Wisely, the ambulance driver stopped, and Urban climbed out. The driver made a lightning-quick about-face and sped back to the rear lines. Urban, limping, scrambled into a huge crater where a half dozen men were dug in. They were immobilized in terror and were squirming for cover. As the German shelling and small arms fire was beginning to pick up intensity, Captain Urban yelled, "Who is in command here?"

One infantryman, hugging an M-I rifle, cringed and trembled in the far end of the bomb crater. The others pointed to him. Urban thought, "This soldier may be a squad or platoon leader," as he was not wearing an insignia. Urban, with his one good leg, scuffed him on the side.

"Tell your men to scatter and move before you all get wiped out!"

Getting no reaction from the soldier, Urban waved his .45, motioned, and yelled over the sound of gunfire, "You men follow me!"

As they made their way to the right flank, he kept yelling to other GI's who were dug in along the roadside ditches to scatter, to move into the field and follow him. Matt warned all of them that artillery shelling had zeroed in on their road area and that it also was heavily mined.

Urban later learned that the soldier he had kicked to motivate was an army reserve, a Lieutenant Colonel. He was in his forties, newly-activated, just arrived from the States and immediately shoved into the fighting lines at the front.

Details of the St. Lo Breakthrough and Matt Urban's exploits were presented in detail by John G. Hubbell. He authored an article in the December 1, 1981, issue of the *Reader's Digest.* It was titled, 'The Hero We Nearly Forgot.'

Excerpts from this story follow:

The men of Urban's Battalion couldn't believe their eyes when they saw Matt limping up the road using a stick as a cane, and 2nd Battalion survivors were never to forget July 25, 1944. Pinned down by German artillery fire, the Battalion seemed immobile -- no one leading, no one giving orders. The men lay in foxholes and ditches; they seemed resigned to being killed or taken prisoner. "On your feet, soldiers!" Matt ordered. "Let's go! Follow me!"

Sgt. Alex Kahn, a replacement soldier, was later to report his personal reaction upon having seen Urban coming up the road and entering the battle:

"One of the craziest officers suddenly appeared before us, yelling like a madman and waving a gun in his hand. He was probably a replacement, never in combat before. He got us on our feet, though, gave us our confidence back, and saved our lives."

ST. LO BATTLE SCENES

- - - - - - - - -

As Urban reached the most forward point he saw the leading American tank was demolished. The following tank was out, heavily damaged, and from the smoking hulk he could hear a continuous anguished cry.

"Help me! Medic! I am hurt bad! Somebody help me!"

One of the soldiers leaped onto the tank and looked down through the hatch, then yelled for help. When no one else responded Urban crawled on top of the turret, reaching down through the hatch to help. He held the wounded tank driver under the armpits in an upright position while the GI climbed into the tank to release the injured man's foot which was jammed into the pedals of the smoldering machine.

The tank driver's right leg was totally mangled with the lower leg almost completely separated from the foot. There was no other choice but to cut him loose since the foot was already hopelessly crushed, and the tank was in imminent danger of blowing up.

9TH DIVISION TROOPS CLEARING MINES

TROOPS ADVANCING THROUGH A BREAKOUT IN THE HEDGEROW

Urban trembled as the courageous soldier amputated the foot of the injured driver who was screaming in pain. In seconds he was free, and they were dragging him out and into a ditch where Urban quickly wrapped the stump of his lower leg with the jacket that he wrenched off his back, and then adjusted the tourniquet. Within seconds, a medic arrived and took over the operation.

In minutes the tank exploded and was totally engulfed in flames. Urban exchanged glances with the unidentified soldier, and they continued the attack. He had developed a fatalistic sense that you can only die when it is your time, so he was unfazed by the close call.

Urban and the unidentified soldier jumped out of the ditch and sprinted in the direction of enemy fire as they could see men pinned down by a heavy barrage. Even as he ran, Urban said a silent prayer that the tank driver would pull out of it, and it occurred to him that he did not know who the other soldier was who had so bravely rescued his comrade. 'Do or die' situations had to be met by each infantryman. Many battle actions were happening simultaneously, and individual decisions were often made in a moment of isolation. Thus, many real heroes never were to be recognized for their bravery.

Captain Urban moved along the right flank, crouching and zigzagging as fast as his injured leg would allow, yelling continuously to stimulate the troops to leave their positions in the ditches beside the road and follow him to the next line of hedgerows.

They were able to move about a half mile to the right flank and then covered approximately a mile forward up towards their objective. As they began to approach the foot of the ridgeline they were suddenly met with a barrage of heavy-caliber machine-gun fire and rounds from an anti-tank gun securely positioned beyond a hedgerow in an advantageous position close to the top of the hillside.

Urban tried advancing by having a platoon work its way over into a flanking hedgerow where they could advance on both sides. The terrain was well covered by enemy fire, and soon they were pinned down.

Time was of the essence with the Germans still regrouping, digging out of basements and shelters, shaking off the debris caused by the aerial bombardment. Urban had no wire or radio to call for artillery support, and their mortars were not near enough to help. The enemy was not yet at full strength, but even what they had quickly salvaged and brought forward had enabled them to gain the controlling ridgeline where they could observe from the dominating position. American GI's were being picked off, and any delay would cost numerous lives. They had to move, but quick, while the advantage was still theirs --- so act Urban did.

Facing him was a farmer's grassy tow road leading through a hedge and up the hill. A disabled tank was sitting near the opening where it had been hit as it tried to go through. A second tank whose turret gunner had been wounded was sitting back a few yards where it was being raked by intermittent machine gun fire. The enemy anti-tank gun muzzle protruded from the right side of the tow path on the next hillside hedgerow with a machine gun placement bristling from the left side. If the tank moved forward it would be exposed to the anti-tank gun. The route of attack was about two hundred yards of a sloping grassy hillside.

Urban located the Lieutenant in command of the support tanks and in a briefing, they decided that an immediate frontal attack was essential. The tank Lieutenant responded that the closest tank was still operable and that the driver was inside. The 50-caliber machine gun mounted on the top front of the turret was the only heavy gun available. Its firepower was essential to effectively combat the two over-powering buttresses of the German defense: the anti-tank and machine-gun emplacements.

The Lieutenant bravely raced to the tank. With a squirming movement he tried to lift himself up into the tank. Immediately he was flung back by a burst of enemy bullets. Urban yelled for a volunteer to get up there. The courageous Tank Platoon Sergeant followed without a moment's hesitation. He was gunned down before he could reach the turret.

There was only one thing left to do. Urban would not send another of his men to certain death. He crawled along the side of the tank, limping on his wounded leg, and pulled himself snake-like up into the turret. Bullets were whining and zinging all over as they slammed into the steel encasement, causing the most frightening ricocheting ever heard.

Amazing! He didn't know why, he didn't know how. But he was in the tank and alive. Urban was convinced that his death was yet to come.

The tank had to ascend a slowly inclining hillside, and it was necessary to get his head and shoulders far enough above the turret to aim the machine gun and fire at both adjoining enemy gun crews.

In that one second Urban scanned over a hundred prayers as thoughts of his loved ones flashed through his mind, and tears rolled down his cheeks, as he fervently prayed, "God help me," and he thought, "Goodbye, world!"

Then all hell broke loose! The tank was off, in high gear, his guns thundering what seemed like thousands of shots directly at the enemy gun crews. Urban was screaming hysterically over and over, "Bastards! Dirty bastards! Here we come!"

His first shots hit their mark. He returned death and destruction to the German machine-gun nest. The Kraut gunner flew back from his guns, killed instantly by the return volley. A concentrated stream of fire raged through the German gunnery positions, killing a number of enemy men and throwing the others into a panic.

The 2nd Battalion catapulted into action, leaping over the hedgerows and following the tank in a unified speedy assault, picking up the tempo and yelling with a vengeance.

Several die-hard Krauts moved into the emplacement and had the German anti-tank gun blasting away. The spattering of the 50-caliber machine-gun bullets Urban was firing toward their position and the unexpected acceleration of Urban's tank threw off the German aim. Shells exploded all around Urban's tank, but did not disable it.

The attacking men dashed over the one hundred yards in a matter of seconds to make the frontal assault on the German position. From his elevation in the tank turret, Urban could see the faces of the Jerries in the anti-tank gun crew. Seemingly bewildered by this turn of events and daring assault, the bolder German soldiers were standing up trying to man the anti-tank gun. Urban continued pouring machine-gun fire into their area as the Germans attempted to get their sights on him high up in the gun turret.

The relentless daring of the American assault and the yelling of the troops plunging up hill soon overran the German lines. Several bayonet skirmishes in hand-to-hand battle put an end to the fighting. Germans not killed in the assault quickly surrendered.

Urban's sense of destiny and satisfaction in this victory was complete. He felt an extraordinary burst of pride for the men of his Battalion, who had so bravely supported him in the successful attack.

Urban's men were keyed up for pursuit of the Germans from their newly-seized objective. A runner from the Battalion Command Post arrived with an order to hold their position until the flanking units could catch up. Reluctantly they settled into the former German fortifications.

The 2nd Battalion Command Post was strategically located close to the top of an adjoining hill opposite the enemy's ridges. There was about a mile between the Command Post and the enemy. The Battalion Commander, Major Max Wolf, was in a position to follow the action of his troops in the valley below. Major Wolf had his binoculars set on the tank assault as Urban spearheaded the 2nd

Battalion St. Lo Breakthrough. He recommended that Urban be awarded the Congressional Medal of Honor. Shortly thereafter he (Wolf) was killed by enemy artillery fire. Sergeant Earl Evans was a member of that Command Post, and he recalled that some of the last words that Major Wolf spoke were of decorating Urban for his valor in the attack and the saving of so many American lives.

Supplemental note: Sgt. Earl Evans was later captured by the Germans. He endured their prisons and constant persecutions against his Jewish faith. He held on and forced himself to survive the agony of the Nazi imprisonment. He was determined to preserve the legacy of the St. Lo Breakthrough and to bear witness to the valor displayed there. Evans wanted the world to know about Matt Urban's being recommended by Major Wolf for the Congressional Medal of Honor. Evans addressed a two-page letter to the Pentagon on July 5, 1945. It was authenticated and ultimately resulted in Urban becoming the last recipient of the Congressional Medal of Honor to be presented through proper channels (although thirty-five years late).

CHAPTER 14

THE HUN ON THE RUN
The Myth of Nazi Superiority Crumbles

A military storm was brewing behind German lines, where a major counteroffensive was being prepared under the personal directive of Adolf Hitler. His deranged leadership was interfering more and more with the efficient operation of the military. This 'Austrian Corporal' pushed aside his brilliant generals. Hitler was leading his forces into tactics that would prove to be the undoing of his Nazi war machine.

In one of his greatest military blunders of the war, Der Fuehrer threw methodical German tactics to the wind. He made a desperate bid to sever Allied supply lines which had been stretched to keep up with rapid advance of the Americans toward Belgium. He ordered a regrouping of armored and other units into a Panzer Division reminiscent of the mighty forces which had terrorized Europe with the original Blitzkrieg. Had he succeeded, the war would have cost many more Allied weapons and lives. Hitler failed to reckon with the determination of the 9th and the other divisions, which demolished his attacking force with light weapons and sheer guts!

The message to Hitler's Germany was ringing through the ranks loud and clear. In the Fatherland, Goebbel's propaganda kept the population unaware of Allied spirit and their numerous victories. In the trenches, the soldiers of Germany were taking great punishment. The myth of invincible German superiority had crumbled on the battlefields of France.

As mentioned in the preceding chapter, the 2nd Battalion Commander, Major Wolf, had been killed by enemy artillery. He had been standing in the doorway of a deserted farm house observing and guiding the battle from this strategic forward position. The loss of this great Commanding Officer was a stunning blow to the men of the 2nd Battalion. Major Wolf had been a good friend to his fellow infantrymen.

The heat of the battle continued. Captain Matt Urban at age twenty-four assumed command of the 2nd Battalion, and the unit moved forward. Later there would be time to reflect and grieve over the loss of Major Wolf.

Colonel Jessie L. Gibney became the Commander of the 60th Infantry and replaced Col. de Rohan. General Manton Eddy, who had commanded the 9th Division with extraordinary ability, was promoted to command the XII Corps of the Third Army. His excellent leadership was needed to bring new life to yet another segment of the American Army. His successor, Major General Louis A. Craig, was designated to lead the 9th Division in their conquest of Belgium and Germany.

Urban's units were hot on the heels of the retreating Nazi troops. They overran German command posts, often finding indications that those troops had pulled out only moments before. Towns and villages were usually devoid of local residents. A few were found hiding in deserted cellars. There were no cheers, greetings or flowers from the liberated townspeople as was to be experienced by the American troops to follow.

Hitler's decree of 'hold at all costs' was transmitted throughout his western defensive front. The Fuehrer's insane strategic decisions now assured total destruction of his army in France. Against the advice of his experienced generals, on July 7 almost every remaining German armored unit in Normandy

This 1939 cartoon by Vaughn Shoemaker of the Chicago Times forecasts Hitler and the German people repeating the same disasters of Germany and its leader, the Kaiser, in 1918 - WW I.

This 1944 cartoon humorously portrays 'The Chase' of German troops across France after the St. Lo Breakthrough.

was ordered to battle on the Mortain Front against the U.S. 9th and 30th Divisions.

On the morning of August 4, the 60th Infantry Regiment, led by the 3rd Battalion, jumped off at 0800 hour. The defending Panzer 'Lehr' Division fought with stubborn courage born of desperation. They were loyal to their Fuehrer's dogma of 'no one retreats --- no one surrenders'. Even such 'do or die' tactics were no match for the American courage. It was instilled in every positive advance of the American's quest for victory. The Germans were annihilated. Victorious young Americans could not help but pause with a feeling of pity and think, "God have mercy on their souls!" The GI's quickly regained composure and were grateful for being alive and for the capture of their objective, the Forest of St. Sever Caluados.

It was at this location that the 3rd Battalion captured one of the largest German ammunition dumps yet discovered. German food and medical supplies had also been left behind. These supplies quickly benefited the GI's as they were outracing their own supply lines. The German field rations were a welcome addition to the diet of Americans who existed many months on C-rations of hash and beans.

The morning of August 6, Urban's 2nd Battalion was ordered to attack the Champ Du Bout sector. The preliminary bombing by the Artillery and Air Corps pulverized the sector. American seizure of the area was completed relatively easily by beating back the enemy rear guard.

At dawn on August 7 detachments of Hitler's 2nd and 116th Panzer Divisions counter-attacked from behind their heavy artillery and mortar barrage. In preparation Captain Urban had tho 2nd Battalion entrenched on the outskirts of town behind the solid stone and hedgerow cover. Urban was imparting confidence with words of encouragement, a pat on the shoulder, a grin of assurance.

Again all hell broke loose! Urban's troops felt as if they were used to HELL. They were now seasoned veterans. They had an element of cockiness built on the many battle experiences from Africa, Sicily, and Normandy. These American infantrymen maintained faith in their ability and victory over the German and Axis forces.

Positions were being held against the power of Hitler's military. The German soldiers were fighting back with a ferocity of men determined to avoid doom of defeat or death.

The Allied forces' achievements resulted from maximum effort in a minimum time. The production of war material, build-up of troop strength and determined battlefield actions blended into a unity never seen before. This total strength would assure victory for the Allied military forces. Coordination between tank, artillery, engineers, communication, medics, infantry, Navy and Air Forces was greater than could have been anticipated in the early days of the war effort. This was truly astounding considering the Allied forces were composed of millions of people from diverse ethnic backgrounds, customs and languages.

Now it seemed that Urban and his battalion needed all of the capability and support possible. Urban later reports that this firefight appeared comparable to a Mini Bastogne!

A communications wire had been strung along the ground. It was to provide a temporary telephone link to field headquarters. This line received decisive use as Matt Urban called for urgently needed air strafing of German positions. Within 15 minutes an Allled fighter plane zoomed in, spitting machine-gun fire into the enemy locations. These bullets were on a trajectory only a few feet above the American troops. They wanted to witness the results --- but for self-protection remained burrowed into the depths of their foxholes.

After this close-firing air support ended, excited shouts of gratitude erupted from Urban's battalion:

"Where in Hell did those pilots get that 'bulls-eye' alm!"

Another yelled: "These Krauts only had 30 yards more to go to chop us down!"

One more called out: "Fly boys, we love you!"

The deadly Allied air attack quickly turned the tide of battle. It drove Hitler's forces from their positions, moving back in full retreat.

Urban ordered his battalion to move out --- to follow him --- and to 'dog' the retreating Jerries. During this chase, an exploding shell fragment (about half the size of a pea) penetrated Matt's jacket. It imbedded itself in his chest next to a rib.

Matt's body stiffened in pain, almost as if paralyzed. A morphine injection by the medic, a blanket for warmth, and careful attention to his wound helped Urban to overcome the misery. His troops provided encouragement and compassion that helped!

Captain Urban refused to be evacuated. He insisted on being with his men. Matt considered his troops 'family'. He knew they were isolated, no help was near, and that they should hang together. The battalion dug in again to repel a German counter-attack. None came.

After a day of rest and cold C-rations, Urban gained enough strength to be mobile. He and his 2nd Battalion moved ahead.

Later, Matt reported that this wound caused him more pain and fright than anything he had previously experienced.

Meanwhile, other units of the 60th and their sup-porting units took tremendously heavy shelling. The German Tiger, Panzer and Mark IV Tanks seemed

COLONEL   KEENE WILSON

Urban reports that Keene Wilson commanded 'K' Company in North Africa and the 3rd Battalion in Normandy.   Wilson continued this command throughout the European Campaign. He was one of the most combat-decorated Commanders in the 9th Division.   Urban also mentions Major Quentin 'Hard-tack' Hardage as another legend in leadership.   Both Keene Wilson and Quentin Hardage prevailed with their 'Don't Quit' attitudes.

Note: In addition to many of the highest American military awards, Col. Wilson received several foreign medals, including the French Croix de Guerre and also the Defense of Leningrad Medal.

to move in from all directions. The blazing guns and cannon-fire were nearly disastrous to the 60th Regiment.

Major Keene 'Slick' Wilson commanded the 3rd Battalion with grit and determination resembling that for which John Wayne was noted. He and his troops were famed for their bold frontal assaults during the African and Sicilian Campaigns.

Major Quentin 'Hard-Tack' Hardage was a legend in his leadership as Commanding Officer of the 1st Battalion. He was noted for his indomitable attitude of 'one who doesn't give a damn'. He and his troops were famed for over-running enemy positions in the Africa and Sicily warfare.

Both the 3rd Battalion under Major Wilson, and the 1st under Major Hardage, were equally experienced and battle-scarred from their years of front-line combat action. Now they were about to face a life-or-death struggle with Hitler's troops. Surging attacks by the German soldiers ended with many of them becoming human sacrifices for the Nazi cause. At one point their reckless charges almost caused the U.S. forces to collapse. Only the individual heroism by Army men of the 3rd and 1st Battalions prevented defeat. The final inspiration for the American troops came from their 'don't quit' attitude and the necessity of fighting for your life.

Approaching the hills above Villedieu, combat-weary Platoon Sergeant Kozar was driven into a fury. He rushed directly at a leading monster German Tiger tank. He was instantly gunned down. Next a GI, in a frenzy over the killing of his Sergeant, charged at the tank. He planned to 'hand deliver' his grenade. He was about to plop his explosive into the open hatch of the Tiger. Just then a Nazi machine gunner popped up. He cut down the American soldier with brutal gun fire. The brave GI, fatally wounded, was draped on the tank.

Heavy supporting fire from the 2nd Armored American Unit instantly hit the German machine gunner on the Tiger tank. He fell from the gun turret. His body dropped across the dead GI. At that instant the grenade (still clutched in the GI's hand) detonated. Both bodies were mashed by the explosion. Blood ran red over the tank. It was a ghastly sight, and never to be forgotten.

Many military men have sacrificed their lives for fellowmen and their country. Many are truly undecorated and unrecognized heroes! All veterans know this. They value and acknowledge it. Everyone else should know this and honor these fallen heroes. They and other fighting men have been and are the guarantors of the freedom enjoyed by citizens of the United States and the free world.

- - - - - - -

The defending German soldiers had been considered the best in the world. They fought valiantly for their cause, however misdirected!

German defense construction had been going on for months. After two days and nights of continuous jabbing and pounding, the American and Allied attacks broke the grip of the Germans. Their full retreat continued again.

Point 302 (302 meters above sea level) had been designated as the next target. It was near the next town and in the area of La Hardonniere. Several tanks had been destroyed in this effort. The 2nd Battalion had been brought up to help spearhead the assault.

A frontal tank attack and a wide left flanking maneuver by Urban's GI's were both failed actions.

SMOKE-FILLED STREET
Typical scene experienced many times by the 2nd Battalion
during their eight campaigns to victory.

Urban tried every maneuver possible during the next two days.

Supporting bombardment by our artillery and aircraft was urgently needed but non-existent. Direct Allied tank attacks failed. Ground attacks --- frontal, flanking, and rear --- were also unsuccessful. For two days the 60th slammed at its objective. The enemy held such a well-fortified position on the slopes of the crest that the 2nd Battalion may as well have been 'banging their heads against a stone wall'!

Captain Matt Urban soon knew the continual pounding of the objective would wear down and defeat the stubborn German defense. The enemy was weakening, but still dangerous! Urban could not convince his Regimental Command Post of this fact. The officer in charge ordered Urban, "Get moving"! He claimed that objective Hill 302 appeared easily accessible on his map. Urban explained that the outdated map did not show the true height, its fortifications or actual terrain. Urban suggested that his C.O. join him at Urban's front line Battalion Command Post on an opposite hillside. There he could personally observe the situation in relative safety, but he did not come.

At the end of the second day one of his junior officers was sent. He was to review details and deliver the rationed monthly bottle of liquor allocated for combat officers. The C.O. figured that should get Captain Urban's battalion to move on the assigned target as the paperwork ordered.

Urban says: "To satisfy my curiosity, someone should investigate. Where did all that liquor ration disappear to?" Matt recalls that in three years in combat, he had never seen liquor made available to any officer in his group! Matt said this bottle brought to him was the first and only American liquor or beer that he had seen in years. Even so, it proved to be the best tonic of the moment. Urban and his troops had just come through hectic days with no sleep! There was just enough for two good gulps for Urban ... and each of his infantrymen at the Command Post.

Another call from Headquarters ordered a massive assault to be launched at the designated goal.

Urban was pushed into a state of frustration. He grabbed his M-I rifle and slung two bandoleers of ammo over his shoulder. Matt started up the hill alone. He intended to get to the top of that big hill and see for himself what the hell up there was so formidable and powerful!

The full moon silhouetted this lone figure quietly trudging along the gravel road. When reaching his front-line outpost, the alert sentry challenged him. Urban ordered the sentry to make the front-line troops aware of his mission. About 100 yards into enemy territory Urban was startled to see a large man running after him. Taking aim with his rifle, Urban challenged the approaching figure. To his amazement this was Sgt. Earl Evans, one of Urban's most dedicated soldiers. Evans pleaded with Urban to turn back. Urban refused.

Again, more emotionally, Evans pleaded, "Captain! Don't go! We need you with us alive. It will be suicide if you go!"

Urban edged forward to move on. Evans grabbed him by the shoulder, "Captain, don't! Don't go! If you do, I am going with you!"

That worked. Urban softened enough to cool off. He thought about the real need, priorities and his impulsive action. The Sergeant had brought him to his senses. Both men returned to their base camp alive!

Urban subconsciously thought Sgt. Evans could have 'cold-cocked' him with a solid right and dragged him back. Earl had been both regimental and division heavyweight boxing champion!

By noon the next day Hitler's main force withdrew. The 60th Infantry readily captured the high point fortifications and its remaining rear defenders, who had been 'covering' the German withdrawal.

During the assault on the German position, Head-quarters insisted that Urban deploy (on front lines) a unit of raw recruits fresh from the States. No way! Urban would not comply! The front was a holl hole! The sky was erupting with shells screeching, flashing explosions and continuous bombardment. The erupting sky surpassed any 4th of July fireworks! In this devastation, Matt's two-year veterans were in a state of high tension.

The veteran American troops hardened by previous battles were well disciplined and 'dug in' in the foot-hills of Point 302. Urban knew a hundred restless young men --- just off the boat, never fired upon, noisy recruits --- would be a dangerous and an unfair burden for his experienced veterans. Inexperienced movements of new recruits quickly draw enemy fire.

Captain Urban typically kept his recruits as reserves in protected rear areas. Field training and experience thus could be gained for deployment in emergency situations.

Again Urban expected a court martial for not following orders, but effective action and saving lives was Matt's first priority. Urban accepted his firing line responsibility, and acted accordingly with competence based on experience.

Urban had previously experienced a similar situation at the Kasserine Pass. There a new inexperienced unit of fresh recruits was assigned. An inexperienced Lieutenant led them. They still wore bright new combat uniforms and shiny polished boots. As they were brought up to the fighting in columns of two, they drew enemy fire power and were annihilated.

- - - - - - - - - - -

Captain Urban's regiment was served by three chaplains: Catholic - Father Timothy Andrysziak; Protestant - Donald Propst; Jewish - Rabbi Irving Tepper. Father Edward Connors and Father Joseph DeLaura were chaplains with other 9th Division

FATHER EDWARD CONNORS

This beloved Priest was known as Father Confessor to everyone of the 9th Division regardless of religious belief.

CHAPLAIN IRVING TEPPER

Rabbi Tepper was a soldier friend to all faiths, counselor, religious leader and medic. Chaplain Tepper refused a corps-level job to remain with the 2nd Battalion. He was fatally wounded 11 August, 1944, near the Falaise-Argentan area in France.

units whom Urban remembered as devoted and ready to serve troop needs at all times.

Captain Irving Tepper was fatally wounded by shrapnel during the Point 302 assault. The Rabbi was in his forties with slight build, and physically not equipped for battlefield hardships endured without support of combat training. He had performed his own private miracle of endurance as he helped stretcher bearers aid the injured --- or provide last rites to the dying.

Urban says, "These Chaplains were most admired and highly respected by everyone. Soldiers turn to religion and faith in God at an incredible rate when facing war zone stress, injury and reality of death at any moment. Many find faith for a lifetime. Respect, belief in a higher power and love for fellowman fuses many denominations into one. This would be a better world today if unified faith (such as seen in wartime stress) could prevail in peaceful living .... throughout the world."

The chase continued across France, as the front roared with the fast rolling 9th Reconnaissance Troop acting as the eyes and ears of the Division.

The 9th Signal Company, the 709th Ordinance Company, the 9th Quartermaster Company, the Unit Supply and the Medical Collecting Companies began to wonder how long the communication and supply lines could stretch. They already were almost to the breaking point. If any of these supporting units failed, the rapid American advance would certainly have to halt. American battlefield ingenuity successfully kept the wheels rolling and the lines of communication stretching across the 403 mile sweep across France. Supply and communication personnel formed a team that played a big role in the Allied victory.

- - - - - - - - - - - - - -

On the 31st of August enemy contact was made near Rozoy Sur Seure, France. Major Hardage led his troops into a stiff encounter with enemy infantry and tank forces. The American thrust was strengthened by the anticipation of the war's end. This power was too much for the Germans, and they again retreated.

September 1, 1944, elements of the 9th Division encountered the enemy at 1300 hour and drove them out of France into the southern tip of Belgium. On the area's eastern horizon was the town of

Phillipeville. It was obscured by the slope of an intervening and dominant hill.

The 9th Division had traversed 403 miles across France in the month of August.

On the morning of September 2, Captain Urban was ordered to seize the town of Phillipeville.

VETERANS' RECOLLECTIONS & DIARY

CHAPTER 15

URBAN IS DEAD
"THE LAST RITES --- GOD HELP ME!"

In September 1944, the 9th Division was the first unit of the United States Army to lead the opening foray into Belgium. The 2nd Battalion Rifle Company of the 60th Infantry Division became the first unit to cross a tributary of the Sambre River. Hitler's 'invincible' armies had been routed from Normandy. Allied forces were racing across Europe in hot pursuit.

The young men of the 9th Division had been transformed from a civilian army into one of the greatest fighting outfits in history. With bravery and hard-earned skill, they demolished the professional German soldiers of Hitler's armies on the western front. 'Hitler's Nemesis' became the well-earned nickname for the young men of the fighting 9th Division.

The Allied High Command was not aware that German forces were concentrated in Phillipeville, Belgium. The German army was ordered to hold their position at any cost.

Phillipeville had to be taken by the Allied forces if the American 9th was to have clear access to cross the Meuse River several miles ahead. Beyond the river was the 'open road' to the Rhine and the heart of Germany.

American military planners had come to rely on the 2nd Battalion of the 60th Infantry Regiment for its toughest assignments. This was based on the many months of front-line battle experience reaching from Africa, through Sicily and now into Europe. So it was that Captain Urban and his men were ordered into the battle for Phillipeville.

September 2, 1944 - Early Morning

With the sun still below the horizon, Captain Urban led his men single file across the one remaining girder of the recently blown bridge. A lingering smell of explosives mingled with the fresh, clean air of the late summer. Each of Urban's men was keenly aware of the dangerous exposure to enemy fire during this crossing. The sounds of the forest and the trickling water remained undisturbed. As Urban's three hundred men crossed the remains of the bridge, they moved silently to the other side.

Each piece of their equipment and every weapon was wrapped carefully. These seasoned veterans from the campaigns of North Africa and Sicily had learned the value of precision performance and movement. Thanks to the strategic brilliance of the 9th Division's Commanding Officer, General Manton Eddy, these men had survived. His motto of 'stealth and sweat' was once again preserved. As a result, the eerie quiet of these experienced moving troops seemed completely natural. Each man was attuned to the one next to him.

Captain Matt Urban took command of his battalion earlier that summer. His men had confidence in him. He was a leader and a doer. He ate, slept and fought alongside his men, and they respected him for this. His courage under fire was already well-known in the European theatre of military action. Matt Urban was the type of officer men of all wars liked to serve under, and men of his battalion would follow him anywhere.

TYPICAL OF GROUND FIGHTING IN AREA NEAR PHILLIPEVILLE

LONG RANGE GERMAN 'NEBELWERFER' ARTILLERY

Battlefield Brotherhood — Caring for Casualties

After the crossing, as if by prearranged signal, these combat-ready troops spread out along the banks of the tributary of the Sambre and Meuse Rivers. They dug into a defensive position. Matt assigned a machine-gun squad to serve as an observation post on the leeward side of the first hillcrest. They quietly watched and waited.

The German artillery remained silent. The youthful Captain Urban decided that his battalion should hold position right where they were. They could cover the summit of the rolling hills along the river bank. They were dug in approximately a mile from the village of Phillipeville. It was visible from this position and appeared to have a 'pentagon' shape.

A narrow, worn asphalt road led from this position to the town. The fertile farm country and gentle rolling hills (of the Hinnault Province of Belgium) were practically treeless. Urban knew that sending his men up the flanks of that road would expose them to the enemy. He thought they would be as easy to spot as a herd of antelope on an open plain. They settled in to wait for their heavy weapons company to maneuver their equipment across the open water. They also waited for their heavy machine guns, mortars and heavy weapons company to catch up with them. This would provide the needed protective cover for any further advance on Phillipeville.

- - - - - - - -

The observation post radioed back to Urban, "Captain! We have enemy activity up here! Two German vehicles are approaching --- a Jeep and an armored car. They are advancing directly toward our position from Phillipeville."

Urban instantly ordered: "Hold your fire, keep hidden, let them pass." At their Captain's signal, riflemen formed an ambush point.

The two German vehicles roared past the hidden outpost. Four green-clad German officers rode in the Jeep. A German major relaxed with his foot on the hood of the vehicle. An armored car followed. Several infantrymen rode on top, smoking cigarettes and laughing as if they were on a Sunday outing. It was clear to Urban that the Germans were not aware that the American troops had crossed the demolished bridge and were on their side of the tributary.

One of Urban's men whispered in astonishment, "For God's sake. I can't believe they're driving into our ambush."

364

As the Germans drove into it, Urban shouted, "Halt! Surrender!"

The German major responded by taking his Luger from his holster and ordering the drivers to speed up and get out of there. Urban again shouted for them to surrender. The major responded with a wild shot in his direction. One of the GI's yelled, "Hey! They're trying to run for it."

At this point the Americans opened fire. Hundreds of shots were fired. In a matter of seconds all of the Germans in the two vehicles were killed.

Matt's men were able to salvage the German Jeep which was still operable and drove it a short distance to Urban's command post. They called out, "Captain, we got you some transportation! You don't have to walk no more!" Urban laughed at this battlefield joke in spite of the horror of the ambush. The German Jeep was then abandoned. He immediately ordered his men back to their foxholes and to dig deeper in preparation for an expected onslaught of German artillery fire that would surely follow the ambush. The attack did not come.

Captain Urban considered the absence of artillery fire a small miracle. His troops held only a sliver of land in Belgium. They were alone up front without heavy weapons of any sort. A concentrated German attack, supported by their artillery, tanks and heavy weapons would have been disastrous to the vulnerable 2nd Battalion.

A Colonel in the rear regimental headquarters called Urban on the field telephone. He first ordered and then demanded that Urban continue moving his battalion forward to the assigned objective, Phillipe-ville. Matt Urban replied, "Colonel, I am not going to send any of my troops to face point-blank shell fire ... to be chopped down! We'll hold our position until we get the artillery cover."

The Combat Unit Colonel responded, "Captain, your orders are to assault Phillipeville immediately! I don't want to hear any more of your objections!"

The three battalions of the 60th Combat Team were often separated from each other with temporary assignments to other units. Urban and his troops had been assigned to units as diverse as the Moroccan Goums, General Patton's tank units, and the British Army. This day the 2nd Battalion, as a combat team, was assigned to another U.S. Infantry Division. Urban did not yet know the officer who commanded the regiment. He was the officer ordering Matt and his troops to move forward. The Colonel in command of the Combat Unit clearly did not know Urban or the depth of Matt's battlefield experience.

"Captain Urban, I'll make sure you are court martialled if it's the last thing I do!" the angry Colonel bellowed into the field telephone.

Regardless of the Colonel's threat, Captain Urban remained adamant. His confidence in holding his position was based upon instinct and combat experience. He also was acting with first-hand information. The Colonel at the rear headquarters was using information based upon old, outdated aerial photographs taken from a mile above the area.

The Colonel was incensed by what he considered Urban's direct insubordination. He ordered the reserve unit of the battalion to pass Urban's 2nd Battalion, which had dug in at its position. The reserves were ordered to assault Phillipeville. The Colonel knew that if the village fell, the U.S. Army would have a clear path to the Meuse River just a few miles beyond. He wanted to receive credit for this accomplishment no matter what the battle cost.

In the morning, the reserve troops moved past Urban's position on their way to Phillipeville. They engaged in good natured ribbing with his entrenched men. "Hey, slackers, the war's that way."

"Ya bunch of goldbricks. We gotta do all of your fightin' for ya?"

Matt was greatly concerned and dismayed as the apparently inexperienced reserve troops moved past. Urban thought that they were bunched much too closely together.

Their platoon leaders appeared to be newly-minted 'Looies'. Clearly they were not battle-experienced. The men were grouped together, leisurely moving along both sides of the road into the face of battle. Also, they were passing much too close to Urban's 2nd Battalion position. Urban believed their movement would draw German artillery fire into his position. After the troops had passed, Urban prayed for their safety with a silent, "God help them."

A terrible barrage of German guns was soon heard in the distance. Hellish artillery shells rained down on the attacking reserve troops. They were devastated by this heavy shelling. Sounds of the violent battle carried beyond the hills from Phillipeville. Soon wounded men were being carried to the rear. It was a pitiful procession, litters carrying injured men, limbs missing, guts spilling out, others crawling or hobbling toward Urban's position. All had agonized expressions and were begging for aid.

Cries of the wounded wretched Urban's stomach. Artillery shelling followed the path of the retreating troops. It was blasting their ranks and flinging bodies in every direction. The retreating reserve troops were frightened beyond terror. They stumbled along, uncomprehending and oblivious to the shellfire. The image of this carnage was torturous. Urban was raging helplessly and trembled with emotion as the young soldiers struggled to escape.

Many of these young men were only moments into their first battle experience --- and being cut to shreds. Captain Urban and his 2nd Battalion were forced to hold position in their entrenchment.

A frightened scream, "Help me! Please! I'm dying!" was too much for some of Urban's troops. Defying orders, several men broke from their positions and rushed out to help. They immediately became casualties in the raging German shelling. It was a holocaust that servicemen of all branches and all wars know so well --- the terrible carnage of mankind's destructive power.

From the wounded and retreating men, Urban learned that the Germans had permitted the Americans to reach within a half mile of Phillipeville before opening their barrage of firepower. The rocorvo battalion was in a perilous predicament. Its remaining troops were now dug in on both sides of the road. They were fighting desperately to hold their position. Though he wanted to help, Urban knew he could do nothing for them without sacrificing too many other American lives.

That evening Urban was summoned for a briefing at the area unit command tent. This location was in a safe area across the Sambre River about three miles back on the northern flank. Matt and his Jeep driver, Sergeant Earl Evans, crawled back across the remaining beam of the blown bridge. They picked up an American Jeep and made the dangerous journey by moonlight. They drove in blackout. Sergeant Evans was a native New Yorker and had never driven before. (In New York City he rode the sub-way.) They arrived at the command tent later than the other battalion and regimental level officers.

The twenty-five-year-old Captain Urban had been assigned command of the 2nd Battalion on July 25, 1944, when Major Max Wolf, the former Battalion CO, was killed by artillery fire. Rank had not yet caught up with Urban. He entered the dimly lit regimental headquarters tent as the lowest ranking officer. Others present assumed he was a Lt. Colonel.

Urban blinked as he entered while his eyes adjusted to the light from the lantern. Matt distinguished a star on the collar of the Brigadier General. Insignia of several field officers included two full Colonels and several Lieutenant Colonels. Urban headed for a corner of the tent and kept silent as the others discussed the failure to capture Phillipeville. They were planning strategy for the next day.

Urban was still filthy from days on the battlefield. As was his habit when leading men in combat, he had removed his Captain's bars to avoid being an excellent target for snipers.

VETERANS' RECOLLECTIONS & DIARY

Urban was surprised when the General turned his way and barked, "Colonel, you've been at the front. What do you think?" It took Urban a moment to realize the General was talking to him. He quickly decided to respond and speak as an equal to the other officers present.

Urban sensed that the General might consider him to lead the mission of capturing Phillipeville. He was concerned that the General might consider him too young. He knew if he sounded like a recent replacement, he would never be assigned to take Phillipeville. Matt did his best to sound authoritative and credible as he spoke: "General, Sir, I must insist on artillery support. Give me cover fire from your artillery and my battalion will kick the crap out of those Germans. We need scouting reconnaissance information and a heavy blanket of artillery fire before zero hour. If we get it, I'll guarantee we'll blast those Jerries out of there for you. If we don't, we will take a lot of them down with us. "

Others present listened intently. The General pondered Urban's comments for a moment, then grinned and nodded approval. The general added: "OK, Colonel, you're going to have to hump it to get into position by morning. You will have your artillery support by 0450. Then it's your responsibility to knock those bastards out of there. Good luck."

To insure that the other officers could not determine Urban's lower rank, he was edging toward a tent flap exit as the General was speaking. He took his order, saluted and was out into the night before the other field officers had a chance to comment. Urban had never imagined himself planning strategy with the brass. He certainly had not anticipated being treated as a Colonel! Matt paused outside the tent. He heard conversation from within. Urban recognized the voice of the Colonel who had ordered him into Phillipeville. "I think you should reconsider, General. That man is a coward!"

The General's voice responded in an infuriated tone, "If he had followed your orders, his entire battalion would be dead or wounded by now. Don't you know who he is? That man is Matt Urban, and assigned to us from the 9th Division. He and his men have one of the finest combat records in this entire damn war. He signed himself out of a hospital to get back to the front at St. Lo. He was instrumental in spearheading the breakout. I had Urban and his battalion assigned here because of his combat experience and ability to get a job done."

As Urban moved away into the night he chuckled to himself. He was thinking, "I guess I'm spared another court martial! I just hope my luck holds."

Sergeant Evans enjoyed ribbing Urban about the mistaken title of Colonel by mimicking GI's and saluting him all the way back to the front.

The men in Urban's battalion quickly picked up on the title of higher brass soon after 'Colonel' Urban arrived back at the front. They all enjoyed a good laugh. In a world of death and exhaustion, men found humor in simple things. People in a safer environment probably wouldn't appreciate or understand this. Urban took the kidding in good spirit. However, he was already preoccupied with planning the hazardous scouting mission to penetrate Phillipeville during the night.

September 2, 1944 - 2300 Hours

Three men crept silently in the midnight darkness over the crest of the treeless hill. They dropped snake-flat onto their bellies and stopped. Senses were attuned to any sound or movement from the houses less than thirty yards ahead.

375

Every shadow seemed to hide unseen danger. A quarter of a mile to their left, close to the country road, concrete gun emplacements could be detected. German soldiers could be heard moving about. The houses ahead were dark and appeared void of activity.

The three waited. Captain Matt Urban had picked only two men from several who had volunteered for this critical scouting mission. These two soldiers and Matt were veterans of the African Campaign. They needed no instruction --- they knew what to do.

They slowly inched ahead to the western edge of Phillipeville. Urban glanced back. In the darkness he could just make out the grim expressions on the charcoal-blackened features of his scouting partners. Their gaunt faces reflected Urban's own tension. If any one of them created a single noise they could expect to be embroiled in a hornet's nest of enemy soldiers. Urban made eye contact with his men. With a slight movement he gestured for them to follow. They moved forward in total silence, sneaking purposefully toward the cover of the houses.

It was unusual for a Battalion Commander to be personally involved on a scouting mission, but this was Urban's way. Sergeant Skertich and Corporal Miller fanned out to the left and to the right. They followed their Captain at a proper distance for night patrol. As they closed in on the nearest house, the three of them suddenly froze. The unmistakable outline of a German helmet was silhouetted against the white wall of the house. A sentry was leaning casually against the side of the building. He stared off into the distance apparently bored and waiting for his shift of guard duty to end.

Sergeant Skertich moved quietly behind the house. He crouched low as he slipped out of sight. Within seconds he reappeared behind the German sentry who was not aware of his presence. The Sergeant quickly moved close behind the German sentry. With a slender wire garrote around the sentry's neck, he snapped his head back. The only sound was a slight rustling and a short "ah" from the sentry. The three Americans fought to control their actions and sound of heavy breathing in the tenseness and excitement of the moment.

They crouched and listened carefully. The quiet that prevailed reassured them that the village was still at rest. In the dim light Urban made eye contact with Skertich and nodded his approval to the Sergeant who had killed the sentry. He motioned for his men to follow him and pointed toward some German emplacements closer to the village. The three moved cautiously in the shadows, from house to house, toward the enemy's main fortifications. They knew they had to complete their reconnaissance before it was noticed that the German sentry was missing. Urban anticipated an alarm at any moment.

This timely mission confirmed what Urban had suspected: that the Germans in the village were at least of regimental strength. Also, that they were dug in deeply with concrete bunkers, and several heavy machine guns were set up on the western area of the town. Four tanks could be seen. Urban knew there must be more in reserve. He also saw something that he had never seen in his months of combat through North Africa, Sicily and across the hedgerow country of Normandy. Anti-aircraft guns were not pointing into the sky. They were pointed down the road in the direction of the American troops.

A cool fog was settling in. Under its protective cover, Urban and his two scouts worked their way back to their own lines.

September 3, 1944 - 0400 Hours

With his scouting patrol safely completed, Urban rejoined his troops and prepared for the attack. Whenever the situation permitted, Urban would counsel with a number of his experienced veterans. He would incorporate their ideas into his own planning. While this wasn't a standard military procedure and not by the book, it was a method which worked very well. It enabled Urban to apply their combined experience. This saved time and lives. It strengthened their camaraderie, teamwork and respect for Urban as their leader.

As zero hour approached, each infantryman in the waiting company felt a hollow in his stomach. Some prayed, some cursed. Others occupied their time by checking and rechecking equipment. Each made sure grenades were attached securely on the webbing for easy access. The soldiers were packing, loading and unloading for the twentieth time. They patted ammunition pouches once more. They talked quietly to one another. Several spoke of loved ones, "If something happens to me...."

Others were restless and exclaiming, "What are we waiting for? We've come this far; let's go the rest of the way!"

Even experienced soldiers were fearful. However, they learned to function in spite of it. They could accomplish a mission even knowing that the enemy was doing everything possible to kill them. Urban was aware of the tension, but they had learned to depend on one another. Matt and the others were now moving with a mutual bonding force that was stronger than any fear.

He felt stress and anticipation as he double-checked his watch. Urban quietly moved among his men. He patted shoulders and murmured words of encouragement. By their attitudes, and without words, the tense and weary combat soldiers indicated to their Captain that they were with him.

The predawn darkness was shattered by the lightening-like effect from artillery shelling behind Urban's troops. The deafening roar of shell explosions echoed back from the German positions. This rolling thunder of artillery pounded the village of Phillipeville. Urban ordered his men to deploy to the right in the direction of the line of attack.

Through his field glasses Urban could see houses being blown up. Men and weapons of the enemy were flung in every direction. Urban pondered momentarily what he was doing, who he was and observing his part in the devastation and destruction of human lives. It was awesome. He prayed silently for those who had become casualties.

Shortly before the 0500 zero hour, the 10-minute artillery barrage ended abruptly. A deadly silence settled across the battlefield. Urban thought, "No! That's not enough to destroy the solid fortifications I saw last night." In the early light of dawn he could just make out the smoking hills in the distance near Phillipeville. Urban kept hoping for another barrage of artillery fire. He knew it wasn't coming, and it was time to move out. Zero hour had arrived.

Urban paused slightly. He was surprised to hear elements of the entrapped battalion bursting forth with thunderous cover fire. Some of the troops had held their position and survived! Their sudden activity added support and deception to the mounting attack by Urban's battalion.

At the 0500 zero hour Urban waved his arm and shouted, "This is it! Let's go, men!"

NEBELWERFER 41 ROCKET GUN

This rocket gun was introduced in 1942. Six barrels were mounted on a wheeled carriage. Urban's troops called this the 'screaming meemie'.

SHALLOW DITCH TO SHIELD INFANTRYMEN

It is from a shallow ditch like this that Urban waved his arm and shouted, "Let's go, men" in the final attack on Phillipeville.

They swarmed out of their foxholes and sprinted ahead. Crouching low, the battalion moved straight toward the fortified town of Phillipeville. The assault had been mounted with full force. The village erupted with return shellfire from tanks, anti-aircraft guns and small arms fire. Battle sounds were punctuated with the drawn-out, grinding sound of the dreaded screaming meemies --- the chief German secret weapon. It was a six-barrelled Nebelwerfer rocket gun. It could fire and then change position so fast that knocking one out was almost impossible. It could move 400 or 500 yards in a few minutes. Only its flash would give away its location. Multi-colors lit the predawn darkness as red, orange and yellow flares of shell fire and tracers illuminated the battle-field.

Enemy machine guns quickly found the range of the Americans. Their deadly bullets were landing without mercy among the American troops. The earth erupted with violent explosions from shellfire. White-hot shrapnel spewed into the air and crashed into the troops. Men fell dying; others were screaming in pain, "Medic! Medic!"

Those who remained on their feet dove for any cover they could find. They scrambled behind big rocks and bushes. They dug in behind low hills and burrowed into shallow depressions in the earth.

Platoon Sergeant Skertich came in low, crawling to his Commander. He edged himself close enough to shout in Urban's ear, "Let me take two men and see what I can do to knock out those German machine guns!"

Urban shouted his reply, "Damn good move! GO! We'll cover you!"

Skertich and two of his men leaped from cover and zigzagged toward the guns. Their dash placed them well out in front of their troops who were pinned down. They were about fifty yards from the heavy-caliber machine-gun emplacement. The slope of the terrain placed them beneath the trajectory of the machine-gun fire. He and his two men were in more danger from the enemy's machine pistols and grenades. Urban watched in dismay as one of Sergeant Skertich's men, Don Clark, was hit by machine-gun fire as they plunged forward in their attack. Skertich and his remaining infantryman dove for cover into a shell hole. They remained there under intense fire from the German troops.

Urban impulsively decided to help. He bolted from cover and sprinted to the left flank in the direction of his men. Matt was attempting to get close enough to the machine-gun nest to blow it up with his two grenades.

He ran a zigzagging course. He felt so close to the ground that his chin seemed only inches from his knees, and knees only inches from the ground. He made good speed! Machine-gun bullets tracked him the entire distance, blasting the ground just behind as he ran. Matt pulled the pin on the grenade as he sprinted toward the machine-gun nest. He heaved the grenade as soon as he was within throwing distance.

As Urban released the second grenade, he felt a hammer-blow to his neck and fell. His throat was torn by a machine-gun bullet. He tumbled forward, rolled over, and landed on his back. The thought flashed through Urban's mind as he stared skyward, "Dear God, I'm finished!" The sky seemed to be an infinite dome of heaven. It seemed so close, as if reaching for him. Matt felt as if two fountains of red spouted from the entrance and exit wounds in his throat. Blood oozed from his mouth and his ears. He began to choke in the ever-expanding pool of his own blood in his mouth and throat, but remained conscious of being alive!

Images of life and many prayers instantly flashed through his mind in those seemingly dying moments. He envisioned the weeping faces of loved ones as if they were leaning over him watching him die. Urban perceived death and its paralyzing fingers reaching for his throat. He tried to say, "God help me!" but could only manage a wheezing whisper.

Bullets from another German machine gun kicked up the ground around him. He was aware that the men he had been trying to help had moved to attack the machine gun positioned on the left flank. Urban's grenade must have hit the mark on the frontal machine-gun nest. In his agony, all of that seemed distant from him now.

One of his enlisted men, Urban's interpreter PFC Aaron Schecter, was a Jewish refugee. He had joined the company less than six months before. Schecter left his protective cover and crawled through the fire storm to rescue his Captain. Schecter reacted in horror as he stared down at Urban. The loyal soldier kept his composure and instinctively stuck both of his thumbs into Urban's neck wounds to stop the blood from gushing. Within a few moments he quickly applied field bandages to the wounds. It was this quick action that saved Urban's life.

Corporal Walter Grabski was from Chicago. He had enlisted at age forty-five and served as the Captain's orderly ('dog robber'). He ran openly to reach Schecter and Urban. Miraculously he reached Captain Urban's side unscathed. His determination and dedication were not to be denied. Schecter and Grabski pulled on Urban's ankles and inch by inch they moved him about one hundred yards while enduring ceaseless machine gun fire. Finally they were able to ease him into a muddy ditch sheltered by a slight knoll. This was a small haven of relative safety in the front lines.

Urban became aware of a flurry of movement around him. GI's crawled near hoping to be of help. Some of his men were sure he was fatally wounded and were now openly and unashamedly weeping as they huddled over him. Some military commanders order their men, others lead by example. None of Urban's troops had ever experienced a Commander quite like Matt Urban! He was always leading and in the forefront of every attack. Captain Urban expected no

THE SCENE OF URBAN'S FINAL BATTLE
GIs from Urban's 2nd Battalion and Major Norman Weinberg with medics providing emergency treatment.

more of others than he was willing to put on the line himself. His troops loved him for it and responded with extreme loyalty.

German mortar fire licked the hills around the hidden ditch. That danger could not keep Matt's battalion surgeon, Major Norman Weinberg, from making his way to the front to administer aid. The two officers had known each other since early training days in 1941 at Fort Bragg, N.C. There they had enjoyed being poker-playing buddies.

Dr. Weinberg worked frantically in this front-line muddy ditch under intense enemy barrage to save the life of his old friend. He started intravenous plasma flowing. He swiftly performed a tracheotomy. He inserted an airway tube into the base of Urban's mangled throat.

Chaplain Timothy Andryziak, another devoted friend from the Fort Bragg days, also made his way to the muddy ditch. Looking into the chaplain's eyes, Urban sensed he did not have long to live. The chaplain turned to Weinberg and asked, "Any hope?" Urban's eyes swung toward Dr. Weinberg who was leaning over him. The surgeon turned to Father Andryziak and solemnly shook his head.

Lying there, Urban's mind again envisioned loved ones, family and troops as clearly as if he were speaking to them. He thought, "I am finished!" Matt struggled to remain conscious. Between lapses of faintness, he struggled to hear Dr. Weinberg's medical verdict. Urban silently pleaded, "No! No! Norm, don't let me die ... YOU CANNOT LET ME DIE!"

Chaplain Andryziak crawled closer to Urban and performed the last rites. Just before drifting into unconsciousness, Urban's mind again flashed back to all of those he had loved at home, to his troops, and his concern for them. A response resulted in a feeling that "He COULDN'T abandon them now!" Urban still had the will to live.

A peaceful feeling engulfed him as he drifted into the oblivion of unconsciousness.

Matt's men tenderly placed him on the hood of a bullet-riddled Jeep. They drove him over and behind the low hills on the Belgian side of the river tributary. As the Jeep passed on its five-mile trip to the field hospital, word spread along the line:

"Captain Urban got it!"

"Captain Urban's been killed!"

"Captain Urban is DEAD!"

CHAPTER 16

RECOVERY

The loss of Urban left a serious gap in experienced leadership. As Urban was carried from the battlefield on September 4, 1944, his troops advanced to cross the Meuse River into Germany. A midnight crossing was planned with small rubber boats. The enemy was waiting in ambush. Heavy casualties were sustained from German flame-throwing tanks, mortar and machine-gun fire directed from above the river-bank shoreline.

German troops closed in on the two columns of American infantrymen attempting to scale the river-bank heights. American prisoners were placed as hostages in front of the German troops! Soldiers of Urban's 2nd Battalion held back firepower --- they could not fire into ranks of their own countrymen! More brave American servicemen were taken as German war prisoners.

PONTOON BRIDGE - MEUSE RIVER
This 9th Division Jeep was first to cross the bridge near Houx, Belgium. U.S. Army Engineers, 15th Engr. Battalion, 9th Infantry Division, fought a raging river to build this important bridge.

394

By evening 80% of the 2nd Battalion was lost — from almost 1,000 Americans who had completed the Meuse River crossing! They had borne the brunt of the German forces using machine guns, mortars and flame-throwing tanks.

Pontoon bridges were finally constructed. A task force of the Third Armored Division roared into action across the Meuse River bridgehead. German armored attack columns and their supporting flame-throwing infantry were thrown back in defeat. The American bridgehead was strengthened and firmly secured. By September 6, the 9th Division had completed the defeat of a German army that had occupied Belgium as 'war lords'.

In these Belgium battles, the 9th Division was joined by the Belgian underground. These civilian fighters had risen up to help American servicemen throw off the German oppressors. Their Army Blanche (The White Army) fought alongside our seasoned American troops. Passionate displays of courage by the Belgian underground gave confidence and strength to the Allied onslaught. Now it was on to the German homeland as the Allied pursuit began anew.

TYPICAL OF PERILOUS BATTLE CONDITIONS

After the heavy losses at the Meuse River crossing, 60% of the 9th Division now consisted of replacement troops. On September 15 at 0900, the 9th Division assembled at the Siegfried line. They smashed their way into the town of Monschau, Germany. Here they occupied the outer line of pill boxes on the west wall of the supposedly invincible Siegfried line.

- - - - - - - - - -

The Matt Urban Story Continues:

As Urban's 2nd Battalion moved through Belgium, Urban was taken from the battle zone to a field hospital tent. He was left in the corner of the tent with other soldiers considered beyond hope. For several days he received a minimum of care while doctors focused their attention on men who seemed to have the best chance of recovery.

Urban drifted in and out of consciousness, barely aware of his surroundings, usually feverish and in a delirium from pain. Lying on his cot in a hospital tent in France, he awoke from morphine which had been administered to relieve his misery. Urban noticed that his muddy combat boots were still on his feet. He was sure he had been in the hospital tent for days. He had no real concept of time. Matt was being fed intravenously in his arm. No one seemed to pay much attention to him.

After what seemed to be forever (he later learned it had been a few weeks, and he had been comatose most of that time), Urban scribbled notes to the nurse saying, "Water, please". He did this several times in the days to come. Each time she would consult with the doctor. Prone and helpless, Matt was a pathetic-looking soldier.

With pleading eyes and facial expressions and a finger pointing to his throat, he indicated, "Dying of thirst. Help me!" Looking up in the shadowy light of the tent he saw what appeared to be two large shadows hovering over him. The nurse and doctor were carrying on what appeared to be a private conversation. Urban, waiting in suspense, wondered what the conversation was about and how it would affect him.

After a few more days of Matt's note pleading and nurse/doctor discussions, action resulted! They finally decided to offer Urban a teaspoon of water to see how he would react. React he did! The trickle of water 'tickling' his shot-up throat brought on heavy coughing. Upon Urban's continued written pleading, they reluctantly continued this trickle of water feeding several times without any success.

Soon afterwards Urban was airborne to a base hospital in England. He was still wearing his combat boots and fatigues. Only later were the boots taken off.

It was evening. As soon as Urban was in bed he was confronted by an unkempt, unshaven, short scrawny looking Lieutenant ... a medical doctor.

Doctor? "Hey!" Urban thought to himself, "Who is this character? He doesn't look like a doctor!" This belief grew as Urban scrawled his note: "Water".

Doc called to his soldier attendant, "Bring the Bourbon out of my room!"

Urban thought, "This guy must be an AA dropout needing a 'snort' before he dives into me!"

Within minutes the attendant returned with a pint bottle of Bourbon and a glass. Urban's eyeballs and heart sure took it all in. He thought, "This is the first bit of excitement since the Battle of Phillipeville. I am only hoping that we drink together. He the booze, me the water. Here's to you!"

Urban nearly had a heart attack, almost falling out of bed when the 'doctor' handed over the glass, one-fourth full of Bourbon.

"Bottoms up!" commanded the doctor --- while Matt was thinking, "He must not have known about the disastrous 'trickle-tickle' experiences. If a trickle tickles with water, what will a gulp of booze do? Kill me? Burn my chopped throat?" Hesitating, and with the help of the doctor's shoving hand, down went the 'TNT'. Holy Toledo!! Results: no cough, no adverse reaction. The 'thing' went down.

That evening and from then on, Matt was able to enjoy a light soup liquid diet. What a lifesaver! The moral of the story being: 'trickles do tickle'! That is exactly what the over-cautious persons caused with cautious teaspoon-size portions. Urban wished his first caregivers had been as ingenious and as prac-tical as this unimpressive looking doctor. Urban now rates this doctor as his #1 nominee for a Nobel Prize! Urban says, "Even risking a gulp of water would have been better than the tickling-trickle I had previously endured from the cautious medical treatments."

Because of the war and the many experiences Urban had with doctors, he still marvels at their abilities and skills. Especially appreciated were the ones who deviated from the book and did necessary innovative and wonderful things under the most impossible circumstances ... and Urban feels the same about the field medics and hospital attendants. With their ingenuity and dedication to saving lives, they 'wrote' a medical book of their own during the war. Urban recalls: "We had the best doctors and they saved thousands of lives. Actions were taken that had never been documented in medical books. New techniques solved problems never experienced in peacetime."

A few days later as the senior medical officer was making his rounds, Urban wrote him a note asking when he could return to his unit. Urban had been reading battlefield reports. He had been listening to men around him who had just returned from the front lines. Matt now knew that practically all of his battalion had been wiped out by injury, were missing in action, or dead.

Urban's chief surgeon read the note and spoke to Matt in very serious tones: "Your war is over, Urban. The only place you'll be going is back to the States. You can do more good there."

Seeing the determination in Urban's eyes, the doctor sat on the edge of Matt's bed. He spoke at length about the severity of Urban's wounds. "You came within a fraction of an inch of being killed. With vocal chords shot up so seriously, it's doubtful that you'll ever be able to speak again."

The doctor's words fell on deaf ears. Men were still dying! As long as Matt could walk, crawl or bo carried, he would somehow rejoin his troops.

In a few days Urban was up and walking around. He spent much time outdoors. Matt began walking the grounds in an effort to regain his strength. He wore a neck brace over bandages. He covered the brace with a scarf. An Air Corps jacket gave Urban an appearance of health and vitality. Urban's mind was concentrated on just one goal ... he had to make it back to the front --- to Germany!

After some weeks in the English hospital, Matt requested leave to join his troops for a visit. He wanted to get his feet on German soil: "I have come a long, hard way since landing with the invasion forces in Africa! I do not want to be 'short changed' this close to the ultimate goal --- Germany, the Reich!"

Matt Urban requested a five- or ten-day pass to France. The reply came: "Definitely no! It would be too much for you during convalescence from such a serious injury. Besides, we are planning a ceremony at which you are to be the award recipient." That ceremony was not the reward Matt was seeking!

Urban's next approach was to request a five-day pass for a convalescent leave in the quiet environs of Scotland. With hesitation this pass was finally approved. Urban, of course, had plans of his own. This did not include any trip to Scotland!

Urban was aiming for a hitchhiking flight to the European continent. He intended to visit his troops at the front line. Unfortunately he planned this at the same time that General Eisenhower had just put a "no unauthorized flights" order into effect. This order was brought on because too many hitchhiking soldiers were being lost and unaccounted for when planes they were aboard were shot down or crashed.

This had been happening at an increasing rate. Also, this was about the same time that Big Band leader Glen Miller's plane went down, and everyone aboard was killed. There was no manifest to record the passengers who were lost.

All sense of reality was smothered by Urban's exuberance at having received his five-day pass. He was practically overcome with excitement at the possibility of being with his troops.

Now just outside the hospital's main gate, Urban shuddered with this uncontrolled excitement. He developed a clammy, sweaty feeling. Normally he was an impassive character. This leave began with a hollow note as he looked over his shoulder. He felt lost. He had a feeling much like the prison inmate must experience when suddenly set free and alone in the outside world.

Matt truly was 'on his own'. He did not know exactly where he was headed. As always, Matt had his fatalistic confidence. This time he also had to overcome having no voice with which to communicate.

A bandage hid Urban's neck brace, so he appeared to be combat dressed. He kept warm with his fleece-lined Air Corps jacket. Matt had acquired this by a trade with the Air Force pilot: Urban's Luger for the jacket.

Urban headed for the corner bus stop enroute to the Air Force base. This 'hitchhiker' faced bitter disappointment. It was cumbersome to have no voice to explain his purpose and to beg his ride by handwriting notes!

For days Urban patiently sat on benches in the scantily furnished headquarter barracks. Fog enveloped the Air Force base. Matt was bucking the new 'no unauthorized flight' order. He was also contending with a shortage of planes. Take-off flights were continuously held down by fog and inclement weather. Airmen were plagued with their own duties, but took time to make sure that Urban had three squares a day although food supplies were limited. A blanket was supplied to wrap around Matt for warmth in his 24-hour vigil in the air base flight barracks.

By noon on the third day the clouds cleared enough for some limited take-offs. No way was Matt going to be given an official OK to board. Matt's analysis of the airmen indicated they were sympathetic to his cause. That was enough to convince Urban to become a stow-away! He play-acted with a look of authority as he fell in step behind a flight crew ready to board. None were watchful. In fact, heads turned the other way, as this determined stow-away --- Captain Urban --- huddled in the rear cargo bay.

The plane landed at an airfield outside of Paris. Urban departed with a sense of accomplishment. A farewell wave and a voiceless "Thanks, guys" followed. They split up, walking in different directions.

With more written pleadings, one of the more sympathetic pilots helped Urban to become a stow-away on a flight to Amsterdam.

Matt arrived in the deep of night. The black-out of this Allied air base gave it an appearance of a ghost town. Chilling drizzle added to the dreariness of the area. Urban despaired in not knowing which way to go, or what to do next. In the falling wet drizzle and uncertainty of his present predicament, Urban stumbled along to reach the protective cover under the wing of a nearby moored plane.

A disillusioned Matt heaped himself upon a wheel, hugging as much of the oval as he could for a bit of warmth. He pondered as to the futility of his purpose, of --- of --- of what he had endured! A realization that perhaps the worst was still to come caused the hard-bitten warrior to 'butt-out' with body quivering and agonizing tears that released emotions and tranquilized Urban into a deep sleep. This was by far the most lonely night of Urban's life!

Upon awakening, Urban headed for what looked like the base motor pool. Drivers and mechanics were hustling in their assignments. There wasn't any time for them to pay attention to this bothersome scuffling onlooker. Matt Urban trudged over to a group taking their military break. Smokers gawked as he neared. Matt handed his written 'calling card' of explanation to the mechanic who was least preoccupied.

His note said: "I have been shot through the neck --- my vocal chords are destroyed --- my voice is gone. I am trying to rejoin my troops: 60th Infantry, 9th Division. I need a ride towards Merode. Can you help me? Thanks! Capt. Matt Urban 0416194."

The reader blurted out: "You won't believe it. This guy wants to get back to the front lines!"

Someone else shouted: "Yeah! He's a Section 8 if I ever seen one." Urban moved away from this unwelcome reception. He was not going to allow them to depress his desire and spirits!

Matt had his own thoughts: "Hey, I am still alive. That's good enough for me." This gave him a lift He swashbuckled to his next quarry. A happy-go-lucky, impetuous looking GI was leaning against a mud-covered vehicle. On reading the message this mussed-up, cigar-chewing GI Joe stomped his foot, swung his arm, with "SOB, this is the best I have ever come across. You wanna fight. You wanna be killed!" Haw haw hawing, ho continued, "Be my guest, hop in. I will take you a good part of the way!"

Another cold December ride came in an open 2½ ton truck. Rumbling across the beautiful Belgian countryside and into Germany was, however, good compensation. This was especially so after those depressing five days hitchhiking. Nearing the war zone, the STOP at the MP barricade came as a shock. As Urban was being hauled into the Military Police Post, he dreaded the possibility of this being his journey's end. He was so close!

What was it going to be — the guard house, a POW or transported under lock and key back to the hospital as a patient? Urban's mind and body were at ease when the Provost Marshal, who was a battle-scarred Major, offered a friendly handshake and told Matt that he understood.

The Major ordered his driver to escort Captain Urban directly to the 2nd Battalion, Infantry Bivouac area in Germany!

GERMANY!!!! I MADE IT!!!!

By nightfall Urban rolled into the area where his regiment was bivouacked. He stepped down from the Jeep and walked toward his encamped troops. Several of them walked out to meet him. The first man to recognize Urban was a good friend. It was George Albert! He had been Urban's heavyweight boxer in England!

Albert stood blinking for a few moments unbelieving ... thinking, "Wasn't Urban dead? How could this be? It can't be him." The big man ran up and grabbed Urban in a gigantic bearhug, lifting him off the ground. "You're alive! God damn, you're alive!"

Another old friend, Charles LiBretto laughed as he threw his arms around Urban. "I thought you got yourself killed; now here you are, big as life. Maybe you are a GHOST!"

By now a number of men gathered around. Most were strangers to Urban. Their spirit, however, was familiar to Matt. It was these men who 'carried the ball' after Urban was knocked out by the bullet in his throat. The faces were new, but the fierce determin- ation and 'do or die' sense clearly showed. Many of these soldiers had been in battle for only a short time. Already they had built an awesome record of performance under fire.

Urban was ecstatic! BACK HOME --- job fulfilled --- once again with his troops! This is where he belonged. "I can make a difference here," he thought. "Get into action with them. Fight beside them for a few days."

He submitted a request for an assignment. There was some talk ... a faint possibility....

The men were ready to petition. "We will be his voice" was their platform. "Let's get a bull horn for him" was another comment.

410

Urban was able to catch up on all of the news and enjoy the company of his friends for a couple of days. The Battalion Commander convinced Matt that he really needed to return to his hospital. He was grateful for the morale boost for his troops who were still at the edge of battle. Nevertheless, he was adamant that Urban would have to depart when the 2nd Battalion moved out.

Orders were orders. Urban's days of frontline combat time were over. Matt had to be honest with himself. He was weakened by his wounds. "Yes," Matt thought, "I am not really ready for combat."

The Regimental CO, Col. John G. Van Houten, with good grace, had knocked some sense into Urbie's head. The CO's personal Jeep was provided to bring Matt to the nearest air base. The Commander's warm and encouraging farewell remarks would stay with Urban forever. Matt's return to England was made easier by the good start in the Commander's Jeep and again meeting with his Air Force friends. As his battalion moved out, Urban departed for the Allied airfield and his final cross-channel trip to England.

While Matt was in Germany, his five-day pass became a boomerang! Ordinarily a fourteen-day extended leave probably would go unnoticed or lightly excused. That was not possible this time. The entire hospital personnel and nearby troops were assembled for an elaborate ceremony. Matt Urban was to be the hero of the day at the presentation in the hospital courtyard. Matt learned later that the flags were flying, the band was playing, and the General stepped forward prepared to pin the bronze star on the hero, but Urban was not to be found!

Where is Urban? The entire situation was in chaos. Finally Urban, the wandering soldier, reported in from his 'quiet Scotland vacation'.

Court martial was a real possibility! Urban was fearful that this might become a reality.

The entire matter was reviewed, and finally a decision was rendered: Urban's outstanding record of bravery and the purpose of his leave were carefully scrutinized. It was determined there should be no taint of dishonor on Captain Urban's military service record because of this episode.

Consideration had been given to the fact that Urban had gone where he felt he truly belonged --- with his men at the front line of action in Germany

CASE DISMISSED!!

VETERANS' RECOLLECTIONS & DIARY

CHAPTER 17

AMERICA, AMERICA

September 1944 marked the 'beginning of the end' for Nazi Germany. British and American troops were smashing at the vaunted Siegfried line. From the east, Russia was regaining the last of her territories and moving rapidly across eastern Europe. The strength of the German armies and the support of the German people still could not be underestimated.

The Nazi troops had been thrown back from all conquered territories, and the front was now in their homeland. The original snarling Blitzkrieg attacks had now become a fierce fight of desperation --- defending homeland Germany.

In some unexplainable way, Hitler still had a hypnotic power over the German people. His promises of a secret weapon (which were little more than veiled hints of atomic weapons) soothed their losses and gave the German people a false faith in this

THE MATT URBAN STORY

madman. Many believed he could still save the Fatherland .... perhaps even bring them a victory over the Allied forces.

Continuous bombing flattened every major industrial center of Germany. It laid waste to her factories and cities. Even so, most captured German soldiers held a firm belief that their Wehrmacht was saving its knockout punch --- that German victory was inevitable for the 'superior German race'.

Meanwhile, Matt Urban was sent home, along with thousands of wounded and battle-weary soldiers, sailors and airmen. They wore joyfully greeted as returning heroes. Nearly everyone in America had been touched personally and deeply by this war: many lost fathers, brothers, sons or friends.

The returning servicemen were recognized with sincere respect and admiration as these honors had been well earned. They were rightfully due for men who had dedicated life and limb to protect the liberty of the American people and their Allies around the world.

Urban boarded the Queen Mary in England (a luxury liner) now converted to serve duty as a hospital ship.

He and thousands of other wounded GI's set sail to cross the Atlantic, bound for home. With a full load on board, the ship headed for the United States of America. At last, the end of hostilities! It seemed fitting that seas were calm and the weather clear during the several days of crossing the ocean to New York City.

It was a physically smashed and broken group of men who were sailing with exuberance and high spirits toward America .... to home .... to loved ones!

As he strolled the decks, Urban saw men who were blinded and those without limbs. In spite of many serious injuries, Matt had a deep-set feeling of how fortunate he was.

Urban wandered below decks and found the inevitable poker games. These would spring up in the same areas of every ship. Urban's luck held up. Matt won close to $800 from fellow officers.

A rush of excitement engulfed their ship as they approached the New York Harbor and Ellis Island. These men yearned for that first glimpse of American soil in many long months.

Entering the harbor, thousands of men crowded the decks to catch a view of the Statue of Liberty (the 'Grand Old Lady') --- the monument to American freedom.

Urban recalled the stirring song: 'America, America, God Shed His Grace On Thee'. To Urban the beautiful city of New York seemed to sparkle like a jewel on the waterway of New York's busy harborfront.

The tired, emotionally charged soldiers ... away for such a long time ... were at last ... coming home!!

They gathered 'top side' on their ship. They filled every deck to the edges of railings. They were staring out of every available porthole. There were many uncontrollable tears, cheers, prayers, kneeling, jumping, yelling and saluting.

Crazy? Definitely not!

Overwhelming? Absolutely!

No returning army had felt such a sense of victory and pride. Called from civilian lives, these men had thrown off the tyranny and slavery that World War II had imposed on the free world. They kept their promise. They gave life and limb to secure freedom.

There was very little resemblance now to the brash young boys who had left American shores some time before. They were then filled with exuberance, confidence and an anxious desire to fight for the freedom of the people and country that they loved.

After four years in the jungles and fields of war, they were back in the States! With maturity developed in war, with excitement as men who earned freedom for all.

America! America! We are here! Home! Imagine that --- and after so many years!!

'Out on the town' in New York, N.Y.: 42nd Street, 5th Avenue, excitement and PEACE! Proudly they strolled down 5th Avenue --- on the pavement. No sidewalk was big enough to contain them and new-found freedom.

Later in the evening a group of ten headed towards the exclusive Club Versailles to 'cap up' a day none would forget! After four years of spartan battlefield existence, war-weary soldiers gaped with eyes popping at the magnificent New York surroundings.

Curiosity was aroused as the GI 'tourists' watched civilian party-goers, 'beautiful people' in elegant costumes. Their happy-go-lucky behavior seemed so strange and unusual to the infantrymen who just came from four years of serious deadly combat.

The GI's were not inhuman. Yes, they were rough on the surface, but a sensitive and sensible group well aware of their tough exterior. They had only recently been released from war's terrible killing fields. Anxiety was a natural reaction. It had been such a long war. This all seemed like a new, fresh atmosphere with its attractions of wine, women and song! Our American soldiers were back in their real world, but they were not yet re-oriented. That was to come later.

These soldiers didn't think of themselves as battle fatigued, shell-shocked or afflicted with any battle neurosis. Urban noticed, however, that he grasped his goblet with both hands wrapped around it --- like a GI cup with no handles! Slurping slightly, he gulped his drink as if he couldn't get it fast enough. Ah, that's go---od!!!

420

"I guess we're trying to compensate for a four-year thirst," they joked. Urban felt good, enjoying the camaraderie of his service buddies.

Several guys were behaving as if they were still 'over there', guzzling out of the bottles, standing in the restaurant aisle and roaming around the open room. Their field manners brought unwanted attention from onlookers.

New-found freedom and excitement were not entirely the cause for the unconventional behavior: Although they had been very early night club arrivals, they had been seated at a remote table. It was in a corner, on the top floor --- near the ceiling rafters! To view the floor show, they would have needed to use binoculars and stand on chairs!

As in wartime, they solved their problem by initiating a small floor show of their own. They confined the action to their own party and to their own table, relaxing and enjoying their friendship. Holding back was the last thing in their thoughts --- as well it should have been.

Three waiters, typical of some New York City hustlers, directed all of their attention and service to well-heeled patrons, who seemed to be the regular customers --- civilians who must have been beyond the draft age. They could not relate to these military guys, nor did they show any desire to do so.

Waiters glared condescendingly. Their service was offered only twice. They filled ice buckets reluctantly. Whenever Matt's men would burst into laughter, enjoying their party, waiters scowled and grumbled disapproval. Maybe these soldiers were not be-having according to protocol. Urban's group thought the stuffed-shirt attitude of those non-military guys was out of line and uncalled for.

The GI's were content to ignore those attitudes and poor waiter service. They were greatly surprised by the bill. $150! Urban thought, "Inflation must be wild!"

Urban picked up the tab. He left a generous tip. It exceeded the standard of 1941 (10%), the expected rate when Matt shipped out for military action four years earlier, thousands of miles from this New York social scene. With recent poker winnings Matt felt rich. He was proud and pleased to share this with his men by paying the bill and leaving the tip. It was a whopping amount to Urban --- more than his pre-war weekly salary had been.

The waiter frowned. He looked on expectantly but with an expression of disdain. Urban had seen enough of that in the faces of the Nazi SS Troops. Several co-workers in tuxedos grouped around, indicating that more money was expected. Fifteen percent, they said, was minimal! "They expected to get it," Urban thought, "for rendering insulting service?'" Urban's men reacted accordingly when he conferred with them.

The waiter spoke sarcastically as he was holding the money: "Where have you been? Perhaps you should go back there!"

All hell broke loose!!!

Urban reacted: Oh hell! Not again! Another beach-head! This action was a miniature one in comparison. However, the next day a sign on the door --- Closed Until Further Notice --- was a good clue to the results. Urban's men could rationalize their actions and easily understood the circumstances of last night's 'mini-riot'!

All now agreed: It was time to train themselves to get along in the civilian world again. It was also time to decide where to be and what to do in this 'brand new' capitalistic world.

In this post-war world, Urban decided maybe he should become a waiter! At tips of 15%, it looked like easy money!

Their reorientation had begun.

- - - - - - - - - -

Now Urban was back In his hometown of Buffalo at last! As he stepped off his train in Buffalo, N.Y., he was winding through familiar neighborhood streets. Urban was savoring cherished memories of long ago. He felt as if he were in a dream enjoying memories of another life.

Urban's exact arrival time was unannounced. He climbed the steps to his home at 1153 Broadway with mixed emotions.

Matt's parents knew he had been wounded in action numerous times. He had not yet told them his voice box was destroyed --- that he was returning from the war handicapped --- and had no vocal capability.

Mother Urban had risen early that morning! Matty was coming home! He had been away so many years in this terrible World War.

Everything had to be just so for this long awaited reunion. Matt's mom (Helen Urban) had baked all his favorite foods. Helen had just returned from the beauty shop. She dressed to look very classy. Everything had to be just perfect! Helen Urban wanted a most wonderful reunion with her youngest son, Matty!

The exciting moment arrived. Matt rushed through the kitchen door with his arms outstretched reaching for his Mom. Helen Urban collapsed in her son's loving arms. In happiness she cried softly as Matt Urban silently held his mother in a warm bearhug.

"How are you, Matty?" she asked when she had regained her composure.

He smiled, and with tears running from his cheeks, his mouth finally opened. Only guttural sounds came out. "Ah, ah, ah!"

Helen Urban realized that Matty, her handsome son, could not speak! Mom Urban went into a silent shock! HE HAD A BULLET HOLE THROUGH HIS NECK!

She pulled herself together quickly. Helen Urban was known to be a great lady and notable for leadership in Buffalo civic and women's organizations. Setting aside her inner sadness, Helen turned the tearful reunion into a most joyous homecoming.

Matt's dad, Stanley Urban, in his excitement, repeated over and over, "You're home! The first of my sons is home!" He rejoiced in knowing that his faithful daily chapel prayers were heard .... and answered! He held Matt in a firm hug for several minutes. Affectionate slaps on the back were unspoken tributes to his joy in having Matt home again. This wordless embrace conveyed Stanley's love for his son.

Matt tells that his father was a friendly, tenderhearted, five-foot-ten, wiry man. Stanley was outwardly friendly but had the ability to sharply put down any questionable adversary. As a businessman, he had a very successful plumbing company and investments in real estate prior to the 1929 Crash. In fact,

Stanley became semi-retired at age forty-five. During the Great Depression, he was forced to start over again in the plumbing business.

When the United States entered the war, Matt's father gave up his plumbing business to become a night-guard at the Bell Aircraft Plant in Buffalo, N.Y. He was proud to wear his uniform and side arm as he shared in the war effort. As soon as his sons were mustered out of the service, and the war ended, Stan Urban stepped down from his patriotic night-guard duties at the defense plant.

- - - - - - - - - - -

Helen Urban's own words regarding her son, Matt, as told in 1974 to Jennie Urban, Matt's wife:

"During the war we had been informed by telegram after each time Matt was wounded. The first couple of times the telegram delivery man came by looking for our house. After that he did not even have to look at the house number or street, he just had to look at the name, and he knew where to deliver the messages.

After the first two telegrams, my husband, Stan, and I knew what it was. The delivery man came a third time ---
then a fourth ---
then the fifth ---
then the sixth ---
and finally a seventh time.

Each time our hearts stood still. Is he hurt again? How badly? Is he dead?

We lived on a rollercoaster of emotion, never know-ing and always afraid. You never knew whether it would be the last delivery or not. Can you just imag ine the feeling in my heart every time the delivery man brought a telegram to our door?!!"

Stanley Urban

Helen Urban

Dr. Stan Urban

Arthur   Urban

Matt Urban

MATT

ARTHUR

EUGENE

STANLEY

FAMILY LITTLE LEAGUE
"BIG HITTERS"

429

CHAPTER 18

POST WAR --- LIFE BEGINS AGAIN
Halloran Hospital - Liberty Magazine -
Youth Work - Cassius Clay

Matt Urban and the troops of his 2nd Battalion and his 9th Infantry Division helped immeasurably to bring a world gone wild back from the disastrous destruction of war to a newfound hope for world peace.

Now Urban's men directed their intelligence into new skills and careers dedicated to deep commitments to their families. Comrades in arms and patriotism supporting the American way of freedom would never diminish. There was a bond of trust unique to Matt Urban's men and the troops of the 9th Infantry Division of the United States Army. This bond continues to this day. Each year these dedicated soldiers gather in reunion --- to honor the memory of fallen comrades and renew friendships of a lifetime.

9TH INFANTRY DIVISION REUNION
Worchester, Mass.

The 9th Infantry Division Reunion was held at this location for several years. The site is the parish grounds of Father Connor's Church. 9th Division attendees come from many states and as far away as California.

Upon returning from World War II service, it was remarkable that practically none of these troops needed counseling to adjust to post-war life. The excellent military orientation programs fitted perfectly with the grateful public and industry acceptance of these homecoming heroes.

Most of the returning soldiers picked up where they had left off from civilian life. Despite some emotional scars and physical handicaps, these conditions were eased by compassionate understanding. This helpful response came from loved ones, employers and the American public. It represented the total and positive response for a war won, and was a form of thanks with sincere respect for those brave men who earned the victory.

At the same time, a dedicated corps of doctors, nurses and medical technicians continued their work. They were doing their utmost to repair broken bodies and save the lives of returning American military men. These professionals remained in military service. They would not be 'mustered out' of service until the critically injured returning servicemen received needed healing care. Countless GI's, Urban included, and their families expressed respect and praise for overworked medical personnel.

These well trained people performed near miracles for many veterans in hospitals across the United States.

The medical case history of Lt. Col. Matt Urban is one example of thousands cared for so well in post-war treatment centers.

Urban received the best treatment possible while at Halloran Hospital, Staten Island, N.Y. His treatment extended more than one year, divided between Halloran Hospital and Tilton General Hospital at Fort Dix, New Jersey.

Urban recalls that he prayed every morning in the Hospital Chapel for his voice to return. He practiced his faith by 'singing' hymns --- mouth open, lips moving, but rendered in silent praise --- with hand gestures for expression. Matt said he had no concern about anyone watching him. These regular efforts were based on belief and faith in God that he would regain his ability to talk. Matt says he also followed the philosophy of one of his Commanders, Major Robert Andrews: "There are no such words as 'DO NOT' and 'WILL NOT.'"

After periodic innovative surgeries and the dedicated work of his hospital speech therapist, Matt experienced another of his life's miracles. Urban was startled one day to hear the beginnings of coherent sounds coming from his throat. It was Matt's first indication that his speaking voice would return! After months of practice he learned to speak in a rasping voice sound.

Night after night Matt would be alone in his room and spend the time trying to read aloud. This continued with the same dedication and determination that were trademarks of Urban's life and character. The effort finally became a success when Matt could speak well enough to be understood. It was years since Urban had been shot in the throat and vocal chords and had lost his voice.

Sounds at first were as weak as a whisper. Every morning Matt was up before anyone else. He practiced by reading the newspaper vocally. He read page after page aloud. This strengthened his voice so he could meet the challenge of the public business world.

Mr. Dick Hyman was Business Manager of the national publication *Liberty Magazine*. After interviewing Lt. Col. Urban, he offered him employment. The job was to read and review manuscripts of War Reports. Urban was then to author a column and apply his own first-hand knowledge. The column was titled 'Old Sarge' and devoted to veterans' affairs, information and stories.

The work at Liberty Magazine was personally rewarding to Matt, because his outstanding military experiences brought authenticity to the weekly column. Matt also knew his depth of knowledge of the campaigns was truly presented to veterans who would read and appreciate the column.

A few months after Urban took over the writing of 'Old Sarge', he converted it to 'Veterans' Bulletin Board'. This more truly indicated the column content. By this time Matt was providing a wide range of information to aid and benefit returning veterans. The magazine and Urban's column reached a weekly circulation of six million readers each week. Matt cherished the privilege of reaching so many readers as a veteran representing millions of men in uniform. He was able to do this column in *Liberty Magazine* while continuing more than a year of treatments at Halloran Veterans' Hospital as an out-patient. Matt's weekends were spent at his boarding house on Staten

Island. Two or three days a week were spent at Liberty Magazine offices in New York City. The time required for treatments at the hospital, boarding home and office work on the column kept Matt busy seven days a week.

It was during this time at Liberty Magazine that Urban felt a special happiness and pride. He received word that two of his fellow militarymen, Major John Ryan and Colonel Keene 'Slick' Wilson, were awarded the Defense of Leningrad Medal from the Russian Army. When Russian and Allied forces met at the outskirts of Berlin, each discovered many mutual war experiences fighting Nazi Germany. The Ryan and Wilson awards were presented in recognition of their heroism and that of their troops in defeating the German armed forces.

During Urban's hospitalization at Halloran Hospital, Urban's military promotions finally caught up with him. These were battlefield promotions which had been pigeon-holed. First, he was advanced from Captain to the rank of Major in recognition of his service as the 2nd Battalion Executive Officer. Then he was advanced to the rank of Lt. Colonel for his responsibility while serving as the 2nd Battalion Commanding Officer. This last promotion was

Here is the DAV story as told by one of the most aggressive fighters in the interest of handicapped ex-servicemen.

Liberty
MAY 11, 1946   10c

VETERANS' Bulletin Board
BY MATT URBAN

Lt. Col. Matt Urban (Infantry, Ret.), veteran of six campaigns from Africa to Germany and holder of the Purple Heart with five clusters, is Editor of the Veterans' Bulletin Board in Liberty Magazine.

MORE than 2,500,000 veterans of World War II have come out of the service physically the worse for it, more or less disabled. To their number must be added unknown thousands whose service-connected disabilities are not yet apparent but may crop up later to blight their lives and livelihoods.

In the present drive to find jobs and homes for all veterans, it is understandable that the peculiar plight of the disabled veteran is temporarily obscured.

During the war, physically handicapped civilians performed remarkably in jobs nobody supposed they could do. There is no reason to suppose that disabled ex-servicemen cannot equally well fit into the normal industrial picture of today.

A recent survey conducted by the U. S. Employment Service yields some telling statistics. In a group comprising some 300 employers and 62,283 workers in varied fields, it was proven that 87.2 per cent of the disabled workers were as efficient as their able-bodied colleagues; 7.8 per cent were more efficient.

These facts need emphasis and re-emphasis. Fortunately there is a bang-up organization which is equipped and prepared to present the case. The Disabled American Veterans, 100,000 strong, under the leadership of Dow V. Walker, has for twenty-five years fought for public recognition of the disabled veteran as a normal citizen with normal aspirations.

The nation-wide staff of the DAV aids disabled veterans in the preparation and prosecution of just claims for medical examinations, hospitalization, disability compensation, vocational training, employment, and other problems of rehabilitation.

In an effort to keep up with the swelling ranks of the disabled and help the Veterans Administration overcome its limitations, the DAV has been setting up intensive six-month training courses at the American University in Washington, D. C. From this program will emerge 400 selected disabled veterans of World War II as full-time service officers.

To finance an expanded program, the DAV is now raising $10,000,000. President Truman, General Bradley, and many other leading citizens and public officials are appealing for wholehearted public support.

If you have a disability problem, be sure to get in touch with a DAV service officer. You will find one in all Veterans Administration regional offices and in 1,300 local chapters throughout the country. The address

We can't scrap warworn men like warworn material.

of the DAV National Headquarters is 1423 East McMillan Street, Cincinnati, Ohio.

Commander Walker has this tip for all prospective veterans. He says he can't emphasize it too strongly:

"Before you are discharged, be sure you consider carefully filing a claim for pension if you believe you have a just case. Remember: the slightly lame back or trick knee that you do not consider important now may well be a serious handicap later on. By putting your complaint on the record at time of discharge, you will make infinitely easier the prosecution of your claim later."

* * *

To maintain the free services of the DAV, contribute to the National Service Fund of the Disabled American Veterans, 41 E. 42nd Street, New York 17, N. Y.

* This cartoon is Mr. Lewis' contribution to the DAV's National Service Campaign. He is editorial cartoonist of the Milwaukee Journal.

OLD SARGE AND VETERANS' BULLETIN BOARD
Liberty Magazine provided Urban's first editorial challenge as author of these columns.

received shortly before his medical discharge from the United States Army.

Urban continued with Liberty Magazine for a year and a half, representing veterans in this critical post-war transition period.

- - - - - - - - - -

Despite his vocal disability, Lt. Colonel Urban delivered a talk to the New York State Legislature. His presentation was recommending a state bonus for New York veterans. By use of voice amplifiers, his message was delivered so all legislators could hear Matt. He related his war experiences and support for the New York State military bonus.

Colonel Urban also was invited to submit a proposal to the U.S. Congressional Committee recommending legislation on a universal military training proposal. Urban participated in promotional drives for U.S. Savings Bonds to help the war effort. He made numerous personal appearances in this effort on behalf of the Armed Forces and U.S. Savings Bond Office.

LT. COL. URBAN JOINS MILTON BERLE
A successful $5,000,000 Bond Drive resulted from the combined efforts of Urban, Berle and nationally-known stars of the entertainment world.

Appearances along the Eastern Seaboard included entertainment stars Nanette Fabre, Edith Fellows, Jinx Falkenberg and Milton Berle. On one $5 million bond drive, Matt Urban was united with his new friend, Milton Berle. Matt's support of the bond drives continued for years with speeches in many states.

The World War II homecoming was not forever 'hearts and flowers'. As years pass, many forget too soon. People drifted into complacency, forgetting that so many young men had given their health, bodies and lives so United States citizens could live in a world of relative peace and dignity.

Urban's history reflected the mood and occurrences of that era. Matt's first two years of Liberty Magazine employment was accepted gratefully, but somewhat as 'spoils of the post-war days'. The opportunity and intrinsic values seemed easy and rewarding.

Urban, with some skepticism (after completing the magazine employment), faced the outside world. He was not able to continue his plan for law studies, because he did not have the voice for it. Next, he turned his attention to the challenge of public service employment. His proven talent was coaching, but Matt found that injuries to his vocal abilities were viewed as a handicap in the sports teaching vocation.

Coaching positions supposedly were 'wide open' to this successful military applicant, a Cornell University graduate ... Lt. Col. Matt Urban.

Interviews at a Prep Military Academy in Virginia and New York Prep School showed good promise. Final comments by the administrators were to the effect: "Your record is intrepid. Your references are exemplary. You are quite a man."

The employment interview usually ended without Matt being hired. Parting words were polite 'encouragement': that Urban was destined for a bigger, better position at some school with greater potential for him!

Dismayed, Matt continued his search for civilian employment. He took a tough route countless handicapped persons have taken to overcome their personal limitations. *A positive outlook, a steady heart and soul, a 'never quit' attitude* will win over all barriers!

To comprehend and adjust was Urban's strategy! Fitness, acceptance, and success were his objectives!

Urban's drive and convictions would carry him through the 'healing' time. Perseverance would prevail for Urban. His handicap would be no limitation in applying his talent and knowledge. Military training and experiences were the foundation for his confidence and ultimate success.

As if by providence (but truly from Urban's hard work), opportunity knocked. A city in need of a capable leader hired Urban over 75 other applicants. Matt Urban became Director of the Monroe Community Center in the city of Monroe, Michigan.

Matt Urban was encouraged by civic-minded members and its Board of Directors. Together they achieved goals beyond expectation of the adult community. Matt demonstrated outstanding achievement working with his 'new army' of teenagers and adult volunteers.

The 'center' began with the restoration of a dilapidated brick saloon. Upstairs rooms had been a brothel years before. Total reconstruction was

THE MONROE COMMUNITY CENTER
Urban provided the leadership and tough love so important to hundreds of young people. Many benefited for a lifetime.

required to create an acceptable recreation center. Internal walls were ripped out. The result: new game rooms and a gymnasium! Civic leaders' dreams, teenagers' desires and Matt Urban's drive melded into the new physical structure --- the Monroe Community Center.

The area environment was rough. This was located in the slowly deteriorating 'east end', often thought of as 'the other side of the tracks'. The Martin and McCoy feuds were trivial compared to those of this area's history. Racial differences, broken homes, poverty, and lack of operating funds presented obstacles to challenge Urban. This opportunity provided Matt a good place to 'cool his heels' and adjust to re-orientation into civilian life. Here in a corner of the east side area of Monroe, Michigan, was a mini-war. It seemed tailor-made for Urban's nature, leadership and experience.

Where else could Matt market his gruff, shot-up raspy voice? Bellowing forcefully, he brought enthusiasm and order to these diverse groups. They soon came to appreciate the tough love of their new director.

Urban practically lived with his new employment opportunity and wide-ranging challenges. Twelve-

RANGER

Commanding General ....Lt. Gen. William H. Harrison	Managing editor .... Sgt. Alene Packer
Public Affairs Officer ....Lt. Col. Jay A. Craig	Assistant editor .... Spec. David Ladines
Command Information Officer....................June Craft	Lewis Life editor ....Marjorie Smith
Deputy Command Information	Copy editor....................................Spec. Ken Blackburn
Officer ....Alicia Garces	Editorial assistant ....Spec. Michele Brown
	Photographer ....Spec. Douglas Stander

L E T T E R S

READER COMMENDS ARTICLE ON 'REAL HERO'

Dear Editor:

I would like to take this opportunity to commend you on such a fine article you wrote about retired Lt. Col. Matt Urban. You wrote about a real American hero. You and most other people know him as only a war hero, but your readers should know that this man's accomplishments after the war made him a hero to a lot of kids growing up in the 50's.

When Jimmy Carter said, "It was only God's will and guidance that extended and preserved this man's life on so many occasions," he knew what he was talking about. God did preserve this man for something, and I believe it was for kids such as I growing up in the 50's. Matt Urban was the director of the Boys' Club, on the East side of Monroe, Michigan. I grew up having a great deal of respect and love for this man. He made the difference for many of us. I was among hundreds of kids that grew up under Matt Urban's leadership, guidance and teaching. I guess you could say that he made the Boys' Club an extension of our families.

As a kid, I spent numerous hours in the Community Center participating in various activities to include softball. Matt Urban personally coached the team. He taught and developed our skills, and allowed us to participate when the skills were lacking. We used to pile into Matt's convertible to go to the ball fields. I think that sometimes there were as many as 16 kids piled into that car. It was while on our way to a ball game that we noticed the scars on either side of Matt's neck. We had questioned him on many occasions as to how he came about those scars. He would tell us that he was shot through the neck during WW II. He also told us that a medic had placed his finger in the wounds of his neck to stop the bleeding and saved his life. I don't think that any of us really believed what he had told us. I think that is why we asked him so many times.

Matt Urban made the difference in so many lives and so many ways. He contributed immeasurably to the success of many kids growing up in the 50's. Retired Lt. Col. Matt Urban was not only a great credit to the military but equally a credit to the community of Monroe. We will always be indebted to this man.

Fred Hoskins, Sergeant Major , U.S. Army

446

hour days, six days a week (and often on Sundays) became the normal Urban routine. His commitment was matched with devotion from a bunch of appreciative kids. They craved attention, recognition and guidance --- in that order. Matt provided all of the above. He had it and shared it!

Matt had a unique advantage in reaching troubled young people. His missions in World War II, military rank and status as a recognized military hero made it natural for boys to adopt Lt. Col. Urban as their personal hero.

Matt's athletic ability and war record quickly earned him respect and influence in his new community of Monroe, Michigan.

Matt's objective was clear: to rebuild a neighborhood that was going from bad to worse. He restored pride and brought prestige to the young members of this neighborhood. Participation in sports and recreation programs provided young folks with beneficial outlets for their high level of energy.

Matt's commitment to fitness and exercising mind and body were transferred to the youngsters through Matt's remarkable teaching and coaching. His intervention changed the lives of many young people. As they grew into successful adults, they all remembered the help and positive influence of their coach and friend, Lt. Col. Matt Urban.

For sixteen years Matt poured his heart and soul into developing the Monroe Community Center. He solicited funds, acquired land, and personally coached football, baseball and basketball teams. He felt his crowning achievement came in originating a free summer camp program for the needy children.

The Wolverine Boy Scout Council made Camp Kansetake available (after their summer season) for his project. In the beginning Matt did all the camp work with a few volunteers. This included the cooking and cleaning. Money and required clothing were contributed by the Ladies' Civic Club.

From only fifteen starting campers in 1947, the camp developed with a well-organized, all-volunteer staff. A total of 80 appreciative, needy campers between the ages of eight and twelve were soon enjoying the camp and its learning experience. Urban was a master at teaching personal cleanliness, nutrition, discipline ... as well as sports! Campers' faces reflected love and pride.

At sunset boys and girls encircled the camp flag pole. They proudly participated in the patriotic flag-lowering ceremony. This setting high on a ridge in the Irish Hills of Michigan touched Matt deeply. He was reminiscing about military formations of long ago. They were so similar in purpose, and yet so different in this beautiful camp area .... worlds apart in distance and the differences between war and peace.

Matt Urban continued to serve as a Big Brother to all youngsters that he could reach: from putting neglected children into bed at camp, to motoring local kids to national marble tournaments, to initiating cub scout and boy scout troops, and through a sports/ recreational leadership program.

Boxing always held Matt's special interest. Through his local programs he trained several national Golden Glove Champions. He was a member of the Golden Gloves and the AAU Midwest Committees. Lt. Col. Matt Urban became Chairman of the Michigan State Olympic Boxing Committee.

Urban was one of three administrator-trainers who escorted the midwest champions to the Olympic tryouts at the Cow Palace in San Francisco.

Cassius Clay

Matt Urban

WELCOME
NATIONAL A.A.U.'s EASTERN BOXING CHAMPIONS
TO **OAKLAND**

MUHAMMAD ALI
WORLD HEAVYWEIGHT CHAMPION BOXER

As a Golden Gloves boxer, 'The Champ' was known as Cassius Clay. Urban was one of three trainers accompanying Clay and the boxing team from the Midwest Region --- the finalists are shown arriving in Oakland, California enroute to the Olympics at the Cow Palace (across Oakland Bay) in SanFrancisco, California

Following a successful showing, they gathered at the airport on a sunny Sunday for their homebound flight. While preparing to board, they learned that their light heavyweight qualifier, a young lad named Cassius Clay, refused to fly back. His tempermental nature balked at the flying, whether from fear, defiance or a display of independence could not be determined.

The three coaches conferred. After a long discussion they decided to give the sulky youngster 'his head'. They left him at the airport lobby and provided him with an escort to the train depot, a ticket and money for his meals.

Years later Matt jokingly remarked that he would have hand-carried Cassius Clay's luggage if he had known that the young fighter would become known as Muhammad Ali, the World's Heavyweight Champion. Even in those early days the future Muhammad Ali looked every bit like The Champ.

- - - - - - - - -

Matt Urban and many military buddies from the 9th Division found true satisfaction in civilian life. They proved to themselves that they could win in this civilian life: by meeting goals, by getting things done, and using brains and initiative. Their unstoppable determination and dedication to duty was the same as they had applied during wartime battles to win and to live.

This formed the foundation for many successful careers in their civilian activities.

CHAPTER 19

MEDAL OF HONOR

When the time came for his belated Medal of Honor recognition, Matt Urban received heartfelt support from all over the USA. At long last his extraordinary feats of valor and service to his country were acknowledged publicly. When Matt received a call from the Pentagon, he learned that his records were being reviewed.   Officials were examining a recommendation for the Congressional Medal of Honor based on heroism under fire in Normandy.

After 35 years of bureaucratic oblivion, Lieutenant Colonel Matt Urban was sanctioned for the Congressional Medal of Honor. This was the last valor citation awarded to date by an official act of Congress. The Medal of Honor presentation raised Urban's battlefield awards beyond the total number of combat medals held by America's best-known GI, Audie Murphy.

FRIENDSHIP

This picture of 9th Division comrades shows the bonds of friendship and respect that continue 45 years after WW II.

Left to right: Matt Urban, George Albert, General Westmoreland, Al Sebock, John Allen, Charlie LiBretto

Years have passed. Daily living challenges dimmed memories of war. The annual reunion of the 9th Division, however, remains a precious event in Matt's life. Relationships bonded in the fiery terrors of war have developed a loyal fraternity of 'brothers-in-arms'. A 'sacred' devotion evolved among these comrades who had shared the absolute worst and best of times. Men of the 9th Division, who knew Matt for his battlefield valor and skill, share a mutual respect and admiration. Long-time friendships and memories are brought up to the minute as the veterans meet in annual reunion.

They meet to keep alive the 'closer than brothers' bond and the spirit of liberty for which they gave so much. Having won the war was in itself not enough. These veterans of World War II demonstrated that continued participation in public affairs was essential. In this manner the lessons learned about freedom's value and individual responsibility could take root in the consciousness of America.

- - - - - - - - - -

Sergeant Earl Evans spent the last months of the war in a German prison camp. He had been captured shortly after Urban's final evacuation from the front.

SERGEANT EARL EVANS
1942

(LEFT) EVANS AT WHITE HOUS
MEDAL OF HONOR CEREMONIE
1980

Upon his release from a German P.O.W. stockade, Earl G. Evans - S/Sgt - 12086058, sent a letter dated 5 July '45 to the Pentagon. He was fulfilling Major Max Wolf's commitment that Urban would get the highest award for valor in leading the St. Lo action.

Evans' letter of 5 July1945 stated: "Urban moved forward, and damned if the U.S. army didn't move forward also. He bellied up to the tank and amid heavy gunfire scrambled aboard and manned the machine gun. The driver took heart with Urban aboard. The tank roared forward, and Urban tore that hillside apart with that gun. The men, once again with 'Urban-itis' scrambled up the rise and gained the objective."

Over three decades after Evans sent his original letter to the Military — he received an official inquiry from LTC Vernon R. Hull of the Department of the Army, requesting confirmation of the facts upon which the recommendation was made for Urban to receive consideration for the Medal of Honor. Earl Evans and others verified these facts during the course of the next year.

After his return from service, Evans on several occasions reminded his former Battalion Commander that the late Major Max Wolf had recommended the Congressional Medal of Honor for Captain Matt Urban's actions in the hedgerows of Normandy and the breakout at St. Lo. Evans said he had properly prepared and forwarded the report through proper channels. He could not understand why Urban had not heard anything .... year after year.

Both Urban and Evans were aware that an authentic endorsement recommending the Medal of Honor receives the highest priority for review by the military, the Congress, and President of the United States. Standard operating procedures called for acceptance, denial, or request for additional information on every Medal of Honor form properly submitted. Each candidate was to receive notification one way or the other. Yet no word had ever been received by Lt. Col. Matt Urban.

For Matt it was 'academic'. He was honored to have been recommended. People around him in civilian life never realized Urban's heroic actions or the extent of his wartime service. Matt, in his quiet manner, just never brought up the subject.

ED MECHER, D.A.V. REGIONAL REPRESENTATIVE
Ed Mecher, the Regional Veterans Service Representative from Grand Rapids, Michigan, became well-acquainted with Urban. After several years of casual discussions, the Medal of Honor subject came up. Ed immediately filled out a form and sent it off to Washington, D.C. The rest is history....................................

During Urban's days of hospitalization at Halloran, he spoke with Sergeant Alex Bennett Kahn, who told Urban that his recognition would occur much later in life; that the essential value of those extraordinary actions would withstand the tests of time. Sgt. Kahn also told Matt that when the post-war flurry was over, his record would come under scrutiny by war historians, and the story would then come to light. Kahn's prediction came true!

Lt. Col. Urban's documented actions and his bravery under fire during World War II were to be officially recognized by belatedly awarding several combat medals earned during those wartime actions. It remained to be seen if Urban would actually receive the nation's highest award as recipient of the Medal of Honor.

A typical question on the delay of the Medal of Honor presentation is asked: "How did all this review get started almost thirty-five years later?"

It 'happened' that a monthly veterans' counseling service was provided by Ed Mecher, a DAV Regional Veterans Service Representative from Grand Rapids. He became a good friend of Matt Urban during these monthly sessions. Urban, as Director of the Holland

Lindsey Nelson

1431 CHEROKEE TRAIL, CHEROKEE BLUFF #82
KNOXVILLE, TENNESSEE 37920
September 23, 1989

Lt. Col. Matt Urban
352 Wildwood Drive
Holland, MI 49423

Dear Matty:

When I think back over the years of World War II
I always conclude that the best thing that happened
to me was the opportunity to serve with soldiers like
you.

You were a great combat soldier and leadership like
that provided by you was obsolutely necessary to our
winning the war. I, of course, was a staff officer and
not a combat soldier. But I had the opportunity to
admire your exploits in North Africa, Sicily, and
Europe.

There were no better soldiers than Matty Urban
and on the wall in my den at home I have kept,
for all these years, a picture of you. And many times
as I have passed it on my way in or out of the house
I glance at it, and it brings an almost invisible
smile. And sometimes, silently, I say to myself, "What a
hell of a soldier!"

I have enjoyed the times we have been able to visit
over the years. I trust that all is going well for
you. And remember always to count me as one who is
appreciative of the great contribution you made to your
country . I am proud to have served with you.

Sincerely,
Lindsey Nelson

LINDSEY NELSON

Lindsey Nelson served as Captain with the 9th Division as its Public
Information Officer throughout World War II. Later he became famous
as a N.Y. radio and TV announcer. He was well-known as the announcer
for the N.Y. Mets Baseball Team and NFL Football Team

Recreation Department and Manager of the Civic Center, often conferred with Ed Mecher at his office during free moments.

After years of leisurely discussions, the conversation turned on one occasion to decorations. Urban casually commented that he had been recommended for the Congressional Medal of Honor just as World War II ended. Ed responded that he would send in an awards form requesting the disposition of the Medal of Honor recommendation.

He promptly pulled out the form, filled it out, and placed it in one of his official envelopes. On his return trip to Grand Rapids, Mecher dropped the form in the mail. This was January 1979.

In February came a call from Chief Warrant Officer Carl Hansen of the Awards Office in the Pentagon. "Colonel Urban, I have some great news for you! On digging through our great volume of files, we located a bona fide application for the Congressional Medal of Honor. It was sent to us by a Sergeant Earl Evans (now of Miami, Florida), dated properly and accepted as of 5 July, 1945."

CW2 Carl Hansen   Urban   Lt.Col.   Earl Evans
Awards Office   Vernon Hull
                               Awards Office

The Pentagon
Presenting documentary file related to recipient's
Medal of Honor.

Hansen was encouraging! "Colonel Urban, I am not going to leave a stone unturned until I see this thing through. I will acquire documentation with verification from several witnesses, men who served with you. I will pass it on to the Senior Army Board for review by the Secretary of the Army and the Army Chief of Staff. It will then go on to President Carter for signature."

CW2 Carl Hansen (now CW4 in the office of Chief of Staff, Washington, D.C.) applied his diligence, dedication and devotion to the Congressional Medal of Honor and all it represents. This commitment to the revered status of the award led Carl into more than a year of rigid investigation and research to support Lt. Col. Matt Urban's belated honor.

Hansen received many phone calls. He spent nerve-wracking hours collecting letters from eyewitnesses and veterans who could substantiate Urban's action. Carl Hansen received many reports, thus validating his judgment that Lieutenant Colonel Matt Urban would be approved, and that the award of the Congressional Medal of Honor was well deserved. Hansen was determined that these facts would be made known to America. He also believed Matt

Urban would exemplify the honor symbolized by this award.

Colonel Vernon Hull and his staff at the Pentagon supported Carl Hansen's research. They offered help and total cooperation on the project with the thoroughness and perseverence they knew was required.

Despite a destructive fire in the Military Archives Building in St. Louis, Missouri, inspired research revealed Matt's courageous exploits. Miraculously, a lone file in the 9th Division records had survived! Its charred remains carried the necessary documentation to confirm Urban's recommendation for the Medal of Honor --- and its deserved award:

DOCUMENTATION:
Lieutenant Colonel Steve Sprindis
Congressional Testimony:
St. Lo Breakthrough - 26 July 1944

In order to fully comprehend Captain Urban's return to the battlefront, one must review the impact and vacuum of leadership created by his untimely departure due to wounds. When he got shot, he left a brave, viable fighting unit. When he returned, he found a frustrated, frightened, motionless mass of soldiers that were supposedly on the attack in the St. Lo Breakthrough. Angrily denouncing any and all leaders, regardless of their rank, Captain Urban, within minutes, ignited the fighting spirit he knew they possessed and rallied these soldiers to attack.

During this crucial breakthrough attack, Captain Urban resumed command of his entire battalion frontline activity. Within a short period of time, the Captain reached the leading elements and found one of our tanks destroyed and burning. Another lead tank was hit and smoldering with an agonizing cry for help coming from within. Knowing that the tank would soon be engulfed in flames, the Captain and an unidentified soldier dashed immediately to aid the stricken GI. In defiance of concentrated enemy fire which was zeroed in on the disabled tank, the aiding soldier made his way into the tank. The Captain was behind the tank, shielded from the enemy fire while machine gun bullets ricocheted from the turret. The injured man's legs were badly mutilated and therefore immobilized. With the aiding GI hoisting the wounded tankman from inside the tank, Captain Urban, maintaining as low a silhouette as possible, crept up on top of the smoldering tank and pulled him to safety. This complete life-saving mission was accomplished under heavy enemy fire and with a smoldering tank seconds away from exploding into an inferno. The tank did, in fact, explode within minutes thereafter.

With the leading elements of that fighting force temporarily halted, Captain Urban moved over to his flanking rifle company for supporting fire. Upon reaching that company's action, the Captain found one of their two support tanks in flames while the other seemed intact but had no turret gunner and was not moving. The Captain quickly located the Lieutenant and Sergeant in command of the supporting tanks and directed a plan of attack with their one remaining tank to lead. As the Lieutenant moved up to man the turret gun, he was immediately killed by enemy fire. The Sergeant tried the same and he too was killed. Here again, the Captain knew quick action had to be taken. The enemy was well dug in with complete observation and overwhelming fire -- so he dashed under the scathing fire and safely made his way into the tank's turret. Captain Urban then gave the tank crew orders to start moving directly at the enemy's gun emplacements. The Captain, at this time, was blazing away with the machine gun directly at the enemy's positions. His riflemen launched their simultaneous attack with inspired valor and overran the enemy force.

It is extremely difficult to put into words the heroics of this great man. His whole concept of combat leadership exhibited time and time again from Africa to Sicily to France, his courage, fearlessness in every confrontation with the enemy, was most positively unparalleled in all of World War II. It was only God's will and guidance that extended and preserved this man's life on so many occasions.

I am extremely proud to relate and corroborate a small part of Captain Urban's frontline actions, his total dedication to all GI's under his command, his disregard for personal safety, his incredible courage above and beyond the call of duty, with the supreme sacrifice the greater possibility but not the eventual occurrence.

As the result of Captain Urban's personal heroics, countless American lives were saved.

If the Medal of Honor is not ultimately awarded to this man, who, in my opinion, was the greatest combat soldier ever, a serious injustice in the history of military awards will have occurred. I should know as

I fought side by side with Captain Urban, and we shared the same philosophy of combat leadership. We, as lieutenants, listened intently as General George Patton addressed us at Ft. Bragg and said, "You cannot push a piece of string from the back, it will wither and stop. You must take it by the front end and pull; it will follow."

In closing, I would like to state that this corroboration of Captain Urban's numerous and distinguished achievements was not made by a rear echelon soldier. All my promotions were received on the field of battle (one from General Patton personally) along with four Silver Stars.

Lieutenant Colonel Steve Sprindis

The Matt Urban Story Continues:

Finally, the bureaucratic wheels turned into full gear. On July 10, 1980, 10:00 AM word came from the White House, the Office of the President: "Colonel Urban, you are the recipient of the Medal of Honor. I relay Congratulations from the President, who will personally present the medal. The date and details of the presentation will be rushed to you in a day or two."

The following morning Matt was informed that July 19, 1980, was the only day that the Commander-in-Chief could free himself for the Medal of Honor award ceremony.

Despite commitments in those months of domestic and world pressure, President Carter had acted decisively. The President would not allow awarding the Medal of Honor to be delayed any longer. Matt Urban was to be draped with his Congressional Medal of Honor exactly thirty-five years and eleven days late.

The sudden announcement and short time until the scheduled ceremony spurred Matt's reaction. He had just a few days to prepare! The notification stated that he could only have ten or fifteen guests, including his family. Matt's response was, "No way! My troops are going to be there with me!"

"Every man in my unit deserves that medal equally as much as I do!" Urban insisted on inviting the men who had fought beside him. Urban's sense of fairness wouldn't allow him to exclude his troops who had saved each others' lives time after time. He submitted a list of eighty names.

THE MATT URBAN STORY

REUNION OF 2ND BATTALION COMRADES

Urban insisted that his comrades of the African, Sicilian and European Campaigns be present at the Medal of Honor Ceremonies. He also included friends and officials from the City of Holland, Michigan.

LEFT TO RIGHT: Earl Evans, Dr. Stan Urban, 'Whip' Miller, Al Sebock, Bernie Huber, Fred Josey, General Dilley, Ben 'Bomber' Murell, John Allen, Terry Hofmeyer (Holland City Mgr.), Charlie LiBretto, Gordon Cunningham (Holland Attorney), George Albert, Roger Stroh (Holland Health Dept), Charles Lindstrom(Holland Police Chief).

470

Over the next few weeks Matt developed a great respect for the Pentagon and the Office of Military Protocol. Colonel Charles Dexter appointed himself as Urban's personal escort, flying twice to Holland, Michigan. The Colonel spent a couple days in Urban's home, briefing Matt. Then he returned three days prior to the ceremony to accompany Lt. Col. Matt Urban on this memorable trip honoring his heroism.

From the moment that Matt and his family arrived in Washington, DC, everything moved like clockwork. Every detail was meticulously handled. Matt and his family were housed in the Penthouse Presidential Suite of the Shoreham Hotel. These are among the finest accommodations possible. The elegant six-room suite had a television in every room, complete bar, and exquisite amenities. All adjoining rooms on that floor were filled with friends from the Ninth Division. Sergeants in Protocol served as escorts. They took care of every detail. When young daughter, Jennifer, wanted a hamburger, they provided her with a military escort to a local restaurant. Her every wish was their command on this special day.

Friday, July 18, began with a Pentagon luncheon. At an impressive ceremony at the Pentagon, Lieutenant

Defense Jennifer Urban President Jennie Chief of Staff
Secretary   Carter   General Meyer
Alexander

A MEMORABLE TIME AT THE WHITE HOUSE

Colonel Matt Urban was presented a series of combat awards which had been lost in a bureaucratic shuffle at the war's end. Chief of Staff General Meyers pinned him with the Legion of Merit, the Bronze Star with a 'V' device and his seventh Purple Heart.

The Croix de Guere, France's highest foreign decoration, was presented by the French Ambassador, his Excellency L. F. De Laboulaye. The distinguished statesman gave an emotional recitation expressing gratitude on behalf of the people of France to all American soldiers and to the American people for their help in the liberation of France.

- - - - - - - - -

The ceremony was followed by a visit to the Hall of Heroes. Matt was overwhelmed by the honor bestowed on him. A visit to the Military Cemetery at Arlington, Virginia, gave Matt an opportunity to pay his respects to all those whom he considers the true heroes. Accompanied by the Cavalry and a military escort, Lieutenant Colonel Urban was granted the honor of placing a memorial wreath at the grave of the unknown soldier.

Saturday, July 19, 1980, Washington, DC, was the day for splendid military celebration. It was a red-letter day --- a commemorative jubilee.

Saturday morning Matt, Jennie and Jennifer met President Carter in his suite for a personal chat. Conversation was friendly and informal. The two men shared a love of country and respect for the military. Another point of mutual interest was love for their daughters of similar age. In this family get-together, the President mentioned how much his daughter, Amy, and Matt's Jennifer were of similar temperament and outlook.

The Urbans felt that President Jimmy Carter was a truly sincere person, the friendliest, and most successful 'entrepreneur' they had ever met. Matt's fondest memories during his private talk with President Carter were discussions of Matt's work over the past twenty years as Recreation Director in Monroe, Michigan; Port Huron, Michigan; and, since 1974, in Holland, Michigan; and as Amateur Softball Association Commissioner for the State of Michigan. Both men spoke of their backgrounds in sports and the military. The sense of comradeship with the Commander-in-Chief was a most happy occasion for Matt.

Matt was very comfortable with President Jimmy Carter. Urban had always related well to every kind of individual. He was the same with the privates and corporals as he had been with the officers. He was equally friendly with hired help as with executives. Matt's 'Ivy League' Cornell University background was totally blended with his humble beginnings. This created in him a unique adaptability to all people. The exhilaration of the fireside chat with President Carter made Matt Urban feel that his life must have reached its zenith.

Zero hour! At 10:00 AM the military escorts ceremoniously swung open the doors of the palatial Presidential Conference Suite. Matt's next steps were accompanied by a sense of drifting into a most beautiful wonderland!

The spacious ballroom of the Shoreham Hotel was also transformed into an enchanting fairyland. The ornate ballroom gleamed. It was resplendent with a luminous rainbow of brilliant color from the stage lighting. The wall and overhead lighting filled the area with colorful radiance. The news media, with cameras flashing and popping, filmed the event for national broadcast. This added to Matt's exuberant feelings that 'America remembers and appreciates'.

The ballroom was overflowing with more than a thousand people: 9th Division veterans and their wives, Generals and Admirals --- all ranks of the commissioned and non-commissioned officers were represented.

Friends from all walks of life, as well as Urban's fellow servicemen, displayed pride in paying tribute to this infantry officer in his hour of recognition.

Majestic flags fluttered in alignment, embellishing the hall with an 'America is Great' atmosphere, with patriotism and esteem for each of the branches of military service. From the beginning to tho ond, thic celebration was exhilarating. Military and popular American music played by the prestigious United States Army Band was spine-tingling. The military did itself proud. Urban was filled with admiration for the excellence of this cherished celebration and awards presentation.

The Medal of Honor Ceremony was elegant. It had all the magnificence of the most elaborate awards presentation ceremony in the recent history of the military. Colonel Matt Urban proudly stood in uniform, looking out on the brothers-in-arms who had come to pay their respects and share with him in this honor. Matt listened as a tearful President Carter read with deep emotion from the Congressional Record:

"Captain Urban's personal leadership, limitless bravery, and repeated extraordinary exposure to enemy fire served as an inspiration to this entire battalion. His valorous and intrepid actions reflect the utmost credit on him and uphold the noble traditions of the United States Army."

Now the moment arrived. Abrupt silence filled the ballroom upon presentation of the long overdue recognition. President Jimmy Carter was about to bestow the highest U.S. mark of distinction for valor upon one of America's greatest combat soldiers, Lieutenant Colonel Matt Urban. President Carter turned and gave Matt a long, warm bear-hug. Wiping away tears from his eyes, President Carter draped the Medal of Honor on the chest of America's newly discovered hero.

Unending waves of thunderous applause rocked the ballroom. Hundreds of people rose to their feet in a rousing standing ovation. Matt's heart was bursting with pride. His eyes glistened with tears. Joyfully he waved to friends and family and to his comrades.

A PROUD TIME FOR THE PRESIDENT AND URBAN

Medal Of Honor

CO. F - 1ST LIEUTENANTS:
Standing: Shuttleworth, Tye,
Urban, Allers, (Morton-2nd Lt.)
Front row: Tallent, Nelson

TOP
Staff Sgt. Kerans,
Ist Sgt. Miller,
Capt. Urban,
Grabski(Orderly)
BOTTOM
Petty (Driver),
Heilman(Co. Clerk),
Etue(Mail Clerk),
Filletti(Radioman)

CAPTAIN URBAN, C.O.

JOHN 'WHIP' MILLER
1ST SERGEANT
(Photo is Jean)

URBAN'S VALIANT MEN

F COMPANY

SHUTTLEWORTH

URBAN, VOLLER, BROWN, SHUTTLEWORTH, SUSSMAN, KENNARD

BROWN

**VOLLER   URBAN   SEVIERS
GAMBINO**

URBAN'S VALIANT MEN

CHAPTER 20

HOLLAND HOMECOMING

After Lt. Col. Urban traveled to our nation's capitol to receive appropriate tribute from the President, armed services, and government of the United States, he returned to Holland. A tremendous outpouring of love, affection, and respect from his close personal friends, veterans' groups, and the general citizenry greeted Urban and his family with a welcome-home parade and civic ceremonies.

Matt's Holland friends, led by Rog Stroh, Director of Holland's Department of Environmental Health, made plans for the surprise homecoming. The intent was to provide a gala celebration such as had never been seen before or since for an individual hometown hero.

Roger Stroh reports:

"We did not have the resources of the Federal government, but intended to show Matt our appreciation

ROGER STROH AND LT. COL. MATT URBAN

for his historic, unselfish deeds. It was our desire to share with him the most significant recognition of any citizen/resident of Holland in its history.

Matt makes friends immediately and easily wherever he goes, if only for a day or a week. Wherever he resides, Urban becomes a part of a community's fabric, whether in Port Huron, Michigan; Monroe, Michigan; or, since 1974, Holland, Michigan. This was an important Matt Urban character trait to realize when planning Urban's community-wide homecoming event. It soon became obvious that everyone wanted to participate, help, donate, work and to be there to share with Matt. He, in a different way, meant something unique and special to each person whose life he touched. Now was their chance to show respect to the man, the friend, the hero.

Matt may have seemed a myth to his wartime enemies, but to all who knew him well, he was real and, in many respects, bigger than life.

When planning for the homecoming, I soon realized that what I personally felt toward Matt was shared by most everyone called on for assistance. It was only necessary to step forward to present the idea, and the volunteers immediately agreed to serve. I first called together a planning group: Chuck Lindstrom (Chief of Police), Terry Hofmeyer (City Manager), and Gordon Cunningham (City Attorney). All were close personal friends of Matt and shared hunting, fishing, and other hobbies with him.

The word spread, and we enlisted support from the VFW, DAV, AMVETS, American Legion, City of Holland, local business and industry, and many of Matt's friends.

Dozens of persons with significant contributions of time and effort could be mentioned. They are all aware that Matt knows who they are and appreciates each one. A few names must be mentioned for special diligence in assisting me to raise funds to pay all the invoices coming in long after the glow and glory of the moment had faded. Veterans John Oleszczuk of the VFW, Harvey Slotman of the DAV, along with the clerical support and record keeping of city employees Marly and Barb should not be forgotten.

With all plans completed and every detail in place, the event became history as recorded by the news media. Most importantly to all involved was knowing they were in the mind, memory and heart of

Lieutenant Colonel Matt Urban, recipient of the Congressional Medal of Honor and always our friend.

The community poured out into the streets, Civic Center, and VFW Hall to participate in the community's showing of appreciation and pride. This was a day to be remembered forever by all those who participated in this special celebration.

- - - - - - - - - -

Peter Luke of *The Holland Sentinel* tells the story in fine detail:

"It was a slice of Americana not often seen since the end of World War II when U.S. servicemen returned home to large and small towns everywhere, marching in triumph following victory in the 'big one'.

Thirty-five years later, one more World War II hero strode home amid a police escort, waving flags and a marching band, as cheering crowds lined the streets expressing their appreciation for his bravery and courage which made him the most decorated soldier of World War II and recipient of the Medal of Honor.

URBAN ARRIVES FOR CIVIC WELCOME CEREMONY

Monday, the Holland community saluted Matt Urban, capping a momentous weekend in Washington where he received the Medal of Honor from President Jimmy Carter and the praises of many.

After landing at Kent County International Airport from Washington around 5:30 PM, Urban arrived by motorcade in Holland. He rode atop an open convertible with his wife, Jennie, and 10-year-old daughter, Jennifer. The parade extended along Eighth Street to the Holland Civic Center.

As the American Legion Band led the way, residents ran from the crowd to shake Urban's hand or pat him on the back. The smiles on their faces were as wide as Urban's and expressed an exuberance in the comforting notion that real heroes still do exist in the uncertain aftermath of Watergate.

At the Civic Center, Urban's workplace as the city's Recreation Director, numerous politicians, military officers and the heads of veterans' organizations offered sincere praise for Urban and his accomplishments.

A HERO'S HOMECOMING

Civic Center,
Holland, Michigan

More than 1,500 Holland residents attending the ceremonies responded by giving Urban four standing ovations.

Colonel Urban sincerely thanked the crowd and said their reaction, coupled with a similar reaction in Washington, was further proof to him that our citizens are together in their nation.

Urban said the country must rid itself of its doldrums acquired in the past several years and restore faith that it is still the greatest country on earth.

'We Americans need to be reminded and have to be told that we are as great and as capable as any people on earth,' Urban said in his raspy Gravel Gertie voice obtained in the last of seven wounds he suffered in the war. 'The American people don't have to be afraid. We are the closest, friendliest people on earth. We have nothing to fear.'

Urban spent about five minutes discussing the positive aspects of a draft.

Later, he said the wait for the Medal of Honor has been like a trip on a yo-yo, with emotions going up and down. 'I never knew when it was going to stop,' he explained. 'Well, it finally stopped Saturday, and it was just tremendous.'

The exhilaration included meeting President Carter who, he said, may have given him 'a few cracked ribs' from the bear-hug received after getting the medal. But Urban also spoke of the compassion and emotion on the President's face during the ceremony.

Despite the accolades and attention, Urban reiterated that his only regret was that his deceased mother and father could not be present to witness his moment of glory.

'I'm sure I wouldn't have come back if I hadn't had the prayers of my mother and dad,' Urban concluded. 'Those prayers made it possible for me to be alive and to receive this Medal of Honor.'

The featured speaker of the evening, Brig. Gen. Arthur N. Phillips of the Michigan National Guard, said Urban's name will be engraved in the Pentagon's Hall of Honor and on a plaque at Arlington National Cemetery.

He added, 'None of the inscriptions are as powerful as those in the hearts of your friends. The courage of Matt Urban is the bulwark of freedom.'"

The Matt Urban Story Continues:

Urban, now a nationally-recognized hero, continued his responsibilities as Recreation Director for the city of Holland, Michigan --- baseball, soccer, basketball, civic events of all types and numerous summer recreation programs to serve thousands of young people.

From 1980 until retirement in 1989, Urban responded hundreds of times to fulfill his obligations at patriotic and civic events. As recipient of the Medal of Honor, Lt. Col. Urban answers the patriotic calls to duty inherent with this award.

In 1989 *The Matt Urban Story* was finally in completed manuscript form. This culminated several years of work by Urban. His book became a narrative of life and World War II experiences as told to family and friends.

Upon publication of the book, Lt. Col. Matt Urban retired as Holland City Recreation Department Director and Civic Center Manager.   In his words, "I started a new career as an author making book presentations and fulfilling speaking engagements."

Urban tells friends that he plans to enjoy the next few years of his 'new career'.   He hopes to encourage young and old to build patriotism, faith in the United States, respect for its military forces, and confidence in the strength and goodness of the United States of America.

REFLECTIONS

Since receiving the Medal of Honor thirty-five years late for extensive World War II heroic actions, Lieutenant Colonel Urban has received world-wide exposure through media and personal appearances.

The Medal of Honor Ceremony was carried by every major network. ABC's 20/20, Real People, CBS Morning News and numerous other television shows have paid tribute to Urban's extraordinary heroism. Articles in *People Magazine, Time, Newsweek,* and many other publications carried Urban's story. The *Reader's Digest* featured Urban in their story, 'The Hero We Nearly Forgot'.

This exposure led Matt to all areas of the United States and to Europe. He has spoken at patriotic and industry programs of all types, meeting thousands of new friends with his messages of patriotism.

'American Hero' was an unexpected title for Matt, and one that he claims must be shared equally by every GI who ever fought for this country. Yet, his story is unique. The qualities Urban brings to the role reflect everything that is good and decent in the American culture. Continuing publicity has kept Urban in full view of the public and created the unexpected responsibility of public personality and model for thousands of appreciative admirers.

Lt. Colonel Urban was certain that the Medal of Honor would not have any lasting effect on his life. However, he soon learned that his service to country and to mankind had not ended with the war, nor his work with children and adults as an educator and recreational director. Receiving his final cluster of military medals clearly opened up the greatest chapter of his life and a new responsibility.

Suddenly life was filled with phone calls and guests. Speaking engagements were scheduled with military and veterans' groups, as well as consultations with industry. Matt has a unique form of leadership which rejected 'managing' people in favor of leadership by example.

At a time when the country was losing pride in itself and withholding support of business and military interests, Urban remains a leader in the fight for national patriotism.

Patriots, the military and veterans are moved by his message, as well as people in business, sales personnel and education. Urban often speaks before conferences, award ceremonies, testimonials, civic and service organizations, churches and schools. Topics are as varied as leadership, determination and motivation presented in a blend of compassion and enthusiasm.

Urban often wondered what he could say to people that would make a difference. He pondered for weeks, searching mind and heart for words that would communicate what he knew by training and experience.

Questions poured in from interested parents, teenagers and even children:

"What about the draft?"

"How do you feel about Libya?"

"Did the Marines in Beirut die in vain?"

"What do you think of our military today?"

"What do you think of our youth today?"

Finally, a frame emerged for his thoughts and feelings. The following words, spoken with compassion and certainty, are put forth with the sincere prayer that "those who hear will respond with intelligence, patriotism and participation to meet the mutual goals of self and country."

In one of Urban's personal presentations, he says:

"I am a war survivor! Shot through the core of the neck! One chance in a million to live! One chance to talk again --- so do realize I am 'myself'; I am not trying to be a Jimmy Stewart or James Cagney.

I am grateful for your invitation and the opportunity to join you as part of your program.

We can be proud on this evening of distinction! We can revel and enjoy our fellowship and the meaningful presence of everyone here. We can console each other as our anxieties are so wrapped up in the festering, mixed-up, 'CRAZY' world situations: Beruit, Nicaragua, the Contras, the Persian Gulf and the Orient.

It seems so simultaneously that it is as if by God's guidance He is helping to bring our people together with greater love for each other and improved pride and patriotism.

Most encouraging is the evident growth of patriotism and political awareness in our youth of today.

Fortunately, our military, political leaders and responsible personnel know the NEEDS. They recognize the problems, are trying and doing whatever must be done! This is being done within our national goals as a peace-loving nation.

They alerted the world that we no longer are a sleeping giant! Our marines in Beruit, Granada, the others: civilians, hostages, did not die In vain! Our fallen heroes were fulfilling their patriotic duty. Whenever there is danger and need, our God Almighty is always with us, to give us that deep-down inner faith, strength and will to do whatever has to be done!

Situations of kill or be killed! Live or die! Anger, despair, remorse, avenge, were all a part of their risks and experiences.

They knew it then, and we realize now that we must always respect and remember those who made the supreme sacrifice. We must remember in our hearts and souls and minds to cherish and preserve what they have achieved for all of us in these years of peace and dignity! In turn, we must achieve for them a world with love for fellowman, individual appreciation, and preservation of world peace for all people.

Our American people must stand together! Through give and take we can establish and preserve the legacy for which so many fought and died. It was their firm belief that they were leaving behind a legacy for the young and unborn: A legacy of freedom and a world at peace and with its people living in peace and dignity.

We must pray that our national and world leaders will remember for generations to come that our greatest strength is in the presence of God. We must unite to remain free; we must be a team with mutual goals of freedom and peace. We must maintain our complete support and faith in our military strength.

In closing, let us consider how our individual doc-
trines and beliefs resemble each other. All of us
revere the same qualities: Leadership, determination, compassion, courage and winning, whether
at war or in peace.

The United States won World War II. As far as I'm
concerned, we demonstrated our military superiority
in Korea and in Vietnam. We did not lose militarily in
any of the major battles. We did not surrender. Our
servicemen in these areas of conflict performed ad-
mirably in carrying out their delegated military responsibilities. Our country had the moral honesty to
examine itself critically before the world in regard to
political implications.

In 1989, the gaining strength of the U.S. system of
freedom and democracy is spreading throughout the
world. We should credit much of these gains over
the communist systems to the results of our military
performance rendered in spite of the political and
public disturbances imposed during the Korean and
Vietnam Wars and post-war years.

May the spirit of the Medal of Honor, the spirit of
America, the spirit of those who have served and

those now serving, and all their greatness, b e contained within each of us and shared by all.

May you always remember that we are each members in a team for unity and achievement. May you prosper in devotion and service, achieving through excellence a better world for tomorrow.

Add to this: Love of God, family, community and country. We do have a great America. I leave you with this closing thought: WALK TALL! HOLD YOUR HEAD HIGH! YOU ARE A PART OF THIS GREAT, PROUD AMERICA!

Thank you very much! God bless you!"

CIVIC--INDUSTRIAL--PATRIOTIC PRESENTATIONS

THE MATT URBAN STORY

ADDENDUM

MATT URBAN'S EARLY YEARS

Matt Urban was born on August 25, 1919, in Buffalo, New York. Only a few months had passed since an armistice halted World War I, the 'War to End All Wars'. Childhood during the Roaring 20's was carefree. Americans enjoyed unprecedented prosperity and personal opportunity. Technology was reaching into most homes in the form of electricity, telephones and automobiles. The mood of the times was optimistic.

Buffalo was a flourishing industrial city. Great Lakes shipping brought grain and iron ore to flour mills and steel plants on Buffalo's waterfront. The second largest railroad network in the country had its hub in Buffalo. The city was mostly populated with many immigrants. They had arrived 'wave after wave' from Europe. First came the Germans, followed by the Irish, Italians, and then the Poles. They were a hardworking, industrious group of people, fiercely proud of their new home, and wise enough to know the value of living in a free society.

Europe was recovering from the horrible destruction of World War I. Her people had suffered enormous losses. However, political division and racial lines were already being exploited. Ultimately, this would trigger World War II. Germany, chafing under the austere treaty of Versailles, was beginning to assemble advanced weapons systems. These would eventually arm the Luftwaffe and the Panzer Corps. A young Austrian politician named Adolph Hitler was seeking to catalyze the bitterness of the German people into a power for world domination.

The U.S. military, armed with ancient rifles and wooden-wheeled, horse-drawn artillery, slipped into disarray during the 1920's. Men like Dwight Eisenhower, Omar Bradley, and George Patton prepared themselves at West Point while most Americans paid little attention to events in Europe.

The stock market crashed abruptly in 1929. A shadow of gloom dimmed the American dream. The Great Depression of the 30's caused Americans to turn even further inward. Europe was left alone to career toward another disastrous military conflict.

Matt Urban was always the organizer, the leader, in his Buffalo east side neighborhood during the 20's. Other neighborhood kids regularly gathered in the back yard of the apartment building owned by Matt's father, Stanley Urban, Sr.

Stanley, a plumbing contractor, ran his business in the first floor storefront of his building. As was common during that era, his family lived on the second floor. During the warm months the neighborhood children spent every hour they could at the Urban home. The yard was threadbare from use. Matt's mother, Helen, was an excellent baker. She kept the kids supplied with cookies and cakes.

Matt sometimes wondered if his friends were there because of his mother's treats or the games he organized. It really didn't matter as all followed Matt's quiet leadership. Matt arranged the teams and set the ground rules for the games they played in his yard on the vacant lot by New York Central railroad yards. When a dispute arose, Matt was the arbitrator. No one appointed Matt as the leader, but it was always so. Art, one of his older brothers, looked to Matt for answers or inspiration.

Brother Stan, four years Matt's senior, was a scholar and a champion in track. As an Olympic qualifier, he had competed against Jesse Owens in the 100- and 200-yard dashes. Later Owens went on to embarrass Germany's Chancellor, Adolph Hitler, by winning multiple Olympic gold medals in the 1936 German-sponsored Munich games. This dispelled the myth of Aryan racial supremacy.

In 1927 Matt's younger brother, Eugene, died of appendicitis at age seven. The family was in grief, frustrated that medicine did not have the cure. Matt felt the loss deeply. This sorrow strengthened his sense of compassion and determination to protect those he loved.

As the third son, Matt usually received hand-me-down bicycles, etc. It was the same with musical instruments. He really wanted to play the piano. The oldest son, Stan, had studied the violin. Brother Art studied piano. When Matt was old enough to take piano lessons, Stan had decided he did not like violin. Art was then determined not to take any more piano lessons.

Matt pleaded with his parents: "What about me? I would like to take piano lessons!" His parents responded: "We tried music lessons with two of you, and it didn't work out." That meant there would be no piano lessons for Matt.

Although Matt directed the neighborhood games, he was an average athlete. He compensated for his lack of natural ability with a supreme effort. Through will, effort, and diligence, he excelled in every game he played. Winning was essential to Urban, and he gave it every ounce of energy he could muster. Matt often extended his own power by discovering that 'spirit' which transcends normal limits of physical endurance.

While dominant among the younger boys, Matt often hung around the edges of the games of the older boys; many times he was pleading to participate. One day the older boys needed an extra for a sand-lot baseball game. They relented and let Matt play first base.

In the bottom of the ninth inning the opposing team tied up the score. There were two outs with runners on first and third. The batter, a left hander, lofted a pop-up into the sunny sky in Matt's direction at first base! Matt shielded his eyes from the sun. By the time he spotted the ball, it was too late. He dove for the ball. It ticked off his mitt and rolled toward the pitcher's mound.

The next thing Matt heard was a bellow from his older teammates. They didn't like losing the game on the error of their youngest player! Several boys approached him menacingly. One picked up a base-ball bat. Matt tore away from the lot as if from a pack of howling dogs and sprinted down the railroad tracks. The tracks stretched for miles through Matt's east side neighborhood. Matt pushed himself, gain-ing speed and a safe distance from his pursuers. Only then did he leisurely run home.

Matt learned something that day. Even if he was an unspectacular first baseman, he could sure run! He discovered something else --- the exhilaration of pushing his body past its limits to outdistance the older boys. Matt liked the feeling. Again and again, in later years, he would call on that adrenalin rush to gain a winning edge.

Matt developed his ability as a runner, and one year he entered the annual Buffalo Turkey Day Run. He told his mother she didn't have to buy a Thanksgiving turkey, because he would have the turkey as his prize for winning the race the next morning. "I guaranteed it", Matt said, "but she bought one anyway (the first year)."

Matt won the race and made good on his promise. That year the Urban family ate turkey leftovers well into December. The next year, in rain and sleet, he duplicated his feat, and the third year he won again.

The next challenge to confront Matt was another annual race: The Buffalo Courier-Express International YMCA 5-mile Derby. The first year he ran, Matt entered a field of experienced long-distance runners, including Mitchell from Toronto who later represented Canada at the 1936 Munich games. Matt was 16 years old and ran the race of his life. He won the event, snapping the ribbon as flash bulbs popped and newsreels whirred. Urban's victory picture made the front page of the *Buffalo Courier Express* the next day. "It must have been a miracle that day. I won it," Matt said later. The next year he came in twelfth!

By the time Matt enrolled at Buffalo's East High School, he had become a strong athlete. He put body and soul into the game of the season. It was football in the fall, basketball in the winter, and track in the spring. Urban played sand-lot baseball in the summertime.

Matt's father's reaction to his son's passion for all sports was, "Stick to one. Why be a jack-of-all-trades and master of none?"

It just wasn't in Matt to limit himself to one sport. He loved them all. Matt could not bear to give any one up to concentrate on another. Everything else was secondary to sports. The game he loved most was the game of the season. Playing on the sports teams kept him so busy that he rarely thought about school work (unless an assignment was due). He never took time for the girls. Matt said he never had a steady girlfriend during his four-year high school career.

Matt was respected by his classmates and involved in only two street fights as a high schooler. On one occasion his brother Art was accosted by the neighborhood bully. When Matt protested, the larger boy turned his aggression on Matt.

Matt surprised the bully as he bobbed and weaved quickly, avoiding the roundhouse swings. By landing several convincing blows on his opponent and knocking him to the ground, Matt was settling the matter 'once and for all'.

His protective urges led to his second fight a short time later. Nineteen-year-old Jerry, a five footer, slender as a broomstick, was the son of the candy shop owner where Urban worked part-time. One afternoon Jerry came in to the store in a panic. "What's wrong with you, Jerry," Matt asked. "You look as if you had seen a ghost." "I'm in trouble, Matty. Schwartz has challenged me to fight him just because I was playing up to his girl. We're supposed to meet at Humboldt Park as soon as it gets dark. Would you come along and act as my second?" "Sure, Jerry. Anything for a friend. But Schwartz is a big guy. You're going to need more than a second."

An early fall darkness and fog shrouded the ap-pointed meeting place. Mist rose ominously from a large pond near by. A large lamppost in the middle of the pond and a number of smaller lightpoles sur-rounding the area cast a shadowy light on the scene. Schwartz and his cohort stood by the shelter building. The park was otherwise deserted.

Duels always fascinated Urban whenever he saw one on the 'silver screen'. He was intrigued by the setting and the formality of preparation. Urban felt excitement as he and Jerry neared the scene of the fight. The fact that it was a fight for honor sparked his interest and imagination.

Bud Schwartz had stripped to the waist. His big muscles and piano size legs stood out in relief against the slender, almost frail form of his adversary. As they walked toward the other two, Matt turned to Jerry and said, "Jerry, you're not going to fight him, are you? He'll kill you!"

Impulsively Matt peeled off his shirt and took over the fight. Not a word was spoken as the two pugilists started to circle each other, feinting and jabbing. Under the lamplight, with only the two seconds nearby, the fighting pace was furious. Matt used his quick reflexes to dodge and leap out of the way of Schwartz's ham-sized fists. As Schwartz grew exhausted, Matt began tattooing punches off the young man's face.

"Hey, let's quit!" Schwartz finally offered.

Matt was agreeable. Having won one another's respect and settled the demands of an honor, they walked away as lasting friends with mutual respect.

Conflicts were part of Matt's preparation for man-
hood. His development was influenced by a close
relationship with his father. Together they fished and
hunted, tramping the beautiful countryside of upstate
New York, studying the ways of nature. From other
experienced hunters, Matt learned essentials of
wilderness survival and the art of stalking. Use of
firearms was a natural part of a young man's education in those days.

One Saturday evening when Matt was 18, he went to
spend some time with his cousin in Depew, N.Y.
They walked along a railroad footpath to a club
across the tracks for a couple of beers. There they
joined another cousin and two friends. When the
others were ready to leave, Matt insisted on staying
to finish his drink. His cousin decided to remain also,
despite encouragement from the others to join them
for an automobile ride.

About ten minutes later Matt and his cousin left.
When crossing four sets of railroad tracks alongside
a parallel walkway, they noticed lights and a com-
motion at a nearby rail crossing. When they went to
investigate, Matt was horrified to discover that the
three boys who had left the club only minutes before
had collided with a train. They had waited at the

railroad crossing for a train to pass. They then accelerated into the path of a second locomotive that came from the other direction. Their mangled bodies were strewn along the railroad bed. The image of the three boys lying in grotesque postures of death imbedded a permanent impression in young Urban's mind.

Matt wondered why he had been spared. At this point he began to believe in predestination. He developed an unswerving notion that a person would die only when it was destined to be.

After graduation, Matt and his high school friend, Lester Murdoch (an all-state high jumper), decided to tour the midwestern states to visit a number of college campuses. They adopted the slogan: 'Go West, Young Man.' On the tour they visited Michigan State University, East Lansing, Michigan; the University of Michigan in Ann Arbor; the University of Illinois in Urbana; and Northwestern University in Evanston, Illinois. They swung through Indiana to visit Purdue University in Lafayette.

Matt and Les had an old Model T Ford for the trip. Each time they stopped, they would have to push to start the old car. Matt would then leap on the right running board and Les onto the other, simultaneously controlling the steering wheel and hand throttle. The hand throttle for acceleration of the Model T was on the steering column. This made it easy for Matt and Les to beat the hot weather by standing on the running boards.

Pedestrians were left gawking at the automobile with no driver inside. Through Detroit, across Canada, the two friends were chugging along. On the last few miles back to Buffalo, the cast iron engine of the old Model T Ford ran hotter and hotter. Even when glowing red, it faithfully kept working.

A hotter situation arose when the two nomads would find their pockets empty. Only one thing to do --- chug along at a snail's pace, conserve gas, and proposition the next hitchhiker into helping finance the next tank of gas. In those days roadsides had many walking travelers. Just as the boys were at the end of their resources, a waving thumb would be sighted. Not to risk stopping and cranking or push-starting the jalopy, the hitchhiker was waved to jog along side the vehicle.

"Friend, do you have at least a quarter to help with the gas?" Several did. They were invited to jump in and ride. One didn't have any money. Obviously, he continued his journey on foot. Les and Matt, being veteran hitchhikers, hated to leave the guy stranded, but it had to be if they and their paying riders were to reach Buffalo.

Matt and Les did not relax until the tall buildings on the Lake Erie waterfront and arches of the Canada/ U.S.A. Peace Bridge could be seen on the horizon. Spitting and sputtering, the old Model T Ford resisted its payload of two big guys in its rumble seat and three more in front! Matt Urban and Les Murdoch happily entered the City of Buffalo aboard their faith- ful Model T Ford.

During the next month, Urban and Murdoch earned expense money to continue their college search. They took a side trip east and made one final stopover at Cornell University in Ithaca, New York. The environment at Cornell was in dramatic contrast to the bustling image of Buffalo, N.Y.

Urban's brothers had attended the University of Buffalo. It was expected that Matt would follow family tradition, but Matt marched to the beat of a different drummer. He couldn't explain the inner sense of certainty that made him feel that he belonged on the beautiful campus at Cornell University.

Matt's father, Stanley Urban, had been a successful businessman for many years. Prior to the Great Depression of the early '30s, he was quite well off financially. During this depression he had lost practically everything. As a result, he knew that he could not sponsor Matt's education at Cornell University.

After much family discussion, Stanley determined that he would be able to sponsor Matt's tuition costs at Cornell. However, it would be necessary for Matt to earn the cost of his room and board. Matt Urban accepted this challenge and promptly became employed with several jobs at Cornell.

Matt was the first son to leave home. He was also the youngest son, and it was not easy for Helen and Stanley Urban to see him leave. It was an emotional time for the family. They all recognized Matt's determination and need to fulfill his desire for an education at Cornell. This proved to be a turning point in Matt's life. It was the beginning of a new and interesting period for Matt Urban.

With the political events of the late '30s, it developed that Urban became a member of the Class of '41. This group of students became known as 'The class that went to war'. In meeting the challenges of those war years, Urban continued to exhibit those characteristics of a daring leader.

His accomplishments ultimately led to his being the recipient of the Medal of Honor presented to him by President Carter. He was also awarded several foreign medals and more than two dozen medals from the U.S. military.

About forty-four years after World War II, the *1080 Guinness Book of World Records* identified Lt. Col. Matt Urban as 'The Most Combat-Decorated Soldier in American History.'

SPECIAL RECOGNITION

To:

My special gratitude to Charles F. Conrad, who volunteered his time as Co-Author, Editor, and Coordinator of finances, business structure and marketing. Also, special recognition to Marian Spyker for hundreds of hours in editing and word processing the manuscript to accurately and effectively tell this story, and to Wilbur Stoltz for his help in editing and proof-reading this narrative.

Ken Morford, friend, artist and illustrator, for several years of creative artistry in the development of the final artwork for the cover and wrapper of 'The Matt Urban Story'....... also, for the creative illustrations that he developed to enhance the story.

VOLUNTEER ADVISORY COMMITTEE
Holland, Michigan

Charles F. Conrad -- Committee Coordinator
Robert Bishop -- Financial Advisor
Gordon C. Cunningham, Attorney
William P. De Long, C.P.A.
William Sikkel, Marketing Manager

SPECIAL ACKNOWLEDGMENTS

To:

Les Murray and his staff in New York and Houston, Texas for his collaboration, research and pioneering the groundwork for the initial rough draft.

Attorney Richard Johnston of Hale & Dorr Law Firm, Boston, MA for the support and advice he has offered throughout the years.

To my wife, Jennie, and daughter, Jennifer, for their ideas, interest and support.

C R & Associates, Holland, MI.: William Cox, Sr., Richard Robinson, William Cox, Jr., for special assistance, training and implementation of our computer system.

For editorial critique: Joseph MacDoniels, Ph.D., Hope College, Holland, MI. - Jim O'Connor, Holland, MI - Bob Scully, Ludington, MI - Dalton E. McFarland, Ph.D., Grand Haven, MI.

For photographs and historical information:
Brigadier General Pat Brady , Department of the Army,
    Chief of Public Affairs, Wash., D.C.,
    and his staff assistant, Gerri Taylor,
Dan Quinn, Secretary - 9th Division Association,
John Marcham, Editor-Cornell Alumni News,
Ken Van Sickle, Sports Editor, Ithaca Sun,
Stan Bozich, Director - Michigan's Own, Inc.,
    Military & Space Museum, Frankenmuth, MI.,
Russell B. McIlwain, Military Historian, Ferndale, MI.,
Andrew J. Sikora, Publisher-Editor, The Polish American,
Thurlow Spurr, Staff and Liberty Concert Choir
Bob Kane, Former U.S.Olympic President
Don Porter, Executive Director ASA
John Greenslit, Executive Director MRPA
Walt Balcom, Former State Secretary MASA
Ed Mecher, Former Veterans Counselor DAV
Associated Press, Readers Digest,ChicagoTimes,TimeMagazine
9th Division official records, photos, technical data; "Eight Stars to Victory", 1948.

SPECIAL THANKS AND RECOGNITION

to those who made it economically possible to print The Matt Urban Story:

Charles F. Conrad, Coordinator of The Matt Urban Story,
Founder of Thermotron Industries (ret.), Holland, MI.

The Henry Wolters Post #2144, V.F.W. - Holland, MI,
(Paul Riemersma, Commander).

Robert Bishop, A. G. Edwards, Holland, MI.
Max De Pree, Chairman of the Board,
Herman Miller Co., Zeeland, MI
Bernard Donnelly, Chairman of the Board (ret.)
Lithibar, Inc., Holland, MI.
F.M.B. (First Michigan Bank), Zeeland, MI.
Terry Hofmeyer, City Manager (ret.) Holland, MI.
Richard Johnston, Attorney, Hale & Dorr, Boston, MA.
Charles Lindstrom, Chief of Police, Holland, MI.
John Ryan, President-Lee & Mason, Inc., Northville, N.Y.
Larry Sandy, Finance Director, City of Holland, MI.
Charles R. Sligh, Chairman of the Board (Emeritus),
Sligh Furniture Co., Holland, MI.
Roger Stroh, Environmental Director, City of Holland, MI.
Thermotron Industries, Holland, MI., a Venturdyne Corporation.
Dale Van Lente, Holland Insurance Agency (ret.), Holland, MI.
Willard C. Wichers, Director (Emeritus), Netherlands Museum,
Holland, MI.
Bud Michielson, Past Commander - American Legion,
Holland, MI.

These friends have contributed hundreds of photographs, documentary information and advice:
John Ryan - Charlie LiBretto - Ben Murell - Col. Keene Wilson - George Albert - John Miller - Ed Mecher - Major General Mike Kauffman - Earl Evans - Col. Steve Sprindis - Brigadier General 'Chick' Hennen (ret.) - Captain Lindsey Nelson (ret.) - Rich Talman - Ben Mintz - Russell Hopkins - Rich Young - Ed Cain - Bob Boven - Rick Oliver - C.E. (Whitey) Reisig, Gilbert Mouw, Peter Radichio.

The City of Holland, Michigan for its cooperation and support in my fifteen years as Recreation and Civic Center Director, and to Carol Hardenberg as Secretary of our City Recreation Department and Civic Center ... also, for the cooperation that enabled me to represent the City and fulfill my obligations to the public and military activities related to my being a recipient of the Congressional Medal of Honor during the past nine years.

EDITORIALS - - - IN CONCLUSION

HOLLAND SENTINEL, HOLLAND, MICH.

This letter, written by Fred Scott, Jr., of Ocean, N.J. (who served with Urban during World War II) is shared as a guest editorial by the Holland Sentinel.

"When I heard about Matt Urban being awarded the Medal of Honor, it brought back many thoughts of this great soldier. These are thoughts, impressions and things I have talked about for more than 30 years whenever the topic of the war has come up. Every word is uttered in praise; I have always felt that just knowing Matt was like my receiving an award.

Life is now complete for Matt Urban. Nothing else will ever be needed. He has the "Big" one, the Congressional Medal of Honor ... This award was really earned; perhaps it was earned several times. Truly, a great soldier. I think from the day he was born the Medal of Honor was predestined. He, more than anyone I ever met, had to earn it.

I was a replacement officer with the Ninth. Matt was in the Ninth all the way, from Africa to Germany. Sometimes I thought Matt was the Ninth. As it was with everyone, I held him in great awe. All soldier from head to toe. During the war I don't think he ever had a thought of anything except what he was there to do, fight a war, kill the enemy, get shot, get up and fight some more. Be with the troops. Be with his men. Help them with the battle.

General Patton once slapped a soldier. Had he ever known Matt, he would have hugged him; he would have kissed both cheeks; he would have proudly saluted Matt Urban. This was his kind of people, made from the same cut of cloth. They both marched to the beat of the same drummer. All soldier, from the day he put on the uniform until the day he stepped out of it.

Like everyone else on the boat and in the hospital, I put him on a pedestal. He had more awards than most of the rest of us put together. Everyone held him in awe. Wounded seven times. Can you picture someone being wounded seven times? Several of these times he went AWOL from the hospital. Why? Why, to get back to the front. To fight some more war. To be with his men. To be leading the battle. To be where he belonged."

IN OUR TIME
By HERB CLARK
TIPTON TIMES -- TIPTON, IOWA

"Last week I saw Matt Urban again. He is a fully authenticated hero. It required more than 35 years for the Army to give him a long-delayed and richly-deserved Congressional Medal of Honor. He received it during the final year that Jimmy Carter was President.

That he is alive can be considered either an act of God or a whimsical turn of fate, depending on how you look at such things.........

Those who knew Matt Urban when he served with the 60th Infantry consider him a special person. It is understood that what he did was probably beyond the courage or physical ability of most of the men with whom he served. When he walks into a room where he is known, voices hush. It is instinctive respect. He grins, somewhat in the way that Gary Cooper did when he played Sergeant York.

But contradictions breed upon themselves. Matt Urban is a gentle man. It is easy to understand why children like him. He is warm and appealing, friendly and gracious...........

He did what he had taken an oath to do. He did it without thinking of the risk involved and, whatever was done, he believes that it was correct and honorable."

BUCK STOPS HERE
BUCK JOHNSON
CHATTANOOGA TIMES - - July 17, 1980

"I met Matt Urban through softball about a decade ago and was impressed by the manner in which he fought for the things he thought softball needed. Through the years I've watched him operate at national conventions and felt he was something special. Now I know he's a special kind of man.

Matt Urban is the central character in another great chapter in American heroism. To a generation far removed from the echoes of that war, what Urban did and the happy ending for him is truly an unbelievable fairy tale. It is true, and it is happening.

Let me tell you about it ....

This is an incredible climax to an incredible story that began on July 5, 1945, when S/Sgt. Earl Evans wrote the War Department. "I am only a S/Sgt," wrote Evans, "but I feel an enlisted man can exercise the right to put an officer in for the Congressional Medal of Honor. I believe such gallantry beyond the call of duty should not go unrecognized."